After Me, Chaos

AFTER ME, CHAOS
Astrology in the Mughal Empire

M.J. Akbar

BLOOMSBURY
NEW DELHI • LONDON • OXFORD • NEW YORK • SYDNEY

BLOOMSBURY INDIA
Bloomsbury Publishing India Pvt. Ltd
Second Floor, LSC Building No. 4, DDA Complex, Pocket C – 6 & 7,
Vasant Kunj, New Delhi, 110070

BLOOMSBURY, BLOOMSBURY INDIA and the Diana logo
are trademarks of Bloomsbury Publishing Plc

First published in India 2025

Copyright © M.J. Akbar, 2025

M.J. Akbar has asserted his moral rights to be identified as the author of this work in
accordance with the Indian Copyright Act, 1957

All rights reserved. No part of this publication may be: i) reproduced or transmitted in
any form, electronic or mechanical, including photocopying, recording or by means of
any information storage or retrieval system without prior permission in writing from
the publishers; or ii) used or reproduced in any way for the training, development
or operation of artificial intelligence (AI) technologies, including generative AI
technologies. The rights holders expressly reserve this publication from the text and
data mining exception as per Article 4(3) of the Digital Single Market Directive (EU)
2019/790

Jacket image credits:
Sword: metmuseum.org/Public domain
Zodiac coins: metmuseum.org/Public domain
Charts: Book of Iskander (edited image): wellcomeimages.org/Wikimedia Commons
Aurangzeb's painting: clevelandart.org/Public domain

ISBN: PB: 978-93-61316-26-5; eBook: 978-93-61318-84-9
2 4 6 8 10 9 7 5 3 1

Typeset in Minion by Manipal Technologies Limited
Printed and bound in India by Thomson Press India Ltd

To find out more about our authors and books visit www.bloomsbury.com and sign
up for our newsletters

For sale in the Indian subcontinent only

To our lodestar, Mallika, and her auspicious constellation of seven stars—Mukulika, Carl, Prayaag, Shanta, Julian, Kayan and Agastya

Contents

A Note on Style and Sources   ix
Preface: Belief, Behaviour, Destiny   xi

1. Birth of an Empire: The Startling Mystery of a Hideous Face   1
2. The Tablet of Divine Secrets   13
3. Akbar: Sun of Felicity and Fortune   47
4. Jahangir: No One Is a Relation to the King   91
5. Second Lord of the Auspicious Conjunction   133
6. The Last Prediction: After Me, Chaos!   169
7. The Rise of Suhail   219

Acknowledgements   243
Notes   247
Index   269
Selected Bibliography   279

A Note on Style and Sources

THIS IS A BOOK for the general reader, not the academic. In the interests of readability, I have modernised and standardised spelling, punctuation and capitalization.

Wherever possible, I have retained the original phrasing of primary sources, including contemporary translations of Persian, Sanskrit and other texts. For Mughal-era chronicles like the *Akbarnama* and *Ain-i-Akbari*, I have relied on both classic translations (for example, Henry Beveridge's 1921 version) and recent scholarly editions (such as Wheeler Thackston's 2015 Harvard University Press translation). Page references are provided for all direct quotations.

In keeping with Mughal-era sources, I have used the term 'Hindi' to refer to the literary language now often classified as Braj Bhasha or early modern Hindi. This reflects the historical usage of the period, where 'Hindi' encompassed dialects like Braj and Awadhi, distinct from modern standardized Hindi-Urdu.

For Persian, Arabic and Sanskrit terms, I have generally followed the spellings in my sources, though with simplified diacritics for ease of reading. Proper names (for example, Jahangir vs. Jahāngīr) are rendered in their most familiar forms.

I have kept endnotes to a minimum, citing them only for direct quotations or contentious claims. The bibliography includes both published works and archival material, with particular reliance on:

- Mughal chronicles like *Baburnama*, *Akbarnama*, *Tuzuk-i-Jahangiri*, *Ahkam-i-Alamgiri*, *Sirri-i-Akbar*, *Ruqaat-i-Alamgiri*) and their translations.
- Recent or contemporary scholarship (for example, Jadunath Sarkar, Audrey Truschke, Munis Faruqui).
- Texts from my personal library and colonial-era translations.

This book is a synthesis of narrative history and original analysis, aiming to make the Mughal world accessible without sacrificing scholarly rigour.

Preface

Belief, Behaviour, Destiny

THE MUGHAL EMPIRE FLOURISHED so long as its monarchs practised faith but rejected religiosity. It became brittle under the martinet Aurangzeb, who fractured the social harmony of the previous hundred years of Mughal rule with divisive rancour, thinly veiled by personal piety.

All Mughal kings, irrespective of differences in character and temperament, believed in astrology. The most famous portrait of Humayun, commissioned by his grandson Salim (later Jahangir) in 1603, shows him kneeling on a beautiful blue carpet to read the poetry of the Persian poet Sadi, beside him is an astrolabe, or al-asturlab. Humayun was both an astronomer and an astrologer. A reproduction of the painting, by Mohan, can be seen at theHumayun's Tomb World Heritage Site in Delhi. Astrologers, both Hindu and Muslim, were elevated to court officials by Akbar. Aurangzeb, cautious about accusations of quasi-idolatry by orthodox elements of the Islamic clergy, disguised his belief in astrology but, like his imperial ancestors, consulted astrologers as a matter of routine.

This book is a social history of belief and behaviour among the elite in the dynamic phase of Mughal rule in northern India. Mughal emperors from Humayun to Shahjahan rejected faith-based puritanism as both joyless and inimical to political stability. Akbar's alliances with the Rajput kingdoms of Rajasthan, which extended to social fraternity, marriage and binding mutual trust, were central to the sustenance of the empire. His son Jahangir's mother was a Rajput princess. Shahjahan's mother and grandmother were Rajput nobility, so he had as much Rajput blood in his veins as Mongol-Chagatai. An evolving shared culture was evident in court behaviour.

Muslim aristocrats enjoyed wine as freely as Rajput nobles, although it is prohibited in Islam. Almost as many contenders to the Mughal throne died of drink as by the sword. Wine was served at feasts, sending a signal against orthodoxy and faith supremacy. Jahangir overdid the indulgence and paid the price in poor health. Aurangzeb's powerful wazir Jafar Khan shrugged off orders to abjure alcohol but remained in office until 1669 or for the first decade of Aurangzeb's reign. His death marked a turning point for he was replaced by officials more obedient to the emperor than to the empire.

The Mughals, proud of their pre-Islamic Mongol ancestry, preserved their traditions against encroachment by doctrine. Religion demanded faith and worship, about which there was no dispute, but survival in this world required parallel loyalties. Most Mughal kings were ardent believers in Sufi saints and syncretic values. Sufism worked because it was as practical as it was spiritual. The ruling minds were broad enough and their sensibility acquiescent enough to let other faiths co-exist. Aurangzeb, a skilled military strategist, won battles but lost an invaluable inheritance because he forgot that the credibility of empires rests on the goodwill of the people. Aurangzeb alienated Hindus, emasculated the Rajput alliance and lost the confidence of his subjects. The empire disintegrated after his death as his astrologer had predicted with remarkable accuracy.

Over three centuries after the death of Aurangzeb, there is amnesia about the powerful hold of astrology on the Mughal imagination. Faith in astrology, or *ilm al-najum*, transcended the various differences in religion, caste, language, ethnicity and geography that dotted the empire's landscape. Trust in astrology existed far beyond the borders of the Indian subcontinent, across the vast spectrum of diverse Muslim kingdoms in Asia.

Astrology, notes the scholar Abu Rayhan Muhammad ibn Ahmad al-Biruni, one of the great polymaths of the 10th and 11th centuries, is only as good as the astrologer. Born near Khiva in 973, Al-Biruni was a student of Abu Nasr Mansur, the Persian mathematician and astronomer who developed trigonometry. In 994, al-Biruni shifted to Rayy, near modern Tehran, where he helped establish a hilltop observatory. By the age of twenty-two, he had written his first treatise, on maps. Over the next decade, he served a range of sultans as astronomer and astrologer. He came to India with Mahmud of Ghazni in 1022, stayed back, learnt Sanskrit and wrote *Tahqiq ma li-l-Hindi min maqulah maqbulah fi al-aql aw mardhulah* ('Verifying All That the Indians Recount, the Reasonable and Unreasonable'), recognised as a classic of the genre. Credited with writing 146 texts, he translated Patanjali's *Yoga Sutras* and introduced Indian mathematics, medicine and the Hindu calendar to the wider world. No one, claims al-Biruni, is worthy of the style and title of 'astrologer' who is not conversant with geometry, arithmetic and the science of numbers. His *Instruction in the Elements of the Art of Astrology*, written in 1029, a textbook of its time, describes astrology as a 'fruit of the mathematical sciences' but adds that it is only as good as its practitioner.

Islamic doctrine spurns astrology, since only Allah can know the future. The orthodox dismiss astrology as *shirq*, or apostasy, citing Surah Yunus, Verse 101: 'Behold what is in the heavens and earth! But revelations and warnings will not avail those who will not see the truth.' Al-Maida (The Table), Verse 3, forbids Muslims from eating carrion and swine and from settling 'disputes by consulting arrows', a form of divination.

Muslim communities of the time did not consider themselves any less Muslim for retaining some practices from the pre-Islamic civilisations of Babylon, Persia, Egypt, Greece and India. In the 8th century, when Caliph Mansur decided to build a new capital for the Abbasid Empire, he summoned his best astrologers: the Persian Naubakht Ahvazi, the Arab-Jewish Masha-Allah Athari and the Arab-Muslim Muhammad ibn Ibrahim Farazi, who invented the first astrolabe in the region. Farazi's astrological predictions reverberated through the Caliphate.

The foundation stone of Baghdad was laid at 2.40 pm on 31 July 762 because Jupiter was rising at the time in conjunction with the ascendant in Sagittarius, writes historian and author Benson Bobrick in his book *The Caliph's Splendor*. The Sun, in trine to Jupiter, was in its own sign, Leo, in the ninth house, in a sextile to Mars in the seventh, even as it moved away from a square to Saturn in the sixth, to use technical terminology.[1] The first of Baghdad's astrological schools was started in 777 by Jacob ben Tariq.

In a previous book, *The Fated Sky*, Bobrick also details the prevalence of astrology in the Christian realms of Europe. Charlemagne (748–814), king of the Franks from 768 onwards, king of the Lombards from 774 onwards and Holy Roman Emperor from 800 onwards, had an Anglo-Saxon astrologer-poet named Alcuin in his entourage. It was said that every leader, whether pope, king or general, had his astrological adviser during the reign of Louis the Pious between 814 and 840. When half a millennium later, Charles V of France died in 1380, almost a tenth of his library consisted of books on astrology.

Pope Sixtus IV (1471–1484), warrior Pope Julius II (1503–1513), Leo X (1513–1521) and Paul III (1534–1549) held important events only at auspicious hours. Leo X established a chair for astrology at Sapienza. In the late Middle Ages, such chairs also existed in the universities of Paris, Padua, Milan, Bologna, Florence, Vienna and Oxford.

Leo X's favourite astrologer, Franciscus Priulus, became so depressed at his own predictions that he committed suicide. Under Pope Urban VIII (the pontiff between 1623 and 1644), street vendors in Rome sold prediction sheets called *Avvisi*. In the East, the coronation horoscope of the Byzantine emperor Manuel Comnenus, who ruled between 1143 and 1180, survives. Andronius II made his astrologer Theodorus Metochites (1282–1328) his prime minister. Cardinal Wolsey studied his master Henry VIII's chart to find out his weaknesses to pander to them.

Catherine of Medici (1519–1589), the queen consort of Henry II of France from 1547 to 1559, can hardly be faulted for her trust in the art. Her parents died within a month of her birth, but her astrologer Cosimo Ruggieri predicted a great future for the orphan. According to him, Catherine's fortunes would rise after her marriage to a prince of France. She did marry one, but he was a younger brother who had no apparent likelihood of ascending to the throne. His elder brother fell ill while playing tennis and died, and Catherine's husband, Henry II, became the king of France. Even more extraordinary was Ruggieri's prediction that three of Catherine's sons would reign in succession (Francis II, Charles IX and Henry III), but none would have children. As 19th-century French novelist Honoré de Balzac later commented, this was enough to drive disbelievers in astrology to despair.

In his book *The Indian Muslims*,[2] the rationalist historian and academic Prof. M. Mujeeb writes:

> Long before Muslim rule was established in India, Muslims [across the world] had come to believe in magic, in the influence of the stars, in the mysterious qualities of precious stones, in signs and omens. In India, astrology had the prestige of a science, and Muslims were completely taken in by the astrologer.

Indian faith in astrology was as visible in the bazaars of 13th-century Delhi as in the homes of the elite. Prof. Mujeeb, quoting from Ziyauddin Barani's *Tarikh-i-Firuzshahi*, adds:

> No ceremony would be performed in any respectable family, and no work of any importance undertaken by any individual without consulting an astrologer. As a result, almost every street had an astrologer, who could be a Hindu or a Muslim, and in this profession were some who 'performed almost miraculous acts by way of discovering secret motives, interpreting the commands of the Unseen and finding things lost'.[3]

Nearly six centuries later, another sultan, named Tipu, consulted astrologers in his southern kingdom of Mysore, seeking to ward off misfortune through ritual. On every Saturday, writes Muhibbul Hasan Khan, Tipu Sultan made an offering to the seven stars of seven different kinds of grain placed in an iron pan full of sesame oil, a blue cap and coat, one black sheep, and money. The British, who defeated Tipu Sultan in 1798, invested in guns rather than stars.[4]

The title of Mrs Meer Hassan Ali's two-volume *Observations on the Mussulmauns of India: Descriptive of their Manners, Customs, Habits and Religious Opinions*

Made During a Twelve Years' Residence in Their Immediate Society leaves little to add, except that the author might have indicated that the 'natives' were from Awadh, although she could not have known that she was describing the last phase of Muslim rule before the upheavals of 1857.

Making no effort to disguise her cynicism, she narrates the influence of *najoomee* (stargazers) on Muslim aristocrats. Astrologers were generally men of some learning, she concedes. Those who feared God more than they loved the vanities of this world distanced themselves from the 'pretended art of the astrologer', but such men were few. The oracle was in demand:

> I know those who submit, with a childlike docility, to the Najoom's prediction. If Najoom says it is not proper for Nuwaub [Nawab] Sahib, or his Begum, to eat, to drink, to sleep, to take medicine, to go from home, to give away or accept a gift, or any other action which human reason is the best guide to decide upon, Najoom has said it, and Najoom must be right. Najoom can make peace or war, in the family he overrules, at his pleasure; and many are the houses divided against themselves by the wicked influence of a bad man, thus exercising his crafty wiles over the weakness of his credulous master.

The Najoom, she notes tartly, was even more influential than the eunuch, the guardian of the palace harem.

The attraction of astrology among the powerful was explicable in an age when the life of a prince was precarious, vulnerable to disease, personal excess, traumatic familial rivalry and war. Akbar was once taken hostage as a child and dangled over the parapet of Kabul Fort by a vicious uncle, Hakim, to face cannon fire during his sibling war with Humayun. Akbar was saved by fate that day. His mother, Hamida Begum, never trusted her in-laws again. At the age of six, when Akbar was troubled by a bad toothache, his stepmother Bika Begum, also called Hajji Begum, offered him some medicine. Akbar recalled that Hajji Begum loved him beyond description, but his mother still feared that the medicine might be poisoned. Hajji Begum understood. She took some of the medicine herself before rubbing it on the child's teeth.[5]

The credibility of astrology could not have survived without the evidence of events as they unfolded. At the end of his life, Aurangzeb told his son and eventual successor Bahadur Shah that his horoscope, cast by Fazil Khan, had been vindicated by every incident in his life. Aurangzeb warned his potential successors that this massive empire would not last long after his death. Fazil Khan, making his predictions at the height of Mughal glory, foresaw doom in just another generation. Aurangzeb's heirs, he said, would be ignorant, narrow-minded and immature, so prodigal towards some courtiers as to drown them and so harsh towards others as to terrify them. After Aurangzeb, there would be chaos.

This is precisely what happened.

1

Birth of an Empire: The Startling Mystery of a Hideous Face

THE BIRTH OF JALALUDDIN Muhammad Akbar at six minutes past one in the morning of 15 October 1542 is convincing evidence of Mughal faith in the cosmic control of astrology over destiny.

His father, Nasir al-Din Muhammad Humayun, still styled himself Padishah at the age of thirty-four, but it was a forlorn gesture to past glory for the illusory comfort of a dwindling band of loyalists. Once the monarch of a rising Mughal realm, Humayun had become a hunted fugitive since 1540, when the Afghan ruler of Bengal, Farid Khan, more familiar as Sher Shah Suri, defeated him in the Battle of Kannauj and became king of a realm from Bengal to Punjab.

Driven into the deserts of Sindh, the destitute and desperate Humayun had found temporary sanctuary in the Umarkot Fort of a Sodha Rajput chieftain, Rana Prasad Singh. Humayun's young wife Hamida Banu was heavily pregnant. Her labour pangs started when Humayun was encamped some 30 miles away in Thatta on a punitive raid designed to improve his parlous finances rather than his political fortunes.

Humayun had left his personal astrologer, Maulana Chand, at the birthplace to keep an accurate record of the time of birth, from which would emerge the horoscope. 'When the royal banners set forth from the fortress of

Umarkot,' writes Abul Fazl, 'Maulana Chand, the astrologer, who had great skill and knowledge of the astrolabe and the details of star catalogues and casting horoscopes, was attached to Her Majesty's court for the purpose of ascertaining the time of felicity and marking precisely the hour of birth.'[1]

Maulana Chand's instructions were specific. The astrologer was commanded by Humayun to determine the ascendant at the precise time of the child's birth. The maulana kept a beady watch on news from the bedchamber. As night fell on 14 October and the queen's labour pains intensified, midwives began their ministrations. Maulana Chand became frantic. It was too early, he insisted. His agitation kept rising. He wanted the royal birth postponed to a time later that night when an extremely rare and auspicious conjunction of stars, of a kind that happened but once in a millennium, would take place. He insisted that the present time was inauspicious, but that a moment would come a few hours later, the likes of which did not come for thousands of years. He began to plead: could the birth be delayed?

The women scoffed at this fatuous suggestion. The act of nature was a command of God. Such things did not happen by choice. What good would it do to worry?

Maulana Chand had a startling, ingenious inspiration. Suddenly, in the dark of the evening, he took a local midwife with hideous looks to Hamida Banu's bed and shoved her face through the curtain. The historian Abul Fazl is amazed by what transpired. The shock of seeing this face in the dark had an immediate impact on Hamida Banu. The urgency of nature ceased. The labour pains stopped.

One crisis had passed, but another hovered. Maulana Chand was assuaged as the ill-omened hour passed but was soon afflicted by a second, worse worry. What if the queen slept through the moment of destiny chosen by the stars? As this preferred time approached, Maulana Chand wanted the queen to be aroused from her slumber. The midwives snubbed him. The queen, titled Her Highness Maryam Zamani, was sleeping after having suffered greatly. It would not be appropriate to wake her. God's will would take its course.

God's will was written in the stars. No sooner had Maulana Chand made this plea than the queen awoke with birth pangs. Her child, described as the unique pearl of the caliphate, appeared.

Maulana Chand sent the horoscope he had drawn to Humayun. His calculations were based on the *Zij-i-Gurkani*, a star catalogue compiled by Ulugh Beg Mirza in Samarkand in the early 15th century. The fixed signs (*thabit*) were Taurus, Leo, Scorpio and Aquarius; the tropical (*mimqalib*) signs were Aries, Cancer, Libra and Capricorn; and the bicorporal (*dhu-jasadayn*) were Gemini, Virgo, Sagittarius and Pisces. Using technical language that would be understood by Humayun, an accomplished astronomer, Maulana Chand wrote that though Virgo was a bicorporal sign, partially fixed and partially tropical, the stability of the ascendant could be ascertained by scrutiny in two respects: first, the segment of the ascendant was in the seventh degree of the first third of the sign, indicating stability; second, the sign had elements attributed to the earth, promising longevity of power on the throne.

It was bold, if not audacious, to promise a resurrection of the empire under a newborn infant at a time when the father had become hunted quarry. Maulana Chand was, however, seeing stars, literally. His optimism was infinite. In his analysis, the harmonious influence of two great lucky stars, Mercury and Jupiter, had blessed the baby with intelligence, knowledge, perspicacity and shrewdness. The regent (*sahib* or master) of the ascendant, Mercury, functioned as a greater lucky star in harmony with Jupiter, also a star of great fortune, which became luckier in conjunction with another star of good fortune. The coalescence in the skies had given the infant perfect intelligence and knowledge, which would solve problems of religion and state with wisdom. The child's life would never be dull. Felicitous Venus had come in the ascendant, ensuring joy and success.

Jupiter would ensure a high-minded commitment to justice, deep faith, an honest nature and leadership that ensured prosperity for the people until the final days of the child's life. The position of Mercury ensured that the child would achieve lofty heights but keep company with men of high intelligence, knowledge and great natural ability. Scholars, sages and wise men of every group would attend his court, and skilled persons would leave their homelands to live in his empire. The child would lay the foundations of lofty buildings, surpassing kings of the past, and spend his time in those palaces rejoicing in various delights.

The Sun, in the third house of a fixed sign, which bestowed order on world affairs, had emerged from descent and was heading towards exaltation. It would ensure marching armies with victorious banners that brought might and glory. Mars, the planet of war, was in the hyleg of the ascendant, ensuring the triumph of world-traversing armies.

The Moon was waxing, which meant good health, physical power and increasing fortune. The eighth house, Aries, with its regent Mars, offered divine protection from danger. The regent of the ninth house, Venus, positioned in the ascendant, was guardian of long journeys, which would increase territory.

There was some bad news. Scorpio, in the third house, indicated scorpion-like relatives, which indeed became apparent soon after the birth as the child was in greater danger from his uncles in Kabul and Kandahar than from political foes. However, with Saturn to help, relatives would be led by infelicity into the valley of perdition and destruction.

Sagittarius ensured success in ventures and adventures, while Aries was a sign of many children. The house of wealth and fortune was in the tenth angle, with Mercury and Jupiter in trine. The native would command the treasure houses of the age. The Dragon's Tail in the twelfth house would destroy all enemies.

Maulana Chand could hardly ask for more from the future. Akbar's vast empire, created by a combination of continuous military victory and peaceful co-option, brought stability to a fractious subcontinent for nearly 150 years. His personal reputation was burnished by wise conduct, shrewd insight and intelligent decisions. No court could claim a better conclave of intellectuals. His legacy includes landmark architecture in Agra, Delhi, Fatehpur Sikri and Lahore.

The notional queen at Umarkot Fort rose to become one of the most powerful women during her son's reign, lauded as Her Highness Maryam Makani Hamida Banu Begum, a saint of her time, mistress of her age, lamp of her family, proud pearl of fortune, angel of holy characteristics, purity of the earth and time, a wave from the ocean of timelessness, proud pearl of fortune and chastity of the world and religion. Being the mother of an emperor has its literary rewards. Hamida Banu, who was born into a Shia family, lived until 1604, or just a year before her son's death, and was a powerful influence in the court.

Akbar never forgot his debt to his birthplace. According to the Sindhi poet Shah Abdul Latif Bhittai's *Risalo*, the emperor exempted the people of Tharpakar and Umarkot from all taxes.

A painting of the birth in Umarkot reflects the astrologer's belief in preordained glory. The caption reads: 'The Rising of the Greatest Luminary and Luckiest Star in the Firmament of Felicity, that is, the birth of His Imperial Majesty the Shadow of God.' The artist depicts in descending panels a shrouded Hamida Banu with her newborn as castanets and tambourines announce the good news. A bearded Maulana Chand, his turbaned head bowed, is seen writing the horoscope. Humayun hears the joyous news from his courtier Tardi Beg, while men sway to music. Separately, women dance in the ladies' quarters.

Abul Fazl expands the remit of poetic licence: jasmine-cheeked, laughing girls with silvery breasts dressed in purple danced to the incantations of melodic singers, while dulcimer players from Khurasan stole the hearts of those difficult to please. In less lyrical real life, a fast-paced rider set off from Umarkot after Akbar's birth towards Humayun's camp. An ageing servant, Mihtar Sumbul, saw the approaching messenger and predicted good news. Humayun promised to make Mihtar commander of a thousand horse if it was. The indigent emperor prostrated before God in gratitude when he learnt that a son had been born. Mihtar was given the title of Saffdar Khan.

Humayun, an expert in astrolabes, believed in astrology. The official historian praises Humayun's expertise in the mathematical sciences, comparing his insightful mind to Alexander's mirror and Jamshed's world-revealing cup. Humayun made his own calculations and found them in conformity with Maulana Chand as well as other astrologers who were consulted later. When naming his son 'Akbar', he balanced the elements in the letters: *a* was fiery, *k* was aqueous, *b* was aerial and *r* was terrestrial.

In his history of the dynasty, Abul Fazl does not evade discomforts in the Humayun narrative, beginning with his catastrophic defeat in the Battle of Kannauj against

Sher Shah in 1540, which destroyed Mughal power. Abul Fazl's logic is plainer than his prose. When the workshop of destiny prepares to award high honours, it first tests the potential beneficiary with extreme trials and tribulations. Humayun suffered because destiny was due to compensate him with a great gift of sublime fortune. Misfortune also averted the evil eye.

The evil eye belonged to a tradition older than Islam.

The Goddess Alanqoa

Akbar, asserts Abul Fazl, was blessed with the divine ray of light from the Tengri-shaman Mother Goddess Alanqoa, laying claim to the seed of a polytheistic ancestor. Alanqoa was a feminine icon of eastern Turkic Khans, divinity in human manifestation, a fountain of miracles, mother of world-conquerors, ancestor of Genghis Khan and Amir Taimur, and, through them, to Akbar. Praise for her is extravagant. Her physical and spiritual beauty was matched by her wisdom. Friend and foe alike believed that she was a great, wise and God-fearing lady. She was married to her cousin Dobun Bayan, ruler of Mongolia, but he died, and Alanqoa became the monarch of her nation.

She was also a virgin mother, like Mary, the mother of Jesus:

> One night she, who had been nourished by divine light, was resting in bed, when suddenly a magnificent light shed its rays into her tent. The light entered her mouth, and she became pregnant by the light, just like Mary, the daughter of Amram. God be praised![2]

Abul Fazl dismisses doubt about a virgin birth with the Quranic explanation for Jesus's nativity: if you can accept the birth of Adam without father or mother, why should it be difficult to accept the birth of Jesus without a father? It is up to God to create, howsoever the means.

Alanqoa, the queen of chastity, knew that cynics might question claims of divine blessing. She asked her nobles to place a watch of devout men as she went into her tent. Suddenly, in the darkness, a blazing light like the ray of the shining moon came down, exactly as she had predicted. The nobles were perplexed until they began to believe.

Alanqoa had three sons: Buqun Qataqi, Bughutu Salji and Bodhonchar Qa'an. They were called Niru'un, or born of light, and considered the greatest of the Mongols. Bodhonchar Qa'an (Khan) was Genghis Khan's ancestor nine generations removed; Akbar was Genghis Khan's descendant.

Alanqoa was crucial to Akbar's cosmic identity. Pride in this heritage was proclaimed in official history, and this was never denied or diluted by any successor. It was not designed to please the orthodox, and it did not.

Humayun's circumstances in 1542, when Akbar was born, taunted such expectations. He was bankrupt, forced to borrow money at exorbitant interest rates from a noble in his own entourage, Tardi Beg. His single invaluable possession was a fabulous diamond seized from Ibrahim Lodi's treasury in Agra after Babur's victory in 1526. Wisely, Humayun kept the jewel on his person. It would soon pay rich and transformative dividends.

Noblesse oblige had its demands, even in straitened circumstances. Jouher, Humayun's faithful *aftabchi*, or ewer-bearer, tells the poignant story. The forlorn emperor asked for 200 *shahrukhi*s, a silver hand-armour (*dastwana*) and a pod of musk left in Jouher's care. The money and armour were gone. Humayun called for a china plate, broke the musk pod and distributed it among his principal followers, saying that this was all he could afford on the birth of his son. But, he added, his son's fame would expand across the world like the perfume that now filled the place where they were seated.

Babur introduced the flat silver coin called *shahrukhi*, first minted by the Timurid ruler Shah Rukh in the 15th century, to India. Its value can be measured by this transaction: Humayun made an adversary pay one *shahrukhi* for a camel in Sindh and five for a horse. Akbar replaced this currency with the Indian rupee.

Maulana Chand compared Akbar's chart with that of his paternal ancestor Amir Taimur and found it better because the power of Mars was more potent. Akbar would not only enjoy magnificence of conquest and power, but the glory would increase the longer he lived. Abul Fazl pays fulsome tribute to Qutbuddin Amir Taimur Gurkan as the exalted person born on the 25th of Shaban in the year 736 (8 April 1336), the Year of the Monkey, under the ascendant of Capricorn, outside the Iranian city of Kish.

As Timurids, Mughals traced their lineage to Alanqoa; as Muslims, they were the children of Adam.

Adam: The First Horoscope

If logic rules, astrology must begin with Adam, the father of humankind in the Abrahamic faiths. In Abul Fazl's historiography, Adam was created 7,000 years earlier. But even God's creation had a horoscope; Adam came into being when the first degree of Capricorn corresponded with the eastern horizon, along with Saturn. Jupiter was in Pisces, Mars in Aries, the Moon in Leo, the Sun and Mercury in Virgo, and Venus in Libra. He describes Adam as tall and handsome, with curly hair and a wheaten complexion. Abul Fazl repeats the Biblical assertion that Eve was born from Adam's right side but is querulous about some claims made on behalf of the first man. He wonders whether Adam was actually the father of 41 children and 40,000 offspring, although nothing admittedly was beyond divine power.

He repeats a view prevalent in the subcontinent that Adam landed in Ceylon (Sri Lanka) after he was expelled from Paradise and, after his death, was buried on the mountain still called Adam's Peak or Adam's Footprint after an illness of twenty-one days. Eve died soon after and was buried beside her husband by their son Seth. Noah took their coffins into his ark during the great flood and re-interred them either in Jerusalem or Najaf.

Noah preserved life, but knowledge survived through Pythagoras, a Greek, and Hermes Trismegistus, the Egyptian builder of Pharaonic Memphis. Abul Fazl quotes a Hermes dictum: truth in the time of anger, charity in the time of need and forgiveness when in power. Noah's eldest son, Japheth, was the father of Turks and Mongols.

Japheth clearly believed in gender empowerment. He left a sword for his sons. The rest of his possessions went to his daughters.

The Mughals did not call themselves Mughal. They preferred *silsila-i-gurkaniyya*, or the chain of sons-in-law; *gurkan* is a derivative of the Mongolian word *guregen* for son-in-law. Genghis and Taimur, acknowledged as the greatest conquerors since Alexander, believed in astrology. Genghis ruled over some 5 million square miles; his heirs would extend this to nearly 12 million square miles. Taimur brought over 2 million contiguous square miles under his sway. The Mughals used the patrilineal honorific Mirza, a variation of *amirzadeh*, or son of an *amir*, rather than Khan.

Faith in astrology was prevalent when Genghis Khan was born. His father, Sughuchijin, believed that his son, named Tamujin at birth, would conquer the world for the stars said so: his ascendant was Libra. All seven planets were in that sign with the Dragon's Head in the third house and the Dragon's Tail in the ninth.

Abul Fazl mentions that when Genghis became leader of his nation and the Niru'un tribe in 1185–1186, the seven planets were also in Libra. Success, however, was not immediate; there were long periods of fugitive existence before the fulfilment of the prophecy. As Fazl remarks, a leader has no companion but his shadow.[3]

Genghis Khan's radical great law, Yasa, was designed to ensure obedience, unity and justice. It permitted freedom of faith, banned slavery, gave widows a share of battlefield booty, decreed every child legitimate whether from wife or concubine, forbade sale of women, stopped dowry, protected animals and ensured that people shared their food with travellers. His innovative military formations like Moving Bush, Lake [charging in waves] and Chisel (narrow in front, deep at back) helped the Mongols conquer wherever they advanced. Armies were disciplined by punitive measures and regimented into squads of 10 (*arban:* six archers and four lancers), 100 (*zagun*), 1,000 (*mingam*) and 10,000 (*tumen*). They conquered wherever they went.

Genghis Khan's ferocious whirlwind destroyed the old order, emptied thriving cities of people, knowledge, civilisation and trade, and drove millions of terrified refugees to whichever sanctuary they thought was beyond Mongol reach. Their rule spread from China and Korea through Turkistan to the Qipchak Steppes north of the Caspian, north to Russia, and west through Persia and Iraq to the boundaries of Egypt. The missing link was India.

Genghis Khan reached but did not cross the Indus. His successors tried. In 1299, Delhi's Sultan Alauddin Khilji (1266–1316) crushed a Mongol army of over 2,00,000 troops at Kili and repelled a second invasion on 30 December 1305. A third Mongol incursion in 1306 was driven back by Malik Kafur on the Ravi River in Punjab. Taimur reached Delhi in 1398, turned the city into a graveyard, and then returned to Samarkand with immeasurable treasure and talent, including craftsmen who helped build the magnificent structures of cities like Samarkand and Bukhara.

The Mughals achieved what their fabled ancestors did not: they ruled from Delhi.

2

The Tablet of Divine Secrets

THE CREDIBILITY OF ASTROLOGY has a single measure: belief in the stars withers unless sustained by subsequent events.

Humayun, whose academic interests included astronomy and astrology, consulted a wide range of practitioners of astrology, inviting 'constant attendees at the hidden gathering' to 'share heavenly secrets' on the basis of 'their calculations of the stars and conjunctions [and] a catalogue of influences on length of life and height of success, as will be recorded in summary'.[1] The 'best astrologer in India' was 'an attendant at the royal threshold'.[2] Abul Fazl was confident that 'what the astrologers of India' said about the infant Akbar was true.

Jotik Rai was the title of the royal astrologer. Akbar made it an official position in court, with a remit that made him influential. Jotik Rai calculated that the near-miraculous revival of Humayun from desolation to restoration was a direct consequence of his son Akbar's birth: 'The regent of the fourth house, Mars, occurs in the fifth house: the Native's glorious father will receive divine assistance through the Native's most noble existence, and his exalted children will live long and have great renown.'[3] 'Native' is astro-speak for the subject of the horoscope. This is precisely what happened despite the widespread conviction after Humayun's fall in 1540 that Mughal rule was irrevocably over.

Jotik Rai mapped Akbar's ascendant as Leo rather than Virgo, citing several 'principles from the books of sages of India'.[4] Gulbadan Begum, Humayun's sister, concurred; trust in astrology ran across the family. She writes: 'The moon was in Leo. It was of very good omen that the birth was in a fixed sign, and the astrologers said a child so born would be fortunate and long-lived.' She used the plural 'astrologers'.[5]

Abul Fazl attributed Humayun's defeat in 1540 to astral signs: the Sun had entered Cancer at the time, which was not propitious. He absolved the vanquished emperor of responsibility for the defeat with some post-mortem consolation:

> The emperor himself charged the foe twice and engaged in action. Although it is not customary for a monarch to participate in battle, how could one follow rules in such a test of bravery? In this engagement two spears broke in the emperor's hand as he showed his mettle.[6]

Humayun's force had become an 'army of hypocrites', the amirs were cowards and his brothers had betrayed their king.[7] The court historian weighs in with some excessive justification for misfortune. When the 'workshop of destiny' wanted to elevate someone, it first sent troubles to elevate the joys of future success.

William Erskine, a British historian of the first Mughal period, blames Humayun's failure on his mercurial character and unreserved faith in astrology: 'He was a man of great quickness of parts, but volatile, thoughtless and unsteady. Personally of distinguished bravery, he was occasionally successful in war, without possessing the higher talents of a general.' The Victorian in Erskine cringes at Humayun's 'astronomical knowledge', which was directed chiefly to the frivolous or pernicious doctrines of astrology and the occult sciences; and the course of his policy, as well as the actions of his ordinary life, was too often regulated by an absurd and childish attention to signs, omens and superstitious observances.[8]

The rational argument against astrology, apart from its dismissal as a pseudo-science, was that it induced fatalism. Erskine narrates an interesting legend from Humayun's youth. Once, while hunting in the company of his tutor, Humayun decided to check his future through the names of the first three people they encountered. They were Murad (literally, 'wish'), Doulat ('domain') and Saadet ('success'). A more careful look at the omens would have revealed the harsh edge: Murad was old and decrepit, Doulat was driving an ass loaded with firewood, and Saadet was tending cattle.

For three years after his defeat in the Battle of Kannauj, Humayun, chased across the plains from the Ganges to the Indus, was often on the brink of death. For another ten, he was trapped in equally dangerous sibling wars across Afghanistan. He suffered deprivation, desolation and poverty, just out of the reach of adversaries who would have killed him without hesitation. A singular belief kept him hopeful through the worst troughs of despair—that the birth of a son would revive the glory he had inherited and lost. Humayun did not possess the timbre of empire-builders. His personal preference lay in ancient science; his sensibility was velvet rather than steel. His survival required infinite good fortune, which is what destiny provided.[9]

If Jotik Rai had been wrong, Mughal rule would be a forgotten asterisk in the history of India, rather than a substantive chapter of it.

Goddess Alanqoa and the Colossal Elephant

On 26 June 1540, Humayun reached Lahore. Amidst depressing perplexities, he had a dream on 9 July 1540:

> [He] placed his head upon a pillow to rest and stretched out on a couch of relaxation. Suddenly he saw on the stage of a dream, which is the private quarters of the unseen realm, that God would grant him a renowned offspring, from whose felicitous forehead would shine rays of magnificence ... they announced that the glorious name of that divine product would be that with which today pulpits and decrees are graced and with which the face of *dirhems* and *dinars* blossom.[10]

Humayun's sister Gulbadan Begum records this vision in her history, which she completed in 1587. The venerable dream figure was dressed in green from head to foot, carried a staff, and told the despondent Humayun, 'Be of good cheer; do not grieve ... The most high God will give you a son who shall be named Jalaluddin Muhammad Akbar.' Humayun asked the apparition to identify itself. 'The Colossal Elephant [*Zandeh-fil*] Ahmad of Jam,' it replied, adding, 'Your son will be of my lineage.'[11]

Shaikh Ahmad ibn Abolhasan Jami-e-Torshizi (1048–1141) of Torbat-e-Jam was a scholar, mystic and poet with dark blue eyes. He was nicknamed the Colossal Elephant for his height, physique and reputation for straight, even gruff, language. His prophecy in Humayun's dream became a talisman for the fugitive king, who exclaimed on waking up, 'Praise God! The lamp of our royal house has been lit ... In my state between sleep and wakefulness it seemed that a bright star rose from that direction,' indicating west. The star brightened the world. 'It is the embodied light of my offspring, and to the extent that the surface of the dusty earth upon which the world-illuminating light shed its rays comes under his control and domination, it will flourish with the light of justice.'[12]

Abul Fazl added a parallel source of this mystic light: the pre-Islamic Tengri Shaman mother-deity revered by Mughals. The light dazzled 'from the loins of that Venus of fortune, Alanqoa'.[13]

Ahmad of Jam's caveat in Humayun's dream meant that the mother of this glorious child would have to be Ahmad's descendant. It took a coincidence to resolve this conundrum. In January 1541, Humayun was camped in the gardens of the ruler of Thatta, Shah Hussain Sultan, in Bhakkar on the western bank of the Indus, when he crossed the caravan of his twenty-two-year-old brother Hindal, travelling north with their stepmother Dildar Begum, Babur's fourth wife. Humayun noticed a beautiful young lady, fourteen-year-old Hamida Banu, daughter of Mir Baba Dost, in their entourage and inquired if she was married. She was unwed. According to Jouher, Humayun's faithful servitor who remained loyal through the years of anxiety, Hindal flared up when Humayun asked for her hand.

Gulbadan Begum offers more details. Hindal was convinced that his destitute brother did not have enough money for a decent *mehr*, the mandatory dower for the bride, essential in a Muslim marriage contract. 'I look on the girl,' Hindal said, 'as a sister and child of my own. Your Majesty is a king. Heaven forbid there should not be a proper alimony, and that so a cause of annoyance should arise.' Humayun was upset to hear this.

Dildar Begum hosted a dinner to enable a meeting between Humayun and Hamida. She refused the invitation, saying, 'If it is to pay my respects, I was exalted by paying my respects the other day. Why should I come again?' When a second emissary was sent, she replied, 'To see kings once is lawful; a second time it is forbidden. I shall not come.'

Dildar Begum tried persuasion: 'After all, you will marry someone. Better than a king, who is there?'

The spirited Hamida had a superb riposte: 'Oh yes, I shall marry someone; but he shall be a man whose collar my hand can touch, and not one whose skirt it does not reach.'[14]

She kept Humayun waiting for forty days. Finally, writes Gulbadan, 'at mid-day [in September 1541] ... His Majesty took the astrolabe into his own blessed hand and, having chosen a propitious hour, summoned Mir Abul-baqa and ordered him to make fast the marriage bond'. Humayun would not take such a major step without checking the auspices with the astrolabe. Conscious of his brother's taunt, he sent the equivalent of 2,00,000 rupees in 'ready money' as dower.[15]

Fortune, notes Abul Fazl in another context, is that which falls into one's lap. Shaikh Ahmad turned out to be Hamida Banu's ancestor.

Stories of divine benediction began to circulate during her pregnancy. While the royal nomads were travelling through the Sindh desert, Hamida Banu asked for a mango when she saw a grove. Her brother Khwaja Muazzam saw a dazzling reflection from her brow when he gave her the fruit and asked, 'Have you hung mirrors on your forehead?' She had not. Looking closely, he felt that her bright forehead was 'shining with a divine light. Perplexed and astounded by that eternal light, he related the incident to several intimates at court'.[16] Hamida Banu's later title would be H.H. Maryam Makani, the name an equivalent to Mary, the mother of Jesus, whose virgin birth is recognised by the Quran.

During their journey, they had been forced 'to eat the seeds and fruit or berries of trees which grew in the neighbouring jungle'. Just before the child was due, Hamida Banu had a craving for pomegranate. All that attendants could find in the desert was a trader selling barley. While showing them his wares, 'suddenly a luscious pomegranate fell from the sack to the surprise and delight of all'. Abul Fazl calls this a miracle and a happy omen, for 'after suffering much difficulty and lack of water, they arrived at the mighty fortress that was the rising point of the star of magnificence and casket of the gem of fortune'.[17] This was the fort of Umarkot.

In another astonishing incident, which reinforced belief in divine protection, Humayun woke up one morning to discover that his sword had been half drawn from his scabbard. Something had alarmed the thief before he could kill and rob the king.[18]

The Lahore dream kept Humayun buoyant:

> Very soon, a fresh flower will bloom in the garden of the caliphate. One nurtured by the light of fortune will come from the inner recesses of magnificence into the realm of existence, and by the star of his magnitude the hearts of enemies to his fortune will wither on the vine. This exalted dynasty will attain glory through his aura; indeed, the dark corners of the world will gain a new brightness and light from his world-illuminating rays.[19]

The omens began to change. Having been rejected or threatened by almost every principality during this exile, Humayun was nervous as he led his motley band towards the citadel of the Sodha Rajput prince Rana Prasad on 22 August 1542. He was palpably relieved when the Rana's brother came out to receive him with provisions and 'a polite message, that the day was not a fortunate one', so it would be better to meet the Rana on the following day. No one argued with the stars. They met as arranged. Rana Prasad wanted a trade-off: military assistance in the conquest of the adjacent districts, Thatta and Bhiker, then in the possession of Shah Hussain Arghun.

The emperor was literally without clothes, with just one dress left. Humayun was bankrupt. Gulbadan Begum describes their bleak situation:

> The treasury was empty. Tardi Beg Khan [a noble in the group] had a great deal of money, and the Emperor, having asked him for a considerable loan, lent 80,000 *ashrafis* at the rate of two in ten [20 per cent]. His Majesty portioned out this money to the army. He bestowed sword belts and *cap-a-pie* [head-to-foot] dresses on the [Rana] and his sons. Many people bought fresh horses here.[20]

Humayun 'waited for a fortunate hour' before he left on 11 October 1542 for his campaigns to honour the pact with the Rana,[21] at the head of 7,000 troops. He established camp beside a large pond in Jun, a town with good water, corn, fruit and gardens.

Steps on the Starpath

Two years and four months after Humayun's dream in Lahore, Hamida Banu gave birth to Akbar, the first Mughal ruler to be born in India. Hamida joined her husband on 22 November 1542 at an 'auspicious hour'. Jalaluddin (Akbar) was thirty-five days old when Humayun first saw him. Jouher says Humayun described him as Badruddin, or the full moon of faith, because the child had been born on the night of the full moon. Predictably, Humayun saw greatness in the newborn, the seventh generation after their formidable ancestor Sahib-i-Qiran (one born under a conjunction of Jupiter and Venus), Amir Taimur.

In 1543, 'the dark corners of the world' were still fraught with life-threatening peril. The alliance between Humayun and the Sodha ruler collapsed when Tardi Beg and Khwaja Ghazi quarrelled with Rana Prasad.

Humayun was soon abandoned by the other local zamindars. A sliver of relief came when the redoubtable Bairam Khan, the 'foremost grandee' of the Mughal court, rejoined Humayun in April. Bairam Khan had suffered great humiliation during the long retreat from Kannauj. In one incident, farmers 'stripped him of his clothing and beat him with a stick saying, "Go on dancing, you Mughal donkey," and the accomplished man did so by swaying his hands and feet, saying "Alas! My destiny"'.[22] Bairam Khan's negotiating skills came to Humayun's immediate rescue. He established a rapprochement with Shah Arghun, who gave the Mughals 30 boats, 2,000 loads of grain, 300 horses, 300 camels and 1,00,000 *misqal* in cash to leave. On 10 July 1543, they headed west towards Afghanistan.

Humayun's enemies included his stepbrothers Mirza Kamran and Mirza Askari, sons of Gulrukh Begum, who had ruled Afghanistan since Babur's death a decade earlier. They were justly apprehensive that Humayun would claim primogeniture rights over Kabul. They dismissed their elder brother as an incompetent who had lost Hindustan while he indulged in the illusion that they would obey their father's injunction never to harbour evil intentions towards one another.[23]

They decided to abort Humayun's aspirations in the traditional manner: war. Humayun did not possess the resources for battle. He had no option but to escape once again, this time with Askari bearing down upon his camp. In the winter of 1543, Humayun and Hamida fled in the middle of the night, leaving the infant Akbar behind because the child would not be able to survive an Afghan winter in the open. Hamida told all her attendants to stay back with their son; among them, Maham Agha Anaka would become his fondest and fiercest guardian. Jouher rejoined his master only when confident that the boy would be safe. Humayun's one hope lay in succour and support from a potential ally, the mercurial king of Persia, Shah Tahmasp I.

Astral calculus was part of Akbar's upbringing, including in the choice of a wet nurse. The 'infant of blessed advent' was handed over to the 'hopeful embrace' of his first wet nurse, Jiji Anaka, 'at an auspicious hour'. The wet-nurse roster for the infant included Hindus and Muslims: Maham Agha Anaka, Daya Bhawal, Fakhrunnissa Anaka, Bhawal Anaka, Hakima, Koki Anaka, Bibi Rupa, Khaldar Anaka and Bicha Jan Anaka. This was a conscious decision: 'Herein lies the divine wisdom of inducing various natures through a variety of classes in order that the regal body might reach various stages and be acquainted with differing types of divine manifestation.'[24] All mothers' milk was equal, a powerful lesson.

Even in that deep gloom, Humayun was sure that 'nothing untoward would happen' to his son as he was 'under the protection of divine favour'.[25] His confidence was not misplaced. Askari gave the child protection when Maham Anaka, with her ward in her arms, appeared before him after Humayun had left. They were allotted a room at the top of Kandahar Fort, which they reached on 15 December 1543. Askari's wife Sultan Begum showered the fourteen-month-old Jalaluddin with love.

Abul Fazl cannot resist gilding the lily: 'That intelligent lady served him affectionately. Externally she was keeping him, but inwardly she was putting herself opposite absolute light to receive its brightness, as day by day the glory of greatness shone more brightly from the prince's forehead.' More realistically, his aunts saw in the baby's features a reflection of Babur.

But the love of women goes only so far against the machinations of men. Abul Fazl does not exaggerate when he describes the uncles as Akbar's 'mortal enemies'.[26] An evocative passage on Humayun's dismal years describes what the birth of his son meant to him:

> It has been heard from close confidants of HM Humayun, who were bedecked inwardly and outwardly with truth and righteousness, that when HM Humayun held the horoscope before his gaze and contemplated it, several times it happened that he closed the doors of his privy chamber and danced with joy and whirled around in glee.[27]

Humayun's resurrection was so improbable that it can only be attributed to the inexplicable. His material wealth as he headed to Persia was a small bag of jewels, which he wore around his neck. They included the fabulous diamond he had seized from the treasury when Agra fell in 1526. Humayun guarded the precious stone like his life, waiting for destiny to offer a bargain that was worth its value.

He crossed the frontier and entered Persia through Seistan with flickering hope, ready to claim the pilgrim's right to travel unmolested towards Mecca if he was denied asylum.

Persian Monarchs: The Khichri Pact

Shiism became the state faith of Persia in 1501 when Shah Ismail, the founder of the Safavid dynasty, conquered Tabriz and unified a country that had been dismembered and destroyed by repeated invasions. In 1524, his son Tahmasp became Shah at the age of ten.

The expansion of Shia influence in Persia was an acknowledged geopolitical priority because of the empire's continual confrontation with the Sunni Ottoman Caliphate to its west. On the transactional side, it had some positive history with the Mughals. Shah Ismail had once helped Babur, who stamped the names of Shia imams on his coins as implicit homage but went no further. In 1506, Babur married Humayun's mother, Maham Begum, the daughter of Sultan Hussain Mirza of Khorasan in northern Persia. It was assumed that this might make him more sympathetic to the Persian cause. On his part, Humayun had learnt, from adversity, the art of being flexible.

Jouher, who was with Humayun, gives a politically astute and acutely observed account of his Persian sojourn.[28] The initial signs were promising. Kara Sultan Shamla, the governor of Seistan, welcomed his unannounced guest with due hospitality, which included the gift of a horse named Leilet al Qadr ('Night of Power'), commemorating the time when the Prophet Muhammad first received a verse of the Quran during the last days of the month of Ramadan in 610. This, however, meant little more than courtesy. Bairam Khan advised Humayun to send a suitably suppliant letter to the Shah, requesting succour from a ruler who included 'Asylum of the World' among his epithets. Jouher sums up the essence of this letter crisply: 'We arrived in your country and await your royal order.' The letter was replete with compliments.[29]

Fortune, once again ready with a smile, was with Humayun. A complex political calculus began to work in his favour as the Shah pondered over how to deal with the unexpected visitor. If Humayun could be converted into a Shia and helped back to his throne, he would become Persia's eastern bulwark in the conflict against the Ottomans. Shah Tahmasp's *firman* (edict) to the governor of Khorasan on the reception of Humayun runs to nineteen printed pages of the *Akbarnama*.

Humayun was asked to proceed to Meshed Sharif. Here, after three years of hardship, he enjoyed the luxury of being a pampered tourist. In Meshed, where his entourage spent forty days, he played the Shia card with finesse, praying at the shrine of Imam Ali bin Musa.

Some part of his prayer was answered when Tahmasp offered a meeting in Cazvin. Humayun then moved through Nishapur, Subzwar (where he spent another forty days), Bustam and Mesmeh, where a messenger from Afghanistan disclosed that his brother Kamran had begun to punish his (Humayun's) followers. Humayun could do little more than advise patience and promise that 'everything will yet turn out according to our wishes'.[30]

Instructions awaited at the fort to send Bairam Khan, a Shia, for preliminary negotiations in Cazvin.[31] Tahmasp, playing psychological games, ordered the Mughal noble 'to cut off his hair, and wear a Persian cap'. Bairam Khan refused, saying that he took orders from only one king. Tahmasp 'tried to frighten [Bairam Khan] into compliance' by executing some prisoners in his presence. The veteran Mughal was unmoved.[32] Having tested his mettle and found steel, the Persians began negotiations.

Humayun, on reaching Cazvin, was told to rest for three days before an audience with Shah Tahmasp. The governor was his host on the first evening, the *qazi* on the second and city dignitaries on the third. Sam Mirza, Tahmasp's son, presented an unbroken horse and a dress of honour, with a catch. The cap was in the Shia style.[33] Humayun wore the dress but ignored the cap.

Shah Tahmasp insisted that a meeting would take place only if Humayun wore the Persian headwear. Humayun obliged and was welcomed by trumpets while the nobility prostrated themselves before Allah in gratitude. Humayun was given accommodation with the Shah's brother Bahram Mirza, where he took a hot bath, got his hair cut, put on a new dress and 'passed the night in feasting and carousing'.

The Persian king took time before his next move. He was clearly affected by an alternative proposal from Kamran, brought to him by three emissaries named Roshan Beg, Khwaja Ghazi and Sultan Muhammad. Kamran, they said, would be a more effective ally than Humayun, who did not possess the talents of a king. Kamran promised to cede Kandahar to Persia if Humayun was made a prisoner. Delay became a tactic in a carefully calibrated game. Tahmasp eventually sent a large quantity of wood to Humayun with a tough message: if they did not become Shia, the wood would become their funeral pyre. Humayun answered blackmail with dignity, saying that life was in the hands of God and requested permission to proceed towards Mecca.

Yet again Humayun was saved from the abyss by an unforeseen and hidden benefactor. Tahmasp's sister Sultanum Khanum argued persuasively that the Shah had enough enemies: Turks, Uzbeks, Georgians, Russians and more. 'I hear,' she told her brother, 'you are now about to raise up other enemies by your intentions of injuring Muhammad Humayun, whose son and brothers will one day seek revenge. If you will not support him, at least permit him to go away, that he may apply for assistance somewhere else.' The Shah was persuaded: 'My chiefs have been giving me unworthy advice; but what you have suggested is certainly more dignified and praiseworthy.'[34]

Tahmasp invited Humayun for a friendly hunt where he reassured his guest: 'Keep your mind at ease, for I shall very soon send you to your own country in a proper manner. Cazy Jehan [Qazi Jahan; or head priest] will mention certain subjects, to which I request you will pay attention.' The deal was ready but not done. Humayun would have to prove that he had become a Shia. Qazi Jahan brought documents and sensible advice: 'Temporize with your oppressors.'[35] Humayun signed one document and became 'tranquil'.

Gratitude, however, had to weigh more than words. Humayun placed the largest diamond from his bag of jewels in a mother-of-pearl box, added some rubies and diamonds on a tray, and sent them as a gift to the Shah through Bairam

Khan. Abul Fazl chafes that the diamond 'would suffice for the expenses of all realms and climes and two hundred fifty Badakshani rubies'.[36] The Shah was dazzled; his jewellers declared that the diamond was priceless.

Abul Fazl describes the hitch caused by Kamran with oblique delicacy: 'During this felicitous time of royal conjunction, there occurred a clouding of the mind on the part of both rulers on account of some mischief stirred up by troublemakers. It did not last long and was cleared up.'[37] Kamran's emissaries were thrown into a deep pit. To the Shah's puzzled surprise, Humayun interceded on their behalf and asked for clemency. Jouher quotes a line from the Quran: 'He who digs a pit for his neighbour shall fall into it himself.'

The final summit in July 1544 was lavish. Five hundred dishes were cooked each day at the Shah's summer camp in Persepolis. Silken rugs and carpets were spread as far as the eye could see. Horses had gilt saddles, and nobles wore bejewelled swords, daggers and furs of sable, ermine and squirrel. Candlesticks were studded with rubies and pearls. A bottle and goblet were placed before each guest at the meal. Everyone filled their own cup and drank as much as they wished.

The Shah wondered during a convivial conversation whether Humayun would host a dinner 'in the Hindustani manner of cooking'. The main course of Humayun's Indian repast was the ubiquitous khichri, a dish of rice and peas, then unknown in Persia.[38] The Mughal court had a long memory. According to Francois Bernier, Shahjahan served khichri to the Persian ambassador at a formal dinner nearly a hundred years later.[39]

The stars were indelible. The monarchs 'bade each other farewell at an auspicious hour in observation of the finest protocol'.[40] Jouher writes that Tahmasp placed his right hand on Humayun's breast and asked to be excused for any deficiency on his part.

Before he left, Humayun paid homage at a very special shrine, that of Ahmad Jam, the Colossal Elephant, on 29 February 1544. His years of despair seemed on the wane when he entered Afghanistan in late 1544 with a force that exceeded 14,000 men, including 12,000 from the cavalry of the Kizilbish, or Army of the Red Heads. According to a Mughal saying, a battlefield is the banquet carpet of warriors. This time, Humayun had something to serve.

The Lucky Ascendant

Kamran's mood darkened upon hearing the news. His first decision was an order to shift Akbar to Kabul from Kandahar. The child, code-named Mirak, was taken 'in the dead of winter in the midst of snow and rain', accompanied by Kamran's sister Bakshi Banu Begum, Shamshuddin Muhammad (who had saved Humayun's life in Kannauj, now titled Ataka Khan), Maham Anaka and Jiji Anaka.[41] In Kabul, Akbar was placed in the care of a grandaunt, Babur's sister Khanzada Begum.

Kamran was petty and vicious:

> Although the prince had not yet been weaned, Kamran ordered him to be kept from suckling, unaware that one who suckles at the breast of divine favour cannot be harmed by such an act and one under the protection of the one true guardian faces no danger from such thoughts.[42]

The two-year-old had become a hostage in a fratricide.

The progress of fortune seems as inexorable as the hurried pace of misfortune in the route maps of the zodiac. Once, Humayun could get nothing right; now he could do no wrong. Even mistakes, bred in complacency, did not exact too harsh a price.

On 21 March 1545, Humayun launched his bid for power, laying siege to Kandahar 'at an auspicious hour chosen by astrological observation'.[43] The astrologers had got it right. Askari surrendered on 3 September 1545.

Bairam Khan brought Askari, who had woken 'from the sleep of heedlessness' but 'lost his nerve', to Humayun with a sword around his neck, but Humayun forgave Askari on the intercession of the family and 'in the interests of the state'.[44] He entered the city four days later but did not tarry. Abul Fazl explains that the 'chief reason for hastening the conquest of Kabul was a desire to see H.I.M. [Akbar], whom he considered the key to all victories', as had been prophesied.[44] Winter had set in, but 'guided by good fortune and his lucky ascendant, the emperor proceeded toward the capital, Kabul' with 5,000 men and his younger brother Hindal at his side.[45] Askari escaped.

Humayun entered Kabul on the evening of 15 November 1545. He was appalled by the conditions in the fort and city. Humayun sent word to Rayke Begum, one of Babur's widows, to check if there was any dinner. All she had was some beef broth and curry. Humayun berated Kamran for having kept their mothers in such an indigent state. Jouher quotes his master:

> Oh unfortunate Kamran! Was this the mode of your own existence? And did you feed the asylum of chastity on the flesh of cows? What! Could you not afford to keep a few goats for her subsistence? This is not fit food even for the devout persons who wait on the tomb of our father. What! Could not we, his four sons, support his [wife] as he did?[46]

In Kabul, Humayun embraced Akbar for the first time in two years. When Hamida Banu arrived with a group of ladies, he wondered if the three-year-old prince, traumatised by separation from his mother, would recognise her. Akbar went straight to his mother to the applause of the assembled.

The years of separation had not been easy. Abul Fazl describes Humayun's torment during the siege of Kandahar. While in private conversation with intimate companions who were telling stories of champions to test their own mettle, Humayun remembered his son

> with great longing, wondering how he was faring, separated from his friends and in the midst of his enemies. What plans did those unwise, envious malevolents have for that sapling of felicity? With uncertain mind and heart mingled with hope and fear he raised his hands in supplication to the court of divine magnificence, which grants success to the perplexed, and prayed for long life and success for that sapling of the sultanate, and by this means he achieved some relief of his distress.[47]

It was Akbar's horoscope that reassured him.

> [Humayun] asked for the prince's horoscope, which was like a tablet of divine secrets, and after studying it contemplatively he found it indicated health, long life, and success for the prince and devastation of enemies, failure on the part of those who would wish him ill, and the miscarriage of dishonest people's plans. Raising his head in joy, he said, 'Thank God, I am completely satisfied on this score. Hopefully we will soon rejoice in the sight of that infant nourished by divine light, and with the fortune of his ascendant we will triumph over all our enemies.'[48]

Humayun had good reason for dread, for Kamran was infamous for his ruthlessness towards women and children, as Abul Fazl records:

> Mirza Kamran, having unleashed his aggression, acted unspeakably towards the men's children and wives. Muhammad Qasim-Khan Mauji's wife was hanged by her breasts. Since the mirza was sick with rancour and envy, whatever act of opposition he mounted against the emperor actually resulted in rebellion against God.[49]

Children as young as three, five and seven were thrown over the walls.

Humayun's worst fears were realised in 1547. In the spring of 1546, he went to Badakhshan, leaving Kabul unprotected. Kamran, with fresh money and troops, pounced. In February 1547, Humayun mounted his second assault on Kabul's Bala-i-Hissar ('High Fort'), stationing his artillery on Koh-Akabain ('Eagle's Hill'). During a cannonade, Kamran was nearly hit by a stray musket ball when he was on the roof of the fort. Enraged, he ordered Akbar to be held over the ramparts and placed in the direct line of Humayun's fire.

Abul Fazl narrates this crisis:

> In order to protect himself, in his folly, Mirza Kamran placed H.I.M., the bud of the orchard of sovereignty, in the face of cannon fire and held him in a position where it should have been difficult for an ant or a locust to get by without being hit by the imperial artillerymen ... What sort of bestial and demonic rite was this?

Maham Agha Anaka, says Fazl, covered the young Akbar with her body to try and save the child. Humayun's chief of artillery, Sumbul Khan, saw what was happening and silenced his guns.[50]

Gulbadan Begum also records this near-calamity and quotes Humayun as saying, 'Some time or other, if we had used force against the citadel, Mirza Muhammad Akbar would have disappeared.'[51] Such barbarism as Kamran's was rare even in a family that never confused power with sentiment.

Bala Hisar, the ancient fortress in the south of Kabul, fell on 27 April 1546. Kamran fled. The city's poor were fed for eleven consecutive days in thanksgiving. Akbar, the 'recipient of infinite divine favour, went out like luck itself to greet him [Humayun] ... and the emperor found a new light and comfort in his heart from seeing H.I.M. What gift could be greater than for Jacob's eyes to be restored by the sight of Joseph?'[52]

Humayun had ignored Shah Tahmasp's advice: kingdoms cannot be held by hands wearing kid gloves. The gloves came off but never fully. In 1548, Humayun made yet another effort at reconciliation with Kamran, this time through his astrologer, the aptly named Nesyb (literally, 'fate').

His letter said, 'Oh my unkind brother, what are you doing? Every murder that is committed on either side, you will be answerable for at the Day of Judgement: come, and make peace, that mankind may no longer be oppressed by our contest.' Kamran's answer was short: 'He shall obtain the bride of the kingdom who embraces her across the edge of the sharp sword.'[53] Nesyb stepped aside.

Kamran was caught in 1553. Gulbadan ends her memoirs on a dramatic note, as if she could not bear to write more, for Kamran was also her brother: 'When he [Kamran] drew near to Rohtas, the Emperor gave an order to Sayyid Muhammad: "Blind Mirza Kamran in both eyes." The sayyid went at once and did so.'[54]

Jouher describes the price of rebellion: a handkerchief was thrust into Kamran's mouth to prevent his screams from being heard. He was laid down on the ground while his eyes were punctured with a lancet (*neshter*), after which lemon juice and salt were squeezed into the sockets.[55] The blinded Kamran was sent to Mecca, where he died on 5 October 1557 at the age of forty-five. Life was short.

At every milestone, personal or political, Humayun followed the stars. Jalaluddin was four years, four months and four days old when his formal education began under Mullazada Mulla Isamuddin Ibrahim on 20 November 1547. Humayun, 'so aware of heavenly sciences' that he 'knew the details of stars, had selected, in collaboration with expert astrologers, a particular hour, the likes of which does not occur over aeons and lifetimes, for the commencement of the prince's instructions'.[56] This day, too, had been dictated by astrology.

Akbar, having survived all the trauma he had endured early in life, doted on his parents who meant as much to him as he meant to them. He never forgot the love and devotion of his surrogate mothers and those aunts who had showered affection on him during his near-orphan years. Memory preserves what matters. Akbar told Abul Fazl how Maham Anaka had forced Askari to toss his turban on the floor, as was the traditional Afghan custom, when he took his first baby steps, and how he was taken to be blessed at the shrine of Baba Hasan Abdal before his hair was cut for the first time.[57]

Maham Anaka became a powerful figure in Akbar's court and remained so until her death in 1562. In one painting, she is shown sitting just below the king, indicating her hallowed status. His mother, Hamida Banu, was called Padishah Begum, or emperor begum, because she took over as the effective administrator when her son was on campaigns. Arif Qandhari, a contemporary historian, praises her as an equal to Sarah, the wife of Abraham, comparable to Asiah, the wife of the Pharaoh during the time of Joseph, and Bilqis, the queen of Solomon, while lauding her for being as dignified as Khadija, the first wife of the Prophet Muhammad.[58] This may be melodramatic but conveys the awe in which she was held. Qandhari adds that Akbar was nicknamed Saad Akbari or 'child of Jupiter'.

The Zodiac Tent

With Kabul under control by 1553, India beckoned. This would have been foolhardy but for yet another improbable sequence of events: within one generation, the formidable kingdom of Humayun's bête noire, Sher Shah Suri, had collapsed.

Sher Shah died on 13 May 1545 from a gunpowder explosion in the fort of Kalinjar at the venerable age of seventy-three. His successors frittered away an impressive legacy. Such was the ensuing chaos that even a radical usurper nearly succeeded: 'Khawass Khan, one of Sher Shah's slaves, who made himself renowned by foolishness and idle talk and by appropriating people's possessions, by giving away the world's treasures to the lowest of the low, and by persuading common riffraff to support his rule'.[59] We are not told much more about this premature Lenin.

As always, Humayun checked the stars: in mid-November 1554, he 'turned his reins toward the realm of Hindustan at an hour so auspicious that the motions of the heavenly bodies would be proud'. The moment had to be exceptional for such an ambitious campaign. With him was his son, 'now twelve years and eight months old'. Bairam Khan followed a little later with the bulk of the army. Humayun vowed to remain vegetarian until victory in Delhi.[60]

Lahore fell without serious opposition on 24 February 1555. A series of engagements at Dipalpur, Machhiwara and Sirhind ended in a comprehensive Mughal victory on 22 June 1555. The Suri commander Sikandar Khan fled to the Sivalik Hills. Humayun took the open road to Delhi, while Akbar was ordered to pursue the remnants of the Afghan army, his first independent command.

Humayun reached Delhi on the first day of Ramadan, 20 July 1555, and was re-anointed three days later as king. He celebrated with a bout of hunting, felled a *nilgai* with his sword but dried the meat because he had extended his vow to remain vegetarian to the end of Ramadan.

The influence of stars on Humayun's administration is quite remarkable. His crown had 'two openings, each of which looked like number 7', for he considered seven to be a lucky number; two 7s made 77, which was the numerical equivalent of the word *izz*, meaning power. In the Qanun-i-Humayuni ('Law of Humayun'), three golden arrows symbolising felicity, fortune and joy were a metaphor for good governance. Felicity represented justice and religion; fortune was determined by management of the nobility, bureaucracy and salaries; and joy was the acquisition of all things pertaining to 'refinement and magnificence'. His government was divided into twelve departments. The twelfth quiver, of 24-carat gold, dealt with royal interests. Every wazir was enjoined to serve God, the state and the people. Corruption and selfishness were unacceptable. There were four ministers for the four elements: fire, air; water and land. Fire was the realm of weapons and artillery; air dealt with accommodation and transport; water included supervision of canals and rivers; and the land minister held the agriculture portfolio.

Stars were the centrepiece of symbolism. Humayun's court, carpets, tents and seating arrangements were designed around the zodiac. He would dress in the colour of the planet of the day: yellow on Sundays, green on Mondays 'and so forth'. Tents were central to Mughal life, from the barqah, which could accommodate up to 10,000 people and took 1,000 men a week to erect, to the sarapardah, which was 150 yards by 150 yards, with 16 divisions.

> [Humayun invented] a tent with twelve parts, like the number of constellations in the zodiac. Every constellation contained apertures so that the lights of the stars of fortune could shine through. There was another tent like the sphere of spheres, which surrounds the sphere of the fixed stars, and it surrounded the first tent on all sides. Just as the sphere of spheres is devoid of designs, this tent too was devoid of apertures.
>
> He created a round carpet of pleasure containing circles for the celestial spheres and the elemental planets. The first circle, attributed to Atlas, was white; the second, blue; the third, black for Saturn; the fourth, sandalwood for Jupiter; the fifth, ruby-red for Mars; the sixth, golden for the Sun; the seventh, light green for Venus; and the eighth, violet for Mercury. The ninth circle was white for the Moon, after which came the orbs of fire, air, earth and water, followed by the seven climes.
>
> The emperor himself would choose the golden circle, and there he would grace the throne of the caliphate. Every class of person would sit in the circle to which his category assigned him. For example, Indian amirs would sit in the circle of Saturn, and sayyids and the ulema would sit in the circle of Jupiter.[61]

Abul Fazl calls Humayun's unique ideas 'inventions'. They included an 'arrangement of shops and markets on boats' on the Jamuna for grandees travelling by river from Delhi to Agra, a garden on the river, a moveable bridge and a portable wooden palace of three stories which could be dismantled and assembled.

Humayun foretold his own death. He had frequent premonitions. When Akbar told Maham Anaka that he had dreamt 'that someone was pulling his black forelock', word reached Humayun, who 'calmly informed H.I.M. of his own approaching death and consoled him'. He set aside a seven-day supply of opium, wrapped it in a paper, and told his servants that this was all he would need for his remaining days. On the morning of Friday, 24 January 1556, he consumed the last four pellets with some rose water. At noon, he told those around him, 'On this day a great injury will happen to one of the great men of our age, and he will pass away from this world.'

He conversed with high nobles who had returned from different parts of the realm and then went to the roof with 'a group of mathematicians, for he suspected that Venus would rise that night and wanted to observe it'. He also intended 'when Venus rose and an auspicious hour came, to hold a royal assembly and promote some persons to high office'.

In the early evening, he started to descend. When he reached the second flight of stairs, 'a muezzin named Muqri Miskin gave the call to prayer at the wrong time'. It was the call of fate. Humayun, in reverence, tried to sit down where he was.

> Since the steps on the staircase were steep and the stones were slippery, as he sat his blessed foot got caught in the hem of his coat and his staff slipped. Losing his footing, he pitched forward and received such a dreadful wound

on his right temple that several drops of blood emerged from his right ear.⁶²

The first official communication declared that the wound was not serious. That was a cover-up to buy time for an orderly succession endorsed by nobles. The nerves of an edgy populace that had witnessed enough turmoil were calmed by a ruse: the 'late emperor's clothing was put on Mulla Bekasi, and he went out on the portico that was the emperor's accustomed place to sit and showed himself to the people facing the river'.⁶³

News of the emperor's death on 27 January was revealed seventeen days after his fall, on 10 February 1556, when the *khutba*, or the sermon preceding prayer, was read in the name of Akbar.

Astrologers, led by Imam Ghaznawi, chose the hour of coronation. Abul Fazl describes the process:

> A diagram of the horoscope of the accession must necessarily be given so that those of enlightened minds may have even greater illumination and so that the shortsighted may acquire farsighted vision ... In casting this marvellous horoscope the following observations have been made. First, the sun sheds its light upon the right angle of the tenth house, which is the house of rule. The main point to observe in ascertaining a time for enthronement is the propitiousness of the tenth house, and then it should be a propitiousness befitting the approach of the ruler of the world. Imam Abul-Muhamid Ghaznawi, who is one of the greatest astrologers, has stated that it is fitting to select for this purpose an ascendant of Scorpio so that the tenth angle will be Leo, which is the house of the sun. Praise God! Here the sun itself sheds its light of felicity and fortune in the tenth house.

A small extract from the extensive detail in the *Akbarnama* is reproduced here to indicate the depth of belief in astrology at the time:

> The moon is in Aries, the sun's house of exaltation. The great men of this art have stressed the importance of the position of the moon in horoscopes of accession, for it is a medium of shedding light from the superior stars upon the inferior bodies. That it should be in Aries is of great importance. The sun is at a right angle to Jupiter, the regent of the tenth house is in the seventh, and the house of the ascendant is aerial. All these things indicate the array of victorious troops and great imperial magnificence and splendour. The Part of Happiness is strong, for it passes through Leo, which is the house of the sun.[64]

The 'Part of Happiness' was tested immediately. The challenge arose from a new luminary of the old order—the charismatic Hemu, who had risen from obscurity to become the ranking amir with the title of Raja Nisbat Rai. Abul Fazl is perforce nasty about the man who nearly drove the Mughals back to Afghanistan, calling him an 'ill-featured, short-statured, ambitious' grocer from Rewari, who was appointed a purchasing agent by Salim Khan, Sher Shah's son, and rose to high office after his mentor's death in a vacuum of talent. But he praises Hemu as courageous and brilliant, 'having performed outstandingly in war', until 'little by little he reached the point at which he turned his face in audacity, daring towards H.I.M.'s exalted train'.[65]

The time had come to discover whether Jalaluddin Akbar would live up to the prophecies of saints and the calculations of seers.

The Arrow of Fortune from the Bow of Divine Wrath

Abul Fazl chose an accurate title for his narrative describing the period after Akbar's accession: 'A Summary Account of Events that Transpired During This Time of Chaos in Hindustan'. The teenaged successor was deemed vulnerable. Charlatans joined aspirants to spark off insurrection.

Akbar celebrated his first Nauruz on 10 March 1556 with a remission of tolls and custom taxes, pleasing merchants and bringing down prices, against the advice of 'fork-tongued slaves', who pointed out the resulting loss of imperial revenue.[66] But reformist policy was hardly an antidote to the myriad ambitions around. To give only an instance, one of Sher Shah's Afghan courtiers, Hajji Khan, besieged Narnaul near Delhi with a large army. He was defeated. The name of a Rajput noble who helped the Mughals came to attention during this conflict: Raja Bihari Mal Kachhwaha. But the significant threat was from the east, where Hemu had amassed a huge army after winning twenty-four battles to establish his suzerainty from Bengal to central India, while Humayun advanced from Kabul to Delhi.

Hemu believed that his moment had come when Humayun died suddenly, or, as Abul Fazl put it, 'he imagined in his shortsightedness that the times were chaotic, and he audaciously decided to step beyond the boundaries of etiquette and do battle with H.I.M.'s retinue, which enjoyed divine assistance'.[67] Hemu did not take his adversary for granted. He 'set out from the east with massive troops and war elephants', reaching Tughlaqabad near Delhi on 6 October 1556.

Tardi Beg, Humayun's companion in exile, was the Mughal commander in Delhi, with Akbar away in Punjab. He had initial success in the battle on 7 October, capturing hundreds of elephants and much booty, which proved to be his undoing. Hemu attacked when Beg's soldiers were busy plundering. Victory was reversed. Tardi Beg fled. Abul Fazl describes this as retribution for the disloyalty that Tardi Beg had shown to Humayun during his travails on the road to Persia.[68]

It was now Hemu's turn to make a mistake. He did not pursue the Mughals but went to Delhi to claim the throne.

Akbar was in Jullunder when he received news of the disaster on 13 October. He remained calm and ordered his courtiers and warriors to 'set forth at an auspicious hour' for the inevitable battle against Hemu. The stars were always a guide to imperial decisions.[69] He sent a conciliatory message to Tardi Beg and ordered him to await further instructions at Thaneswar while he established his position at Sirhind by 23 October.

Tardi Beg never reached the king's camp. He was killed by his rival Bairam Khan. Khan invited Beg through a common friend to his tent, went out excusing himself for ablutions, and had his guest murdered by servants. Abul Fazl writes derisively that the two deserved each other: 'In addition to such enmity, which results from lack of wisdom and springs from jealousy and envy, they were twins in deceit and deception.'[70]

Akbar was out hunting with sparrow hawks in Sirhind on the day of the murder. His reaction was wiser than his years: 'When it was reported to him, no change in his countenance occurred, and he entrusted retribution to almighty God while observing destiny without a wrinkle of complaint on his brow.' Bairam Khan sent an emissary offering profuse apologies and a forensic argument: the deceitful, disloyal, hypocrite Tardi Beg had maliciously chosen the dishonour of flight during battle, and if such shortcomings were ignored, major affairs would be affected. The rationale was clever. He had not sought permission to deliver such exemplary punishment, for which he was 'wholeheartedly ashamed'. Akbar's nature, he added, was 'a mine of kindness and affection'. Akbar would never have 'agreed to have him killed'. If the emperor had expressly forbidden this, 'to countermand the order would have been brazen beyond measure, while to adhere to his command would have been detrimental to the state and the army'. Akbar was astute. He needed Bairam Khan. He 'received Bairam Khan's emissary kindly and pardoned the khankhanan'.[71] He forgave but did not forget.

Bairam Khan now had to prove that he could lead an army to victory over Hemu.

Hemu, reinforced by the upbeat spirits of his men and substantial booty from Delhi, including 400 war elephants, headed towards Punjab. The decisive battle would take place in Panipat, where Babur had won an empire three decades earlier.

Hemu had one deficiency, which he never fully recognised. According to Abul Fazl, he had not learnt to ride a horse in battle. Instead, he 'was carried about in a box on an elephant'.[72] He believed in the power of the elephant. In his typical style, Abul Fazl suggests that Hemu 'was unable to comprehend that he who relies upon elephant keepers will sooner overwhelm his enemies than he who relies upon elephants'. If that was a reference to destiny, then it was accurate.

On the night of 4 and 5 November 1556, Mughal scouts reported that Hemu had reached Panipat, 'about thirty leagues' from Delhi and ten from Jullundur. Hemu sent forward his heavy artillery under his best commanders, Mubarak Khan and Bahadur Khan. He himself followed 'with amazing speed' at the head of the centre, mounted on his elephant Hawai instead of his favourite, Kali Beg. His left division was commanded by Shadi Khan Kakar and the right by his nephew Ramya, 'a fearless warrior'.

The pride of his army was an array of 500 'mountainous, dragon-breathed elephants that had been collected by so many rulers of Hindustan and been assembled by heavenly fate around [Hemu] ... each one of which was outstanding in swiftness of foot' and 'exemplar of nimbleness of limb, ferocity, and bravery'. These 'running mountains' could outstrip a Persian horse, uproot trees and hurl horse and rider into the air with their serpentine trunks, breaking the ranks of a large division. They wore mail and armour, had daggers and spears attached to their trunks and were mounted by musketeers and crossbowmen. Hemu assigned the most renowned elephant, Ghalib-Jang, Gaj Bhaunr, Jaur Bunyan and Fauj-Bidar, to Hasan Khan Faujdar, Mangli Khan, Ikhtiyar Khan and Sangram Khan respectively, all of them 'lions of battle'. His cavalry consisted of 30,000 'pugnacious Rajput and Afghan horsemen'. Everyone had a station in a well-designed battle order.[73]

Abul Fazl, who could hardly afford to be fully non-partisan in such a context, comments, 'The ill-starred Hemu had acquired so many reasons for intoxication, as has been summarily reported, that he had vain imaginings and allowed himself to have destructive thoughts.'[74] But the chronicler does not disguise the fact that the Mughals were unnerved. Morale wavered as 'trepidation found its way into the minds of the friends of fortune through the machinations of empty-headed rumour-mongers, with which armies are always filled—indeed, they make up armies'. Akbar had 10,000 men, but only half of them could be described as warriors. He ordered an immediate march, protected by the 'helmet of divine fortune' and 'the breastplate of divine protection', as he 'placed the foot of fortune in the stirrup of determination'.[75]

Bairam Khan took charge of the battle, rallying the men with 'promises of kindness and threats of wrath ... The two armies so clashed that they stirred up fire from water.

You'd say the air was continually planting tulips, that rubies were constantly raining down from steel'.[76]

Hemu's elephants began to bear down on the right and left wings of the enemy until the Mughals pulled off a classic feint: they went diagonal and rushed their foe while 'platoon after platoon of [Mughal] archers advanced into the fray from all directions'. Aliquli Shaibani, commanding the Mughal centre, took up position in front of a ravine, which Hemu's elephants could not cross, and counterattacked 'until the elephants retreated from the sides of the centre, and then they set out in pursuit of the enemy, shooting arrows and wielding swords'.[77]

Hemu, directing action from atop Hawai, gathered a group of *musth* (inebriated) elephants and charged 'audaciously ... breaking the ranks of the imperials', despite losing some of his best generals like Bhagwant Das and Shadi Khan. It was at this point that destiny intervened to protect its chosen beneficiary.

> Suddenly, in the midst of the fray, an arrow from the bow of divine wrath hit Hemu in the eye, went straight through the eye socket, and came out the back of his head ... when the troops around him saw that the arrow of fortune had hit its target, the arm of their ambition went limp and they lost heart. In total confusion they could offer no further resistance, and defeat befell Hemu's army.

His troops began to flee.

A Mughal officer called Shahquli Khan Mahram reached Hemu's elephant without realising who was on it. The mahout pointed to the wounded Hemu. Shahquli Khan 'thanked his lucky star for this great windfall and threw the hat of happiness into the air'. He promised the keeper a reward, captured several elephants, brought Hemu to Akbar's presence and 'received many regal favours'.

Hemu refused to utter a word. Bairam Khan asked the emperor if he could behead Hemu and was surprised by Akbar's answer: 'Exalted high-mindedness does not allow the killing of the captive.' He refused to change his mind despite the entreaties of his commanders. Abul Fazl has a remarkable explanation for Akbar's behaviour. He wonders if this 'elevated comprehension' meant that Akbar wanted a talent like Hemu in his own administration at some point in the future. Was there some foresight on his part 'to keep Hemu in prison and prepare him for service at the imperial threshold. Truly he had been an outstanding servant and possessed high-mindedness. Had he been patronized by such a great person [Akbar], what deeds would he not have performed?'[78]

Bairam Khan ended any speculation with the sword. Hemu's head was sent to Kabul and his body to Delhi for display among the people.

The time of Akbar's return to Delhi was determined by astrologers: 'The next day the imperial retinue set forth, and, at an hour chosen by the astrologers, the emperor arrived in Delhi, spreading the light of justice over the expectant population.'[79]

Delhi, always obeisant, greeted victors with rapture. Grandees and men of every craft and trade went in groups to offer their congratulations to the young conqueror. Majnun Khan Qaqshal, a hero of Panipat, reminded the king about the valour of a Rajput noble in Narnaul in an encounter with the enemy before the Battle of Panipat. Raja Bihari Mal Kachhwaha and his sons were invited to Delhi and honoured with robes. When they came to seek permission to depart, 'the emperor was mounted on a *musth* elephant. In its intoxication the elephant was careening in every direction, and the people were running away. Once the *musth* elephant ran toward the Rajputs ... they remained standing where they were.'[80] Akbar was deeply impressed by such valour.

The bond between Emperor Akbar and Raja Bihari Mal would shape the course of Mughal history. Abul Fazl writes:

> What a variety there is in the effects of destiny! What an assortment there is in the signs of fate! Not a plant rises from the ground without there being wisdom therein. Not a leaf moves on a tree without there being many interests involved. Who can count the mysteries hidden within the events and occurrences that are involved in the motion of the world?[81]

If there was any hint of what was to come, it was in the glint of the stars.

3

Akbar: Sun of Felicity and Fortune

JALALUDDIN AKBAR, LIKE HIS father Humayun, believed in both Allah and astrology without any sense of contradiction. He used the titles Sahib-i-Qiran ('lord of the conjunction of two superior planets, Jupiter and Saturn') and Zille-Ilahi ('shadow of Allah'), echoing Taimur, their all-conquering Uzbek ancestor. The state was secular in the context of its era. He fought Muslim and non-Muslim rulers with equal panache and aggression and converted a collapsing kingdom into an empire that unified the northern expanse from the border of Persia to Bengal in a series of military triumphs, which Abul Fazl ascribes to the stars as well as to his personality: in his words, exactly as astrologers had read in the emperor's natal horoscope and as the farsighted had seen on his illuminated brow.[1]

Akbar's reign began when he was only fourteen, at an 'auspicious' moment determined by the astrologer Imam Abul Mahamid Ghaznawi. Akbar ascended the throne at Kalanur, near Lahore, at midday on a Friday, in Al Hijri year 963, or the 15th of Tir by the Yazdgirdian calendar, equivalent to 14 or 15 February 1556. Abul Fazl explains the reason for using an astrological calculation for fixing the time of the coronation: the greater illumination of enlightened minds.

Fazl's account is replete with technical astrological references. The tenth angle of an ascendant Scorpio was in Leo, the house of the Sun, when Akbar, clad in a golden robe and with a black crown on his head, ascended the throne to the cries of congratulations from six directions.[2] 'Praise God!' he writes, 'Here the sun itself sheds its light of felicity and fortune in the tenth house.'[3]

After drawing up the chart, Ghaznawi detailed the implications. The second house, Cancer, which was the 'house of hope', indicated that the keys of treasure houses of the world would fall into Akbar's hands. Leo, the third, ensured obedience. Virgo guaranteed stability and Libra brought affectionate children. Jupiter in Sagittarius ensured eternal felicity. Sagittarius, in direct opposition to the ascendant, was the house of enemies, but because it was 'devoid of a planet of felicity', all foes would be defeated. Capricorn secured perfect inheritance. The ninth house, Aquarius, indicated true ideas in affairs of religion and state. Pisces enhanced sovereignty and splendour, while Aries, brought hope and friends. The malevolent impact of Taurus was negated by the absence of planets; enemies would therefore 'drink blood from the sword'. The Moon, in the eleventh house and regent, promised the fulfilment of hope.[4]

Abul Fazl's invocation of the goddess-ancestor Alanqoa, as mentioned earlier, was a revealing departure from orthodoxy. Her divine light had remained hidden for generations, he wrote, until it found the perfect manifestation in the person of Akbar.[5]

Beginning with Humayun, royal horoscopes were cast according to both Indian and Persian systems. As monarch, Akbar created a formal position of Jotik Rai or Jyotish Raja ('lord astrologer') to have a scholar versed in Indian astrology formally recognised at court. For three generations of Mughal rulers this position was held by Brahmins. They played a thoroughly political role and were handsomely rewarded, often receiving their weight in currency. Some of these astrologers also wrote texts for the Mughals, such as Paramananda, who composed a Sanskrit work on Indian astrology for Jahangir. In the 1630s, a high noble, Asaf Khan, commissioned Nityananda to translate a work of Persian astrology, the *Zij-i-Shah Jahani*, into Sanskrit, which is one of the rare Persian-to-Sanskrit translations known today.[6]

Azududdaula Amir Fathullah Shirazi, described as the 'most learned man of his time', forecast with formidable accuracy details about the character and achievements of Akbar. His most unusual prediction was that Akbar would consolidate his power through a marital alliance with Indian rulers when still young.[7]

Akbar's first marriage, at the age of fifteen, to a cousin called Ruqaiya Sultan Begum, was traditional. His second, in 1561, to Salima Sultan Begum, Bairam Khan's young widow and mother of a four-year-old son Abdur Rahim, signalled reconciliation with the kin of a mentor he had to defy and defeat. Akbar's third marriage shifted the landscape of Indian geopolitics. It was the first link in a chain of marital alliances that knit Rajput aristocrats into an elite Mughal network, absorbing over time the most powerful martial class of north India. The Suryavanshi Rajput nobility of Amber [equivalent to modern Jaipur) brought the best cavalry in India into the Mughal army and was rewarded with exceptional privileges. The descendants of Surya, or the Sun God, became powerful generals, governors and bureaucrats; they were the only group of *jagir*dars with hereditary rights on their land in the Mughal dispensation.

In early 1562, the twenty-year-old Akbar was out hunting, a sport he called the 'elixir of the intelligent'. At Mandhakur, midway between Agra and Fatehpur, the young monarch chanced upon pilgrims singing the 'virtues and glories' of Khwaja Muinuddin Chishti, the

13th-century Sufi saint whose shrine in Ajmer had become a place of pilgrimage.[8] Akbar was struck by a sudden urge to pay homage at Ajmer. He sent word to Maham Anaka at the Agra Palace to bring his family members to Ajmer, and on 14 January 1562, he set out for his first visit to the shrine. This marked the onset of a revaluation of Mughal ideology, which thus far had taken spiritual sustenance from the Naqshbandi order of Muslim Sufis, who were dominant across Central Asia, had come with Babur to India and looked askance at Akbar's outreach to other religious sects. The Chishtiya order was more indigenous, with Ajmer a popular centre of pilgrimage.[9]

At Kilaohi, a camp stop, an official, Chaghatai Khan, reported that the governor of Mewat, Sharfuddin Husain Mirza, had driven Raja Bihari Mal Kachhwaha of Amber out of his capital to the hills by collusion with Suja, the raja's nephew. The pedigree of this Kshatriya dynasty went back to 967 when Dhola Rai established the kingdom. The people described Mughal intervention as tyranny and fled as Akbar approached Daosa. Akbar was surprised. He had nothing in mind, he said, but favour and clemency towards the common people. He wanted to know the cause of this terror.[10]

Akbar invited Bihari Mal to Sanganer, greeted him graciously, raised his rank and enhanced their relationship through his marriage with Bihari Mal's eldest daughter, 'a girl of great chastity and wisdom'. Bihari Mal and Chaghatai Khan were told to go ahead and make arrangements for the marriage as soon as possible. Akbar left for Ajmer, which he entered 'at an auspicious hour'.[11]

The bride's name was Hira Kunwar Sahiba Harkha Bai (1542–1622); her later title was Mariam-uz-Zamani ('Mary, mother of Jesus, of her age'). Raja Bihari Mal became one of the grandees of the realm, surpassing in rank all the rajas and rais of Hindustan.[12] His son Bhagwant Singh and grandson, twelve-year-old Man Singh (1550–1614), were part of the imperial retinue that reached Agra on 13 February 1562.

This Sun Alliance, welded into a syncretic, strategic framework, evolved into something far greater than the sum of its parts. It became the hallmark policy of one of the great emperors in history and inspired a phase of cultural harmony across the subcontinent that entered folklore. The Timurid–Rajput association sent a potent message, reassuring Hindu rajas that they could be partners in power rather than passive subjects vulnerable to the predilections of victors.

In an absolute monarchy, the monarch's behaviour is more influential than any edict he might issue. Akbar used to drink 'the water of immortality' brought from the Ganga in sealed jars to Agra via Sorun, the nearest point to Delhi, or from Hardwar if he was in Punjab.[13] In early 1564, within two years of his marriage to Harkha Bai, he abolished *jizya*, the hated tax levied on Hindus and other non-Muslim subjects. He was only twenty-two.

Abul Fazl praises this radical decision, which had far-reaching implications, as magnificent, and notes that the amount of tax remission could barely be measured. He describes this decision as a 'headline for order in the world', pointing out that the edict was issued against the wishes of the nobles, despite much remonstrance on the part of those who did not know the value of the social bargain. *Jizya* represented 'deep-seated enmity' against Hindus imposed by those whose hearts were 'set upon insulting and killing opponents'. Akbar believed that peace and justice beget loyalty: those of other faiths became as loyal as those who shared the emperor's religion.[14]

An infuriated clerical establishment instigated insurrection in what was still a fluid environment. In Jaunpur, Muizzul Mulk and Muhammad Masum obtained a fatwa from the chief priest Mulla Muhammad of Yazd, declaring rebellion to be lawful against a king who had, in their view, contravened Islamic law. Akbar defeated this uprising in the summer of 1565. Mulla Muhammad was drowned in the Jamuna.[15]

Akbar took a less known but equally significant decision in 1564 while hunting in Mathura, where he heard of a tax, called karmi, on Hindus visiting temples, measured by the status and wealth of the worshipper. He forbade karmi, describing it as reprehensible and a stumbling block in the path of Hindus to the threshold of unity and worship of God.[16] Abul Fazl comments that the farsighted emperor forewent revenue amounting to crores throughout the realm.

Social reform came in consistent steps. Muslim clerics were stopped from passing judgement on Hindus. Cases between Hindus were decided by learned Brahmans and not Muslim Qazis.[17] Forcible conversion was banned. Hindu widows were allowed to remarry. Muslim men were permitted a second wife only if the first was barren. Akbar wanted to abolish sati, which he considered cruel, but held his hand for fear of alienating Rajput allies. He made it voluntary, which had to be confirmed through due diligence by the kotwal, the local police chief. In 1591, beef was banned. Justice became a counterweight to belief. The emperor based his laws upon 'great truths' that would please God.

A high point of Akbar's reforms came on 8 March 1582 when he summoned a special session of his court and asked his ministers to cleanse their minds of flattery before announcing a transformative change: the abolition of slavery. He set the precedent by releasing several thousand imperial slaves, for slavery of captives was beyond the boundaries of justice and good conduct. It was the culmination of a process which started in 1562, when the emperor began to free his slaves and re-employ those who wished to remain in palace jobs at regular wages. They were renamed 'chela', a term for follower.[18]

Akbar gave the ownership of change to court nobles through the simple expedience of making them announce the new laws. Jahangir, then Salim, proposed the abolition of child marriage. Mirza Aziz Koka announced the end of capital punishment—then a power held by governors—for life had been given by God. Raja Todar Mal made charity compulsory for nobles. Raja Birbal challenged corruption in the bureaucracy by the creation of a non-partisan cadre at the palace gates that would take public grievances directly to the king. Abdur Rahim restricted the hunting of small animals, birds and baby fish. Muhammad Qasim initiated the construction of inns for travellers. Shaikh Jamal asked for ombudsmen to monitor welfare programmes. Shaikh Faizi proposed market inspectors to prevent price gouging. Hakim Abul Fath, the emperor's doctor, sought hospitals for the people.

Three Hindu luminaries in Akbar's court became the most powerful of nobles: a Kshatriya, Raja Man Singh, his nephew through marriage, and two Brahmins, Raja Birbal and Raja Todar Mal. Man Singh is credited with having fought sixty-five battles from Bengal to Kabul. He was twenty-six when he led the imperial forces against Mewar at Haldighati with nobles like Raja Ram Sah of Gwalior, the Sayyids of Barha, Rai Lonkaran, Ghazi Khan, Madhav Singh and Jagannath under his command.[19] Man Singh was sent to quell a rebellion by Akbar's brother Mirza Hakim Mirza, evidence of the highest levels of trust and friendship. He served on the Indus when his father, Bhagwant Singh, was the governor of Punjab. Lahore's Jami Masjid was built during this period.

Man Singh was always forthright. When some Muslim nobles, seeking to create tension, suggested that he change his faith, Man Singh refused. Prof. Mujeeb writes: 'Religion did not make any difference to the Rajah's position in the court and among the dignitaries of the realm. Given the title of Mirza Rajah and Farzand [son], Man Singh was the first mansabdar to be given the rank of Seven Thousand.'[20]

Todar Mal (1500–1589), from Awadh, was the finance minister who rationalised revenue collection between 1574 and 1575 through a system in which a *karori*, assisted by a *fotedar* (treasurer) and *karkun* (clerk), oversaw an area yielding one crore *tankas*. He defeated the Jaunpur rebels in 1565 after the *jizya* revocation and won plaudits after the conquest of Bengal.[21] Akbar's economic reforms would have been lauded in the 21st century. Todar Mal reduced tariffs like tamgha, rahdari, sarana, peshkash and taxes on the entry of people and goods into the territory or on forest dwellers. Various forms of cess, including those extracted by landholders, were either removed or reduced.

Maheshdas Brahmabhat, a poet-warrior of many talents, including diplomacy, wit and poetry, was first appointed the Kavi Rai ('poet laureate') in Akbar's court before being honoured as Birbal ('one with great comprehension'). He was recognised for his *hikmat* (wisdom), *shujaat* (courage), *siffat* (individuality) and *sadaqat* (discrimination). One incident indicates the emperor's affection for Birbal. On 17 October 1583, Birbal fell from his horse during a polo match and lost consciousness. Akbar rushed to his side and breathed on him until he regained his senses.[22] When Birbal was killed in a war against the Yusufzai tribes of the northern frontier, Akbar did not want to believe the report. Stories spread that Birbal had been sighted in the hills of Nagarkot walking with jogis and sannyasis. Akbar mourned a second time when the death was confirmed. Birbal was as renowned for his liberal views as his wit. His short verses, bon-mots and jokes became immensely popular.

Abul Fazl narrates how Man Singh saved the emperor's life during a drunken night in March 1573. Excessive drinking, described as the vice of the age, was a common affliction, and the casualty rate in the upper echelons was high: two sons of Man Singh's, Bhao and Jagat Singh; Yusuf Khan, the eldest son of Jiji Anaka; Shahnawaz Bahadur; Zayn Khan and Mirza Jani Beg of Thatta. The price paid by the first family was considerable. All three of Akbar's sons, Salim, Murad and Danyal, were alcoholics. Murad, considered a natural genius by his Jesuit tutors in Agra, imbibed with abandon when sent to Malwa at the age of twenty-one in 1591 and became a disruptive drunk in Gujarat and the Deccan. In 1598, Akbar sent Abul Fazl to bring the errant son back to the capital. Murad eluded his father's emissary but could not escape death. He died of alcohol poisoning in 1599. Danyal died in April 1604 at the age of thirty-two.

Since a loyalist scribe is hesitant to recognise weakness in his master, Fazl finds a ponderous excuse for Akbar's own indulgence in drinking: ancient rulers used to get their nobles drunk to discover their inner thoughts, for wine robbed one of sense.

One evening, Akbar's courtiers got a glimpse of his dark side. As the wine circulated, conversation drifted to the courage of the Rajputs, who claimed they were so fearless that they would charge at each other with *barcha*, a double-headed, body-piercing spear. Akbar, inebriated, placed the hilt of his sword against a wall and said that he could outdo the Rajputs. There was a stunned silence. 'Everyone was overcome by a strange state: no one could speak or even breathe. At this point, the devoted Man Singh ran forward and nimbly knocked the sword away in such a way that the area between the emperor's thumb and forefinger received a slight cut.' The enraged king threw Man Singh to the ground and began to kick and hit him.

Saiyid Muzaffar separated the two but accidentally twisted Akbar's wounded finger. When the effects of the wine cooled, His Majesty recovered his equilibrium.[23]

The Shield of God

Shirazi, who foresaw that Humayun would die early, promised the successor a glorious rejuvenation of the empire before Akbar reached 'the age of discrimination' because of the influence of Gemini. He would rule across India since the Sun, in partnership with Saturn, was dominant over the ascendant. Mercury assured wealth, Virgo's position pointed to perfect intellect while Jupiter would ensure that wealth was spent for the common good in ways pleasing to God.

Jotik Rai was equally upbeat. Akbar would rule 'the world for long ages' with correct and precise plans and ideas. The fourth house, Mars, signalled military triumph and stability on the condition that Akbar personally supervised policy. Mercury in the third house made the 'native' skilled, hardworking and displeased by idleness. The Leo child, monarch for forty-nine years, built an empire that grew from an uncertain patch of territory around Delhi to a geography greater than any since Ashoka's death some eighteen centuries before. Panipat, Lahore, Multan and Ajmer were conquered by 1558, followed by Gwalior (1559–1560), Malwa and Chunar (1561), Gond (1564), Chittor (1568), Ranthambore and Kalinjar (1569), Gujarat (1572), Surat (1573), Bihar (1574), Bengal (1576), Kashmir (1586), Sind (1590), Orissa (1592), Berar (1596), Gawilgarh and Narnala (1598), Ahmednagar (1600) and Asirgarh (1601).

Shirazi was certain that the king would be exceptionally courageous because Venus was dominant in the eighth house and Pisces had Jupiter as regent, in partnership with Mars at exaltation. Akbar exhibited a fearless temperament from childhood. He was less than three when he wrestled a bigger cousin, Ibrahim, for a kettle drum, which the latter had received as a present from his father, Kamran. A painting of the scene is in the Bodleian Library. He flirted with danger, whether speeding on camels as a child or charging in battle as a young man, and seemed blessed with divine protection even when ill. Smallpox pustules appeared on his body when he was nineteen, compounded by high fever that caused great anguish. God, the 'almighty physician', did the healing. After several days, the boils finally broke.

Jahangir recalls that people were continually astonished by the impetuous monarch, so oblivious to danger: 'His courage and boldness were such that he could mount raging, rutting elephants, and subdue to obedience murderous elephants which would not allow their own females near them—although even when an elephant is bad-tempered he does no harm to the female or his driver.'[24]

Akbar was entranced by elephants, by their kindness, fury, lofty comprehension and vengeance. They were the strangest of animals, mountains with impeccable beauty of form, wrathful in battle, swift as the wind, incomparably wise, and capable of breaking an enemy's ranks. Tripping occasionally over his own praise of Akbar, Abul Fazl tells the story of how the young monarch mounted an elephant named Lakhna while it was at the height of fury and urged it to fight another in an equally ferocious mood. Lakhna won and, in its frenzy, chased the opponent. Suddenly, its foot sank into a narrow and deep hole. As it lurched, the *bhoi* (expert mahout) fell. As cries rose and the loyal began to tremble with fear, Akbar fixed his foot in the rope around the elephant's neck, called *kalwa* in Hindi, and restrained Lakhna.

Attendants helped the emperor dismount. Lakhna's foot became free, but its pain and rage persisted. Akbar calmly mounted the animal again and set off for the capital. Bairam Khan distributed alms to ward off the evil eye. The customary laudatory phrases do not diminish facts or their impact on the people, which is recorded in a painting captioned 'His Imperial Majesty's Fascination with Elephants and Elephant Fights'.

Three episodes from Akbar's twenties, varying in time and circumstance, can be cited as evidence of his abnormal bravery: a sudden, unplanned onslaught against brigands in 1563, a battle against rebels in Malwa in 1564 and the remarkable re-conquest of Gujarat in 1573.

In 1563, Akbar was hunting near Agra with Raja Bhagwant Das when they came across a cluster of eight villages called Ath-kanya ('Eight Daughters'), infamous as a nest of outlaws. A Brahmin named Hapa complained to the king that some criminals had killed his son and plundered his property. Akbar, promising immediate retribution, set off at dawn for Paronkh, where about 1,000 outlaws had set up fortified positions. Akbar had only around 200 men as he entered the village, advancing against a screen of fire with Raja Bhagwant Das and Raja Badichand alongside. His troops were hesitant, but Akbar spurred his elephant Dalsingar against a fusillade of arrows, clubs and rocks from all directions. Dalsingar stepped into a grain pit and was hit by the elephant behind, but it trampled a brigand who aimed a sword at its tusk.

Suddenly, a fifteen-year-old boy fell on Dalsingar from a roof above. A Mughal soldier, Jujhar Khan, was about to kill the boy when Akbar intervened, noting that he was just a teenage bystander. The emperor led the charge. Seven arrows struck his shield, and five pierced it, some by five fingers and some by three.

One of his men, Tatar Khan, cried out, 'Where is my emperor going in this rain of arrows?' Akbar was heading into the midst of battle. The brigands were destroyed.

If such heroics were rash, they were also characteristic. As Shirazi noted, this king sometimes needed God's protection from his own inclinations. Abul Fazl concluded that the king's breastplate was divine protection.

In July 1564, the imperial standards marched amid heavy rains towards Malwa to chastise a rebel, Abdullah Khan Uzbek. While on the march, Akbar enjoyed hunting during the day and spent evenings listening to stories about Hamza ibn Abd al-Muttalib, a companion and relative of the Prophet Muhammad, nicknamed Asad Allah ('Lion of God').

Akbar was in Dhar, contemplating whether to accept an apology proffered by Abdullah Khan, when a terrified woman came to him, complaining that she and her adolescent daughter had been assaulted and their home plundered by Abdullah Khan's arms bearer, Muhammad Husain. Akbar reassured her that justice would be done.

The encounter at Bagh took place in August 1564. A part of Akbar's vanguard, which had moved too far ahead, was surrounded by hostile troops. Akbar set out immediately, literally hitting his officer Khaksar Sultan when he advised the emperor to cease his gallop. In the intense fighting, an enemy arrow passed by his head but did no damage. Akbar ordered the drums to roll for attack. His commander Munim Khankhanam was taken aback when Akbar began to loosen the reins of his horse, for they had no more than 300 troops against at least 1,000, and advised that this was no time to be riding alone. Another officer, Itimad Khan, tried to restrain his twenty-two-year-old king by holding the latter's horse's reins but was angrily repulsed.

Akbar led the charge with Mirza Aziz Koka, Muhammad Qasim Khan Nishapuri, Raja Todar Mal and Rai Pitr Das riding with him. Abul Fazl attributes victory to divine assistance, which made numbers irrelevant.

The first person to be executed after the encounter was Muhammad Husain.

The fate of life and the empire was in the balance for Akbar in the third episode. Gujarat had broken away from the Khilji Empire in the last decade of the 14th century. In 1443, its rulers, enriched by trade with the Ottoman Empire and Africa, shifted the capital to Ahmedabad, the Shahr-i-Muazzam ('Great City'), and created an army famous for its stealth warriors from Abyssinia, known as the 'Habshi'.

Decline began with the Portuguese advance and increasing mercantile power, followed by the Mewar king Rana Sangha's successful incursions. Humayun took Gujarat in 1532, but it was a pyrrhic victory. Gujarat protected its independence until Akbar's victory in 1572. In early 1573, Mirza Aziz Koka, the son of Jiji Anaka, was sent as governor to Gujarat. That summer, Sultan Muhammad Hussain Mirza recaptured Bharuch and Cambay and besieged Aziz Koka in Ahmedabad. News reached Fatehpur Sikri that Aziz Koka would not survive.

Jiji Anaka was distraught. Jahangir recalls that his father was so upset by her distracted state that he set off immediately for Gujarat without waiting for a regular army to be assembled and covered some 600 miles from Fatehpur to Ahmedabad in nine days, a journey that normally took two months. Accompanying the emperor were Bhagwant Singh, Sayyid Mahmud Barha, Man Singh and the emir of Malwa. Raja Bihari Mal was left in charge of the capital.

On 23 August 1573, a Sunday, Akbar mounted a 'bow-necked' camel, 'swifter than an arrow' and, trusting in God, set forth on the long road accompanied by a small entourage on horses and camels. Rest was no more than a few hours. Abul Fazl, relapsing into poetry, compared the pace to that of a cloud, as swift as patience fleeing from lovers. They reached Ajmer by Tuesday mid-morning, where the emperor prayed for success in this audacious enterprise at the shrine of Khwaja Muinuddin Chishti. At Bhagwanpur, Akbar ignored the near-unanimous advice to take the safer route and chose a terrible road because it was shorter. A lion was spotted on Friday morning, but the emperor would not let any harm come to the majestic animal, lest it should invite misfortune. On 29 August, Akbar observed the new moon at Bansiwara and sped ahead without rest until the end of Sunday. Incredulous officials en route refused to believe the speed. Shah Ali Lankah closed the gates of a Mughal city, Disa, until he realised his mistake. Akbar rejected the consensus view to wait for reinforcements at Patan. He believed that surprise would be lost by delay.

From Mehsana, about 45 miles north of Ahmedabad, the march was in array, with the emperor surrounded by a hundred nobles and chieftains. A messenger was sent to inform the besieged Aziz Koka that help was imminent. Abul Fazl's list of 'loyal champions' indicates a composite army: Abdur Rahim (Bairam Khan's son), Birbal, Saif and Zain Khan Koka, Man Singh, Husain Khwaja, Abdullah Khan, Jai Mal and his son Rupsi (who had come without appropriate armour and, fuelled by opium, wanted to fight without protection until chastised by Bhagwant Singh), Jagannath, Raisal, Jagmal Panwar, Mir Ghiyasuddin, Raja Dip Chand, Muhammad Zaman, Shaikh Abdul Rahim, Ram Das Kachhwaha, Ram Chand, Bahadur Khan Qordar, Sanwal Das, Jadon Kayath Darbari, Surkh Badakshi, Dwarbhala, Hari Das, Tara Chand Khawass and Lal Kalawant.

The imperial advance halted a little short of Ahmedabad. The odds were poor, but the omens kind. Bhagwant Singh offered congratulations before the battle, reporting that he had seen three signs of victory: the emperor's horse had stopped at an auspicious moment, the wind was blowing in the enemy's face, and ravens and kites were accompanying their army. Each sign, he said, was considered propitious by the people of Hindustan.

Jahangir records that his father consulted a diviner called Hazara, who saw the future in shoulder blades and promised success but predicted that a high dignitary would die in battle. Advisers proposed a night attack in view of the numerical imbalance. Akbar rejected this as cowardice, the resort of the faint-hearted and deceitful.

In Ahmedabad, Muhammad Mirza, disbelieving stories that Akbar had reached the city, came out to reconnoitre the area. His spies had reported seeing Akbar in Fatehpur fourteen days before. How could elephants move so fast? Akbar had not travelled by elephant. Ironically, the beleaguered Aziz Koka did not trust such reports either. He thought they were a ruse by the enemy to draw him into the open.

Akbar's strategic advantage was surprise. He ordered an immediate offensive. He was the first to ford the Sabarmati River on 2 September 1573, shrugging off caution. In his hurry, he forgot to put on his pish-ruy (face guard). When this was called a bad omen, he replied that it was an excellent omen, for it had revealed his face.

The initial phase of fighting went to the better-equipped and larger Gujarat army. Akbar's self-belief did not waver. Watching from raised ground, Akbar told Bhagwant Singh that God's favour would be with them. He targeted Muhammad Mirza, who had ridden ahead of his battalions. Akbar's orders were designed to convert weakness into strength: do not charge from afar or break rank, for it would achieve nothing against numbers; attack with one face, one heart, one aim. A punch delivered by a closed fist was more effective than a slap by an open hand.

Hapa Charan, positioned next to the king, gave the battle cry. Akbar drew his sword and raced at the head of his troops amidst cries of 'Allahu Akbar' and 'Ya Muin'. The enemy broke through on the Mughal left wing but was held in the centre and the right. Divine assistance arrived just in time. The Gujarat army had a firework called kuhukbans in its arsenal that hit one of its own elephants, which ran amok, causing substantial confusion in the Gujarat ranks.

Akbar, riding in front, witnessed Man Singh engage successfully in hand-to-hand combat and Raghu Das Kachhwaha sacrifice his life. He was recognised. An enemy sword landed on his horse, and another on his thigh before the assailants were dispatched. News spread that Akbar was wounded. Akbar dispelled potential demoralisation, raising his voice and urging his men to fight. The Mughal forces rallied, and the breeze of victory began to blow. Muhammad Hussain Mirza was captured while trying to flee. Akbar wanted the death of this 'ingrate', but his innate clemency prevailed.

The prisoner was handed over to Man Singh to be taken to Agra. Akbar, grateful to God, bowed in prayer. The Buland Darwaza ('majestic gate'), the highest doorway in the world at the time, was built in Fatehpur Sikri to commemorate this improbable victory. Ready by 1575, it faces south, towards Gujarat. On its walls are verses from the Quran and a quotation attributed to the Prophet Isa (Jesus): 'The world is a bridge, pass over it; build no houses upon it. He who hopes for a day may dream of eternity, but the world lasts but an hour. Spend it in prayer for the rest is unseen.'

Akbar looked after those who had fallen in this campaign. In 1573, when he heard that two soldiers, Saif Khan and Shaikh Muhammad, who died in Gujarat, had left heavy debts, he paid all their creditors. The phrase *fath-i-Akbari-mubarak* ('victory-of-Akbar-greetings') became part of public salutations.

Akbar's breathtaking disregard for danger, his military successes and his humanist policies justified the title of *mujtahid* ('inspired man of religion'). His realm was considered a sacred monarchy with divine protection. This divinity was multipolar, for the emperor participated in spiritual practices of other faiths, such as memorising 1,001 names for the sun and restricting himself to a tantric diet, leaving the more conventional of his Muslim nobles perplexed or critical in private.

Ultimately, his detractors remained in the minority and proved unable to undermine the power or status of a successful king. Akbar's claims were burnished by a royal cult and the compendium of panegyric writings of Abul Fazl, who effusively established the emperor's reputation as the *insan-i-kamil*, the perfect man.[25]

His subjects began to believe that Akbar's destiny could protect them from celestial malevolence. On 9 November 1557, when the Sun was in Scorpio, a comet with a long tail appeared, remaining visible for five months. Astrologers, reports Abul Fazl, said it was a sign of upheaval, price rise and disturbances, adding that the ruler of Iran would die, leading to disturbances in Persia and Khurasan. It came about exactly as they had predicted. Not long thereafter, a caravan brought news that Shah Tahmasp had passed away, Sultan Haidan had been killed and Shah Ismail had become ruler. India was safe because Emperor Akbar had been blessed with divine protection. Even when such terrible phenomena appeared, no great harm came to the kingdom. Akbar's star would never fade, said Jotik Rai.

Astrology was intrinsic to imperial ideology, and its practice extended to European kings. It was studied systematically in the Muslim world. Astrological tradition stressed the vital significance for events on earth of the conjunction of the planets Saturn and Jupiter. Akbar was hailed as the 'lord of the conjunction' and the architect of a new era in mankind's history.

By 1578, with Akbar having been on the throne for close to a quarter of a century, people began to attribute miraculous powers to his person. Abul Fazl mentions one such story. In March that year, the rains were so heavy that the perturbed people and soldiers began to cry out in despair. It is not explained whether Akbar's response was based on advice or sprang from his own ingenuity, but he breathed on a mirror and put it in a fire. Through the 'mysterious workings' of his breath, the clouds obediently ceased their heavenly rumblings. This was seen as evidence of divine power.[26]

In December that year, Akbar was hunting when Sultan Khwaja presented him with horses that had just been imported from Arabia. Sultan Khwaja also told the story of a child who had fallen from the ship carrying this freight, and though its cries could be heard by the distressed passengers, it could not be located by the search team. Khwaja made a vow in the emperor's name, and at midnight the rescuers returned with the child safe and sound. The chronicler claims that these 'miraculous incidents' had been noted with an 'objective eye'.

The miracles grew more amazing. On 7 September 1579, Akbar left for Ajmer, hunting along the way as was his habit. On 8 October, the imperial banners rested at Khawass Khan's Pond, where villagers reported that a traveller had been accosted by a 'strange beast' that rose to kill him. With presence of mind, the traveller drew a line round himself and began to pray for the 'world lord' (the emperor). Hearing the 'imperial name', the beast stopped and the man escaped.

Such adulation seems credible because a perceptible rise in prosperity had also raised admiration for their monarch. Abul Fazl notes as much. On 10 December 1579, Akbar stopped in Fatehpur, where

> the marketplace of the world acquired a new splendour; and esteem of goods enjoyed a brisk market. All classes of men and groups of people turned their faces in supplication toward the exalted threshold, and the rulers and governors of all regions sent tribute.[27]

The Promise of Other Stars

Azududdaula Shirazi had ascribed Akbar's defiance of danger to the influence of the eighth house, whose cusp was in Pisces, with Jupiter as regent, Venus dominant and Mars at exaltation. His other predictions were more salubrious. Every star had its promise. Aries, in the ninth house, with Mars as regent, assured the native success in travel and conquest of territory. Taurus in the tenth, with Venus ascendant, indicated happiness, pleasure and exalted esteem. Gemini gave abundant wealth. Cancer and its regent, the Moon, destroyed enemies who would always suffer disaster. The Dragon's Tail in the first degree of this house further strengthened this assertion. God would extend the life of the 'lord of good fortune' and his good nature, which was necessary for sovereignty and statecraft, would attract the affections of both the elite and common people.

Shirazi settled a debate between astrologers over the ascendant in Akbar's birth sign: 'since the royal horoscopes appeared to be in disagreement, it was hoped he would study the matter and arrive at the truth … employing Persian and Greek principles to extract the ascendant [he] ascertained that the ascendant was Leo'.[28] There are five pages in Fazl's history on the mathematics of stars, followed by an 'explanation of the results of this marvellous horoscope', which stretches to another twelve printed pages. This was Shirazi being concise. If, he said, the 'gifts of the planets, the felicity of their gazes, the special characteristics of the signs, and other things were to be recorded completely and perfectly, assuredly many registers would be filled and volumes would have to be made'.

Shirazi drew a portrait of his subject: large head, broad forehead, wide chest, power, gaiety, fearlessness, magnificence, courage, strength of mind and goodness of outlook. This agrees with the description that Jahangir has left of his father: of middle height but inclining to be tall; wheatish in hue; dark eyes and eyebrows; lion-bodied (*shir-andam*), with a broad chest and long arms. On the left side of his nose, he had a fleshy mole the size of half a pea. Those skilled in the science of physiognomy considered this mole a sign of great prosperity and exceeding good fortune. His voice exuded a richness; his actions and movements were unique. The son repeats that the glory of God manifested itself in the emperor.

Every chart, whichever system it was based on, predicted greatness and the emergence of a spiritual icon in Akbar. Abul Fazl explains the differences between Indian astrologers and 'Greek stargazers'. Shirazi used Greek principles and Persian rules. Shirazi was the wisest, he avers, but Jotik Rai was the best.

Jotik Rai was certain that Akbar would be a benevolent, philosophical, firm, charitable, measured and equitable ruler. The downtrodden and the poor would enjoy his munificence and generosity. This reading was based on the presence of Venus in the second house. Akbar started free kitchens in 1583. Since each faith had its own dietary rules, Muslims were assigned Khairpur ('Care-town') and Hindus Dharmpur ('Faith-town'). On demand, a third centre called Jogipur ('Ascetic-town') was opened for sadhus.

Jupiter, the greater lucky star, would ameliorate the people's worries; the Sun would increase the emperor's circle of friends and reduce his circle of enemies. With the Sun, Saturn and Mercury in one sign, Akbar would become the greatest of the great and emperor of emperors materially and spiritually, innately and coincidentally. His renown would spread across the world, his empire from shore to shore. Sovereigns and rulers under his command would submit to him because Mars was in the house of Jupiter and the Sun looked at him in sextile. Since the Moon was in the sixth house, his enemies, however great, would not be able to touch him. Instead, they would seek his friendship to save themselves from calamity. Akbar's armies would 'reduce to nothingness all upon whom he gazes in wrath'. Akbar would possess exceptional memory, said Jotik Rai, because the regent of the ninth house, Mars, was in the fifth, the house of Jupiter.[29]

Akbar was illiterate because, as a dyslexic child, he refused to take lessons. His tutor Mullazada Mulla Isamuddin Ibrahim soon discovered his student's preference for truancy. The prince often disappeared, preferring to play alone, away from the gaze of his tutor. Bayazid Bayat confirms the prince's indifference to studies in *Tazkira-i-Humayun-o-Akbar*. Humayun would admonish Akbar, but the boy paid little heed.[30]

Obedient students, on afterthought, decided that this child, who had been selected for divine beneficence, was not destined for the formal knowledge of the world. Even if you set aside hyperbole, the adult Akbar would surprise sceptics with his understanding of subtle points of Hindi and Persian poetry, and would recite long passages from the *masnavi* and *divan* of the Persian poet Hafiz and even dictate some verse in Hindi.

Poetry was ingrained in Mughal culture and heritage. Babur wrote verse in Chagatai Turkish. Akbar invited

Persian writers and poets when the Safavid court went through a period of intellectual relapse. Jahangir makes an important point: although his father was illiterate, he had spent so much time with sages and learned men in discussions that no one could guess he was unread. His comprehension of the subtleties of prose and poetry was exceptional.

Never one to scrimp on encomiums, Abul Fazl describes his master's evolution: the wine of adolescence matured into spiritual might, external beauty and inner kindness. He repeats Jotik Rai's analysis of the horoscope, indicating that the 'good-looking' king would be measured in speech, charity, social graces, sublime wisdom and lofty thoughts of piety and theology. He would investigate various religions and differing sects, focus on righteousness and desire to extricate the people from the slippery slope of blind tradition.

Questions of doctrine constantly troubled Akbar. He sought answers where he could, including while hunting in the forests, especially through conversations with *jogis*, sanyasis and *qalandars* living in unassuming solitude. Not every ascetic was immune to temptation, notes Abul Fazl. He is derisive about sycophant mendicants who joined fawning court doctors in promising the emperor that he would live three or four times as long as a normal human being.

The conundrum for Akbar was: do religions and human tendencies have nothing in common? Akbar wanted emotional integration and repudiation of 'customs that appeared to him cruel, unjust or harmful', in the words of Prof. Mujeeb, author of the finest sociological study on Indian Muslims. As a ruler and an Indian, Akbar sought to encourage debate between Sufis, Sunnis, Shia, Ismailis, Shaivites, Vaishnavites, Sikhs, Jains, Jesuits, Jews and materialists as a means to intra- and inter-religious resolution of doctrinaire conflict. He participated in the religious practices of other faiths, like Christianity and Zoroastrianism, and asserted that the wisdom of Vedanta was the wisdom of Sufism. To him, the Sufi ideal, expressed in the worship of Allah and service to the poor, was exemplary. Even the lion, it was said, became tame in the presence of a Sufi shaikh like Shaikh Salim Chishti, Akbar's spiritual mentor.

Sultans had armies; the mystical dervish had the power of popular support. Akbar's great leap forward was *sulh-i-qul*, the philosophy of universal accord, a fusion of religious freedom with cultural sensitivity. Astrologers had predicted Akbar's quest for knowledge of the hidden and fascination with the depth of the unknown.

Akbar's intellectual embrace did not dilute his Islam. In addition to the ritual public congregation on Fridays, he prayed after the evening meal. In 1582, Akbar's aunt Gulbadan Begum brought back from Mecca what was purported to be an imprint of the Prophet's foot on an immense stone, so heavy that it could be transported only on the back of an elephant. Akbar kept any scepticism to himself and walked some 9 miles to greet the returning pilgrims. Grandees carried the stone on their shoulders to the city.[31]

Abul Fazl records that during a Friday prayer at Fatehpur Sikri's Jami Masjid, the emperor recited a verse he had composed:

The Lord has given me the empire,
And a wise heart, and a strong arm.
He has guided me in righteousness and justice,
And has removed from my thoughts everything but justice.
His praise surpasses man's understanding.
Great is His power, Allah-u-Akbar![32]

Akbar told Jesuits who professed horror at seeing him enter a mosque, having mistaken his pluralism for conversion to Christianity, that he was a Muslim. As Wendy Doniger points out, Akbar understood the Jesuits; they could not encompass him. The Jesuits[33] construed Akbar's respect for the Sun as distance from Islam and misunderstood his interest in the West as belief in Christianity.

Doniger quotes the famous inscription by Abul Fazl for a temple in Kashmir:

> O God in every temple I see people that see Thee, and in every language I hear spoken, people praise Thee. Polytheism and Islam feel after Thee. Each religion says, 'Thou art one, without equal. If it be a mosque people murmur the holy prayer, and if it be a Christian Church, people ring the bell from love to Thee. Sometimes I frequent the Christian cloister, and sometimes the mosque. But it is Thou whom I search from temple to temple. Thy elect have no dealings with either heresy or orthodoxy; for neither of them stands behind the screen of Thy truth. Heresy to the heretic, and religion to the orthodox, but the dust of the rose-petal belongs to the heart of the perfume seller.[34]

Akbar was intrigued by Zoroastrian fire-worship, practised by the Parsis from Navsari in Gujarat. Fire and light were complementary to the Sun, the torch of God that illuminated the universe and was the source of the origin of life.[35] Every evening, the emperor would alight if riding, or be woken up if taking a siesta, one *ghari* (twenty-four minutes) before sunset to meditate, laying aside the splendour of royalty and finding harmony with his heart.

At sunset, attendants would light twelve white wax candles, three yards high, mounted on candlesticks of gold and silver, while a vocalist would sing hymns for the 'auspicious' reign. During the first three nights of the lunar month, eight wicks would be used for each flambeau (or branched candlestick). The wicks were reduced by one a day until the tenth day, when one was sufficient in the moonlight. After the full moon, the reverse process would begin. The heat of Surajkrant, a round, white, shining stone, could set a cotton wick on fire at noon; and water would begin to drip from Chandrakant, a similar stone, when exposed to moonbeams. On the eighth day of Virgo, the emperor would wear a tilak on his forehead before entering the audience hall, while Brahmins tied a string of jewels on his hand.[36]

Basawan's painting of a Jain ascetic, dated circa 1600, now sits in the Cleveland Museum of Art. Jain texts claim that the leader of Kharatra Gaccha, Jinachandra, taught the emperor Jainism over a full monsoon season in Lahore. It is recorded that Akbar was deeply impressed by the demonstration of *avadhana*, a mental feat of simultaneously focusing on multiple things, up to a hundred.

The orthodox Abdul Qadir Badauni (1540–1615), compliant in court and caustic in private, indicts Akbar for dismantling the edifice of the true faith in *Muntakhab-ut-Tawarikh* ('A Selection of Historical Narratives'). Unable to conceal his bitterness, he reports that Akbar raised his hands in prayer before the Sun, sometimes as many as four times a day, reciting the 1,001 names of the Sun from memory. The orthodox worried that Islam would be replaced by a hybrid Din-i-Ilahi ('Religion of God'), but this term is not found in the *Akbarnama*. A cynic like Badauni barely mentions it, suggesting that the idea had little resonance.[37]

Badauni was scornful of Akbar for showing greater reverence for Sufis than for the Prophet. He scoffed at Sufism as nonsense and dismissed Abul Fazl as a liar. But he was impressed by the emperor's devotion to meditation and mysticism and his practice of spending whole nights in prayer and adoration, chanting 'Ya Huwa' and 'Ya Hadi', lost in lonely thought. Akbar slept little, for he counted the night as an addition to his life.

In 1575, grateful for a succession of victories, Akbar built numerous places of worship and one of contemplation, the *ibadatkhana* (house of worship), near a water body called Anuptalao, where religious scholars gathered on Thursday nights for discourse. During one discussion, Akbar told Badauni to report any instance of a cleric speaking nonsense. Sotto voce, Badauni replied that most of the ulema would have to leave if such a condition were applied. Akbar was 'highly pleased'. The hypocrisy of a leading light like Maulana Abdullah Sultanpuri was hardly helpful to the orthodox cause. He was caught evading *zakat*, the annual payment towards charity incumbent in Islamic law, by transferring his wealth to his wife each year just before the due date and then taking it back.[38] Akbar promoted a Sufi like Shaikh Tajuddin, who preached the philosophy of immanence, *wahdath al-wujud* (unity of being), which reaffirmed humanism as the bridge between every creation of God.[39]

Akbar understood that it would be politically unwise to exile the orthodox Muslim priests, for they had an audience,[40] but he challenged them. In 1573, when Maulana Abdul Rahman, a visiting preacher from Transoxiana, asserted in a Friday sermon that the Prophet Muhammad's ancestors would go to hell because they were not Muslims, Akbar interrupted, saying: 'This does not contain a grain of truth, for when intercession for so many sinners has been granted through him, how could his mother and father remain deprived? How could they be consigned to everlasting perdition?' The people applauded.[41]

In another instance, a Sunni cleric declared that Hajj was no longer obligatory because both routes to Mecca from India were in the control of heretics and infidels: one passed through Shia Persia by land, while the seas were ruled by the Portuguese. Akbar dismissed this as nonsense. His mother, Hamida Banu, was a Shia.

Jotik Rai identified traits in Akbar that escaped others, such as his deep interest in music. Venus, also in the second house, enabled Akbar able to discern the finer points of music, musical modes and the mysteries of songs. Akbar, a connoisseur of Indian classical music, brought a sublime quality to his court with the genius of Tansen, a *kalawant* from Gwalior unique in his time for his voice. He began his career in the service of Ram Chand, raja of Panna. In 1563, Akbar heard of his unparalleled reputation and dispatched Jalal Khan Qorchi with a friendly letter to the raja. There was only one advisable response to such an overture. The raja sent Tansen to join the corps of singers in court, along with a homage of precious jewels and elephants. In return, he received gifts beyond his expectations. Abul Fazl adds that Tansen became a constant member of the emperor's retinue.

Some predictions were oblique but not opaque. Wealth was easy to indicate, but black animals required inference. Saturn, in Libra and at its exaltation at the time of Akbar's birth, made him master of all the treasures of the world. Since it was in the shadow of the world-illuminating Sun, the wealth would be stable. With success and prosperity assured, there would be black animals of immense size at his gate.

As mentioned earlier, Akbar was mesmerised by the size, gait, form and loyalty of elephants, as well as their benign and aggressive aspects. His first elephant was Dalsingar, which he rode on the way to Delhi with Humayun. His expertise in handling elephants was such that he mounted ferocious beasts that experienced mahouts left alone, each with enough power to put a city in turmoil. His favourites had charming names: Dalbai, Damodar, Fattuha, Faujbidar, Gaj Bhaunr, Ghalib-Jang, Hawai, Jag Mohan, Jaur-Bunyan, Jhalpa, Kali Beg, Lakhna, Palta, Ranbagh, Sabdaliya, Takht-i-Rawan and so on.

The Lucky Capital

On 9 October 1558, the twenty-six-year-old king boarded a boat on the Jamuna for Agra, a metropolis of felicity and fortune, which, says Abul Fazl, put Baghdad with its Tigris and Cairo with its Nile to shame. Nobles built mansions by the Jamuna, whose soft and tasty water had few equals. The weather was an equilibrium between heat and cold. Its trees and fruits matched those of Khurasan and Persia.

On 30 October 1558, the imperial banners were raised atop the finials as the king settled in the citadel. Agra was deemed to bring good fortune. The shift initiated a remarkable expansion of territory. Gwalior Fort was conquered within less than four months. Abul Fazl pays due homage to the 'lucky stars', which were always gazing with felicity upon the emperor's 'ascendant', adding that the strong and impregnable Gwalior Fort could only have succumbed to the 'might of luck of such a lord of fortune'. Akbar received the key to the Gwalior citadel in January 1559.

Akbar continuously improved his military machine, adapting to regional needs with impressive flexibility. He built the first Mughal fleet for the rivers and swamps of Bengal. The Mughals were land people; the water was never their forte. When Akbar moved to Lahore for nearly five years, he ordered the construction of a ship in Himalayan timber, with a keel of 93 feet, for the Indus. Built to cross shallows, it was commissioned on 21 June 1594 for a downstream journey of 650 miles on the Indus.

Akbar did not waste sentiment on battle, punishing resistance when necessary, but he preferred to use military capability was as a form of leverage. Those who accepted co-option into his hierarchical system were allowed to retain much of their local power. This policy was particularly successful in Rajasthan.

While strengthening Agra Fort between 1565 and 1573, Akbar introduced the *jharoka* (ledge) on the ramparts, where he would sit each morning for darshan, a concept borrowed from India, which was also an implicit affirmation of a quasi-divine status. On a more prosaic level, he sometimes kept in touch with street sentiment by wandering through bazaars in disguise, a form of personal due diligence. Abul Fazl records that he was once recognised by the people near Agra. The emperor rolled up his eyes, squinted, contorted his countenance and continued to watch the 'kaleidoscope of human destiny'. The impromptu ruse worked. On 29 December 1577, he slept over at the hut of Bhura, the headman of the village of Lalna in Palam, near Delhi. Bhura was later given a land grant for offering the king shelter.

Star-shine extended to the imperial wardrobe, which contained 1,000 suits, 120 of which were kept in readiness to wear. Like Humayun, Akbar dressed in the colour of the influential planet of the day. The *Ain-i-Akbari* mentions that court language became people-centric in stages. The *burqa* (veil) was also called *chitragupita* (concealed portrait). The *kulah* (cap) was termed *sis sobha*. *Muy-baf* (hair ribbon) translated to *kesh-gan*, *shaal* (shawl) to *parm-narm*; and *pai-afzar* (footwear) to *charn-dharn*.

Abul Fazl's translation bureau, the *makbatkhana*, was more than a department of record. It bridged literatures to help the people understand official communication better. Akbar increased the use of Sanskrit and Hindi words in court diction and named a suburb created for aristocratic leisure near Agra as Nagarchain ('City of Calm'). In 1577, the emperor heard, while in Amber, of an ancient city that had been reduced by time to a mound of earth. Astrologers were summoned to find the best moment for new foundations, which were laid on 10 November. He named the city Mul-Manoharnagar after Manohar Das, the son of the zamindar of the land, Rai Lonkaran.[42]

Playing cards got Indian motifs. According to *Ain-i-Akbari*, His Majesty played with a suit of cards in which Ashwapati, the lord of horses, represented the Mughal king on horseback beneath an umbrella (*chatr*) and *alam* (standard). The full suit included Gajpati, the king of Orissa, whose strength lay in elephants; Narpati, the ruler of Bijapur, famous for infantry; Garhpati, seated on a throne over a fort; Dhanpati, the lord of treasure; Dalpati, the hero of battle; Awapati, the master of the fleet; Tipati, the queen on a throne surrounded by maids; Suryapati, the Sun God or Indra; Asrpati, the lord of genii, along with the master of genii, Solomon; Vanpati, the king of forests with a tiger and leopard; and Ahipati, the king of snakes.

Art flourished. Akbar had learnt painting as a boy. As an emperor, he went to the imperial studio once a week. The Mughal school he inspired began producing illustrations for the stories of Amir Hamza, which the emperor loved to hear, and blossomed into one of the great hubs of world art. Abul Fazl is not exaggerating when he writes that minute detail, general finish and boldness of execution were incomparable. The artists belong to a rare hall of fame: Mir Sayyid Ali of Tabriz (who was also a poet using the pseudonym 'Judai'), Khwaja Abdus Samad (styled Shirin Qalam or 'sweet nib'), Daswanth (the son of a palanquin-bearer, discovered by the emperor, a genius who went mad and committed suicide), Basawan (considered even better than Daswanth by many critics), Kesu, Lal, Mukund,

Mushkin, Farrukh, Madhu, Jagan, Mahesh, Khemkaran, Tara, Sawla, Haribans and Ram.

The emperor was contemptuous of clerics who condemned portraiture as akin to idol worship, calling them bigoted followers of the letter of the law: 'There are many that hate painting; but such men I dislike. It appears to me as if a painter had quite peculiar means of recognizing God.'[43] Illustrations were done for the Ramayana, *Chengiznama* (history of Genghis Khan), *Zafarnama* (history of Taimur), *Nal Daman* (from the Mahabharata, translated by Abul Fazl), the *Kalilah Damnah*, *Ayar Danish*, *Razmnama* and *Hamzanama*.

With temporal success, the spiritual dimension began to increasingly occupy Akbar's mind. He moved towards simplicity, solitude and prayer. By the 1590s, the hunter who had notched over a thousand kills on just one gun named Sangram decided that his stomach would no longer be a tomb of animals. Meat went off the royal menu on Fridays, Sundays, the first day of every solar month, solar and lunar eclipses, days between two fasts, the whole month of Farvardin (February–March) and the month of his birth (Rajab by the Hijri calendar). Having established peace within his realm, the emperor was in quest of peace within himself.

In 1571, the capital was shifted to Fatehpur in honour of the Sufi saint Salim Chishti. Akbar also sought the blessings of Khwaja Muinuddin for the change on 24 July 1571 and ordered construction of a third capital from 9 August 1571. In effect, Fatehpur became a twin city to Agra rather than a separate entity, with the roughly 40-kilometre road between them lined with shops. Agra reclaimed its pre-eminence in the 1580s.

The Power of Mothers

The astrologers were right when they said that justice would be a fulcrum of Akbar's administration. His beloved wet nurse, Maham Anaka, who became a power in the land because of her political acumen, discovered that the emperor's justice was impervious to sentiment.

Akbar, haunted by the trauma of maternal deprivation as an infant and child, loved his two foster-mothers, Maham Anaka and Jiji Anaka. As fiercely protective guardians, they had provided him emotional and even physical security. There is no parallel in Mughal annals to their influence in Akbar's reign.

His mother, Hamida Banu (1527–1604), who had remained in Kabul when Humayun set out on his campaign for Delhi in 1554, joined her son in 1557 after the defeat of Hemu and lived to see her son rise to greatness. She is buried beside her husband at Humayun's Tomb in Delhi. Her titles included Mahd-i-muqaddas ('Sacred Cradle'), Mahd-i-mualla ('Exalted Cradle') and Mahd-i-ulya ('Loftiest Cradle'). A surviving portrait, painted during Shahjahan's reign, shows her wearing a pendant in the central parting of her hair, long pearl earrings in four strands accompanied by a cluster of jewels at the earlobe, multiple bangles and rings, and glittering bands above the elbow. Her hair sweeps down her forehead, above large eyes.

There was competitive jealousy between Maham and Jiji when Akbar was a baby. Maham accused Jiji of using sorcery to ensure that the baby would go to her for his feed. Jiji claimed she heard Akbar say, when he was just eight months old, that he would always shed the light of joy on her if she was in distress, but that she should keep this promise a secret. Abul Fazl, always eager to attribute supernatural powers to his benefactor, headlines this story 'H.I.M. performs a miracle in the eighth month after his birth as a preface to his later saintly miracles'.

A third wet nurse, Bicha Jan Anaka, reported that one morning she suddenly felt as if a great light had settled on her lap. She thought it was the sun, and such was her astonishment that all her limbs trembled in ecstasy. That ecstatic premonition was borne out when she was hired to raise Akbar.

Maham Anaka's loyalty and devotion to the child, evident during the siege of Kandahar and in hostile Kabul, was complemented by great intellect. She was a mature, skilful lady who became a political force in a male world. She outmanoeuvred the formidable Bairam Khan in the crisis that transformed Akbar from figurehead to monarch. In slow steps, Maham Anaka tried to whittle away the power that Bairam Khan had usurped for himself after Akbar's ascension. She is described as being utterly attached both physically and spiritually to her king. By 1560, she was overseeing all administrative and fiscal affairs although Bairam Khan, as *ataliq* (mentor), remained the dominant force in the kingdom.

The tension between Bairam Khan and Akbar took many forms. In 1557, Akbar was watching a fight between two elephants, Fattuha and Lakhna, when the press of spectators reached Bairam Khan's tent. He thought that rowdies had been sent on royal instructions. He asked Maham Anaka: had troublemakers created such disfavour that mad elephants had been set upon him? Maham Anaka soothed his suspicions.

Shared power was not sustainable. By 1560, Bairam Khan became certain that he was indispensable in the management of the affairs of Hindustan. Akbar was equally convinced that he would never be able to exercise the powers of a king if Bairam Khan remained in office. The simmering tension surfaced again when an elephant from Akbar's stable gored one belonging to Bairam Khan. In a fit of fury, Bairam Khan killed the keeper, an act considered beyond the bounds of convention, etiquette and devotion. Despite the provocation, Akbar opted for discretion, but he could not remain indifferent when informed by intelligence agents that Bairam Khan, or 'Khan Baba', had begun to entertain 'destructive thoughts' and was conspiring with nobles like Wali Beg Dhul-Qadr and Shaikh Gadai Kambo to replace Akbar with his cousin Mirza Abul Wasim, Kamran's son. The wine of success is so heady, writes Abul Fazl, that but one in a thousand has the capacity to remain sober.

The emirs were watching to see who would prevail in the power struggle. Akbar decided that the knot needed to be cut. He conferred with Maham Anaka, now recognised by him as a marvel of strategy and devotion, and Mirza Sharafuddin Hussain, who would become the emperor's brother-in-law later that year upon his marriage to Bakshi Banu Begum. Maham Anaka played a crucial role in the ensuing counteroffensive.

She persuaded the governor of Delhi, Shihabuddin Ahmed Khan, to join the royal banners. She was at the king's side when Akbar left Agra on 18 March 1560, purportedly for hunting. Her second move, however, was a mistake. She took into confidence her son Adham Khan's father-in-law Muhammad Baqi Baqlani. This 'ill-starred wretch' betrayed them, but an overconfident Bairam Khan refused to believe Baqlani. Akbar put out word that he was heading for Delhi to see his mother, Hamida Banu, who was slightly indisposed. Shihabuddin Khan joined the king as he neared the capital.

Akbar entered Delhi on 26 March 1560 at an auspicious hour determined by an astrologer. An unambiguous edict was issued, which Abul Fazl records:

> Since Bairam Khan has deviated from the right path due to the onslaught of worldly occupation, he has been banished from our sight and we have settled in Delhi. Anyone who turns to us in loyalty or knows a good deal

when he sees one and wants to reach salvation and reach his goal will, upon the receipt of this world-obeyed edict, come to the court of world refuge in order that we may elevate each and every one with exalted offices, for this is the beginning of the time of the appearance of our eternal fortune.[44]

Bairam Khan, still unwilling to believe that the chess game of fate had turned against him, ignored the royal command until the governors he had appointed turned cool towards his emissaries. He went to pieces, lost control, and then resorted to sorcery and incantation in the hope that magic might save what imprudence had lost. It failed. Bairam Khan then tried abject submission. It was too late. The only options were war or exile. He decided to mobilise. As camouflage, he announced he was leaving for Hajj but instructed the commander of the Lahore Fort, Mahdi Qasim Khan, to hold the citadel against any imperial force.

Akbar chastised Bairam Khan but stopped short of pronouncing a traitor's fate: death. In deference to past loyalty, Akbar reduced the punishment for his mentor's rebellion to exile and pilgrimage. Privately, Akbar admitted that such generosity might boomerang.

Maham Anaka took control of affairs, prepared for war, and appointed Shihabuddin Ahmad Khan and Khwaja Jahan as her assistants. She calmed minds troubled by high-stakes turbulence, as nobles and troops joined the imperial army from all directions. A woman had become the effective executive, writes Abul Fazl, in a role where a man had to be ready to kill his father to protect the emperor. He chastises men who worship the physical form, which was only external strength. Leadership required wisdom and patience, virtues that Maham Anaka possessed to perfection.

On 8 April 1560, Bairam Khan left Agra for Alwar, gathering support where he could, including emirs who had been imprisoned for sedition in Bayana. Ten days later, Akbar sent a force towards Mewat, where Bairam Khan was camped. The ageing renegade tried another feint, claiming in an apologetic letter that all he wanted was to leave for Mecca. He went to Bikaner, where he stayed as a guest of Rai Kalyan Mal. Then, suddenly, he veered towards Punjab. Rebellion became open, the final provocation being a wounded male ego.

Bairam Khan sent a message to the emirs on hearing that Maham Anaka had been exulting over his banishment. He was on his way to Hejaz for pilgrimage, he said, when he learnt that his exile was due to slander by certain persons, particularly Maham Anaka, who thought that she had become autonomous and boasted of having ousted him. He claimed he was now absolutely determined to destroy her and then resume his 'blessed journey'.

Akbar replied with a long epistle. Bairam Khan's vision, wrote the king, had been clouded by pride and conceit; he had become a puppet of a corrosive, seditious group. A sentence summed up the theme: anyone who tried to blow out a lamp lit by God would get his own beard singed. Akbar ordered Bairam Khan to lower his head in entreaty and bend his neck in obedience before the just ruler. Bairam Khan refused to bend, let alone bow.

Akbar left Delhi on 12 August 1560 for Sirhind. Maham Anaka, after due discussion, selected the field commanders for the impending battle. They included her son Adham Khan. Bairam Khan was defeated at Gunachar. Victorious troops pursued and killed Bairam Khan's men, for there was no other fate for rebels. The world, which had been in chaos, calmed down again, wrote Abul Fazl. On 9 September, Bairam Khan's fur robe and mantle were displayed and his officers paraded in chains before the emperor at Sirhind. The booty included a jewelled banner intended to be sent to Imam Riza's shrine in Mashad, which was considered a good omen.

Bairam Khan fell at the king's feet, weeping. Akbar, displaying the courtesy due to an elder, raised his 'Khan Baba', embraced him, sat him at his old place to his right, presented him with a gorgeous robe and gave him permission to leave on the long-mentioned pilgrimage. Despite appearances, it was a steely, regal dismissal.

On 31 January 1561, Bairam Khan was killed in Patan by Afghans with a memory, settling old scores. The assassin, Mubarak Khan Lohani, had avenged the death of his father, killed in the battle of Macchiwara between Humayun and Sikandar Suri in 1555. Bairam Khan was buried in the Persian city of Mashad. His son Abdur Rahim, then four years old, was brought to Agra. Akbar treated him like a son.

It was not long before Maham Anaka realised that the demands of justice took precedence over love and service. On 16 May 1562, her intoxicated son Adham Khan killed Ataka Khan, appointed Mir Wakil the previous November, during a council meeting in Agra Fort. The murderer then rushed towards the private chambers where Akbar was resting. Woken by the clamour and informed about the crime, Akbar struck the drunk killer so hard with his fist that Adham Khan fainted. He was thrown over the ramparts on the emperor's orders but survived the fall. He was dragged back by his hair and pitched again until his neck was broken and his brains were dashed.

The ailing Maham Anaka heard that her son had been caught for some act of immoderation. She rushed to Akbar, whose response was stoic: Adham had killed Ataka. Justice had been done. Maham Anaka began to wail when she learnt the facts. Akbar tried to calm her, but she did not recover. Maham Anaka died in the following month, June.

She was entombed beside her son in a mausoleum called Bhul Bhulaiyan, north of the Qutub Minar in Delhi.

The Magic Knife

By 1569, Akbar's eminence was recognised far beyond his empire. One admirer, the raja of Cochin, famous across the land for the extent of his wealth and territory and impressed by stories told by wandering mendicants and yogis about the resurgent Mughal emperor, wanted to send Akbar a unique gift: an ancient knife made in Cochin that was believed to have medical qualities and act as a shield against sorcery. A swelling on the body would disappear at the touch of this plain-looking knife.

No one was willing to undertake the difficult journey north until the raja's wazir's young son accepted the mission. In Agra, however, he could not get access to the court until Birbal heard about him. Akbar received him graciously and accepted the gift. Abul Fazl reports that the knife was kept in the imperial treasury and heard the emperor say many times that more than 200 persons at death's door had been restored to health by a touch of this omnipotent knife.

Admiration abroad could not prevent machinations at home. The knife was no cure for sibling envy and ambition. Maulana Chand had warned against kin: 'The third house, which has to do with relatives, is Scorpio, which indicates scorpion-like relatives, but with Saturn there, distant relatives will be led by infelicity and disaster into the valley of perdition and destruction.'[45]

Such viciousness was part of family history. Humayun's brother Kamran had combined the bite of the scorpion with the venom of a snake. Akbar would wish he did not have a brother, wrote Jotik Rai after studying his horoscope. The good news was that such relatives would not live long, nor would brothers achieve any level of capability because the ascendant star of surviving brothers was occulted. An elder brother, Al-Aman Mirza, born in 1528, died long before Akbar's birth, at the age of seven or eight. Akbar's younger brothers, Mirza Farrukh Fal and Mirza Hakim, were sons of Humayun's third wife, the astute Mah Chuchuk Begum, who effectively ruled Kabul after Humayun's departure for Delhi in 1554 until her death in 1564. Farrukh Fal died in 1553 at the age of six. Hakim, born the same year, became the focal point of two failed rebellions in 1574 and 1582 before alcohol killed him when he was thirty-two.

Sincere friends would compensate for brothers, said Shirazi, of which Man Singh is evidence. They would risk their lives and receive happiness and fortune from the emperor. Akbar's closest friends and associates passed away before he did: Birbal in 1586, followed by Tansen and Todar Mal in 1589. Abul Fazl was killed on the orders of Salim. The death of two sons from alcohol and Salim's fluctuating rebellion through the 1590s were the cause of great distress in a life of sustained success.

In 1604, a year before his death, Akbar's envoy Asad Beg Qazwini brought gifts from Ibrahim Adil Shah of Bijapur. They included a bejewelled hookah. Smoking had become common in the south after the Portuguese introduced tobacco in India. The beautifully coloured hookah pipe was three cubits in length, with a Yemeni mouthpiece and a golden burner for lighting tobacco packed in a golden box. Among the advocates of smoking in Akbar's court was Aziz Koka, who argued from experience that it was widely prevalent in Mecca and Medina.

The emperor's physician, Hakim Ali Gilani, had a different view, asserting that it would be injurious to His Majesty's health. Akbar took a few puffs and asked if tobacco had any peculiarities, noting that it was not mentioned in Indian books. Hakim Ali insisted that it was unfit for consumption. Akbar argued that there were wise men among Europeans as well, who could not have prescribed it for their kings without due research. Hakim would not budge, arguing that it was not necessary for them to adopt a European custom that had not been sanctioned by the wise men of India, without experiment and trial.

Qazwini retorted that every custom was new at some point, from the age of Adam; that was the law of invention. He gave the example of a newly imported 'China root' that had proved useful in the cure of diseases. The emperor agreed, remarking that one should not reject anything merely because it did not exist in 'our books' or progress would be impossible. But Akbar did not smoke again in the year that was left of his life.

The confetti strewn by astrologers created great expectations. Akbar was hailed as the promised ruler of one-fourth of the world, giving protection to his people in the manner of the Persian king Jamshed. He was extolled for being as wise as Solomon with a realm as well ordered as a garden, whose achievements were a bejewelled garland that would adorn future generations. Praise is easy currency in a courtier's hand. But this much cannot be gainsaid: four centuries after his death, Akbar is recognised as one of the great monarchs of world history. A recent book written by Dominic Lieven, Honorary Fellow and Emeritus Fellow of Trinity College, Cambridge, Honorary Academician of the Russian Academy of Sciences, *In the Shadow of the Gods: The Emperor in World History*, has a cover with a painting by Bichitr, done circa 1630, showing Akbar passing his crown to Jahangir and grandson Shahjahan.

Jalaluddin Akbar would live long enough, Jotik Rai promised, to enjoy the love of grandchildren who would grow grand under his patronage. Shahjahan, born Khusrau, was his favourite grandchild.

Akbar enjoyed good health throughout his life but for that early attack of pustules and an ailment in 1591. Such was the family's confidence in his recuperative powers that his doctors, Hakim Ali Gilani and Hakim Jalaluddin Muzaffar, were accused of neglect when, in October 1605, the emperor did not recover from fever and diarrhoea. Critics accused Hakim Ali of prescribing a meat broth, hardly the best antidote.

Jalaluddin Muhammad Akbar's empire flourished for a century after his death on 27 October 1605 until a great-grandson wrecked the harmony that had sustained the empire.

Appendix: Sayings of Akbar (Selected from *Ain-i-Akbari*)

The bond between Creator and creature cannot be expressed in words.

No harm will befall the heart if it preserves the balance that Hindu (Indian) women do when they fetch water from the rivers, tanks or wells, carrying several pitchers at a time, one above the head, others in hands, and converse freely with companions while walking on uneven ground.

It is easy to transit from real asceticism to unlawful beggary.

When trials befall, do not scowl with knitted brows but accept them cheerfully as a physician's bitter remedies.

Most worshippers are intent on the advancement of their own desires, not on worship of God.

Clean the rust of your heart with the grey of your hair.

Each person gives the Supreme Being a name, but to name the Unknowable is vain.

To impute the existence of evil to Satan is to make him a partner of God. If he is a robber, who is responsible for making him one?

A man is a disciple of his own reason.

If imitation was commendable, the prophets would only have followed their predecessors.

The vulgar believe in miracles; the wise accept nothing without adequate proof.

The welfare of children lies first in obedience to parents. Alas, Emperor Humayun died early, giving me no opportunity to show him faithful service.

The world is amenable only to kindness. No living creature deserves rejection.

Guidance means showing the road, not collecting disciples.

Knowledge is regarded as the summit of perfection, but becomes worse than ignorance unless displayed in action.

Men are blind to everything but their own advantage. If a cat claws a pigeon, they get angry, but rejoice when it catches a mouse: in what way has the mouse done them wrong?

A man is wise when he can distinguish between what is truly his own and what he has only borrowed.

Although sleep is healthy, the night should be spent awake, for life is the greatest gift of God.

To love children is to obey God.

A rope-dancer performs with feet and hands; a poet with his tongue.

The three causes of aberrant judgement are: incapacity of mind; enemies disguised as friends; and duplicity of friends pursuing their own interests.

My constant prayer is that when my thoughts and actions no longer please the Supreme Giver, he should take my life.

The hair of the head turns grey first because it appears before the hair of the beard.

If a man's wish prevails, he wants a daughter in the image of his wife; if the wife has the stronger affection, then she wants a son in the image of her husband.

Miracles occur in every religion; the truth can be but one.

The ear is the sentinel of the voice. When you become deaf, you lose the need of speech.

It is not right that a man should make his stomach the graveyard of animals.

A wise man was asked to explain the reason for the long life of the vulture and the short life of a hawk. He replied: the vulture never injures a live animal, while the hawk hunts.

It is a strange commentary on men that they should seek deliverance through the self-sacrifice of their wives on the funeral pyre.

Tyranny is unlawful, especially in a sovereign, who is the guardian of the world.

A king should not be familiar in amusement with his courtiers.

The words of kings resemble pearls. They are not fit pendants for every ear.

4

Jahangir: No One Is a Relation to the King

THE LAST PUBLIC EVENT arranged by Emperor Akbar at his palace grounds was a metaphor that would seem over-crafted in fiction: a fight between two elephants, one owned by his thirty-seven-year-old son Jahangir and the other by his eighteen-year-old grandson Khusrau. It was a confrontation between the nominated heir and the putative challenger.

The audience understood the context. When Jahangir's elephant began to prevail, supporters from both sides 'leapt into the fight to assist their champions and the event disintegrated into an unruly and embarrassing brawl'.[1] In the always difficult and dangerous battles of succession, Jahangir's claims were being contested by his eldest son.

That evening, Akbar developed a high fever. As it persisted, palace intrigues too intensified—a contest for power that could have created a schism and destabilised a vast empire still only as old as one lifetime. Khusrau had substantial support, most notably from his maternal uncle Raja Man Singh and his father-in-law Mirza Aziz Koka. A mature coalition of nobles persuaded Akbar to pre-empt war by anointing his son as successor.

Just before his death in October 1605, Akbar bestowed the robes of office upon the child of his prayers, his cherished Shaikhu Baba ('Little Shaikh'), as he had named Salim after a Sufi saint, who would be known in history as Jahangir.

There is some dispute about the exact date of Akbar's death, but there is no ambiguity over this in the opening sentence of the *Tuzuk-i-Jahangiri*: 'By the boundless favour of Allah, when one sidereal hour of Thursday, Jumada-s-ani 20th, AH 1014 [24 October 1605], had passed, I ascended the royal throne in the capital of Agra, in the 38th year of my age.'[2]

Akbar had been king without an heir until the age of twenty-seven. Five years earlier, his twins, Hassan and Hussain, had returned to the 'pleasure park of the other world' within a month of their birth. People had begun to fabricate tales and gossip about Agra, saying the capital was unlucky for the realm. God, writes Abul Fazl, had granted several children but taken them away. Unwilling to be too critical of God, the court historian attributes this misfortune to 'a thousand wise reasons', the most convenient being that the existing sorrow would enhance the joy a future pearl would bring.[3]

The 'God-worshipping' Akbar, desperate for a son who would share the 'secrets of the imperial banquet, be worthy of the emperor's address, and share in the ocean of divine effulgence that had been achieved in the person', sought the intervention of a pious Sufi mystic, Shaikh Salim Chishti of Sikri, a village near Agra. Chishti promised the king three sons. With elegant discretion, Abul Fazl records that within a 'short time signs of the attainment of this wish appeared' when the queen Harkha Bai (1542–1623) became pregnant. Two courtiers, Shaikh Muhammad Bukhari and Hakim Ainulmulk, persuaded Akbar to send the expecting mother and her retinue to the saint's care in Sikri. Akbar vowed to walk barefoot in gratitude to the 13th-century shrine of Khwaja Muinuddin Chishti, the founder of the Chishti *silsila* (lineage), in Ajmer if his wish was granted.[4] On Wednesday, 31 August 1569, Muhammad Salim came 'into existence from the hiding place of nothingness' after 'seven *ghari* of the aforesaid day had passed, when Libra [Mizan] had risen to the 24th degree.'[5] In Abul Fazl's words, 'the market of rejoicing flourished, and the eye of fortune was brightened'. Akbar waited before going to see the child of his hopes, as popular belief held that some time should pass before the first viewing of a new-born if God had granted the child after a long wait. The baby was named Salim after the pious benefactor.

Astrologers from both the Indian and Greek schools drew the child's horoscope by 'imperial command'. Maulana Chand was still in service: 'Since the horoscope cast by the astrologer Maulana Chand according to Greek principles was found to be more reliable, it will be given first.'[6] Abul Fazl reproduces the charts[7] that were drawn at Salim's birth.

Akbar kept his vow. He left for Ajmer on 20 January 1570. Travelling ten to twelve leagues a day, he reached the shrine with the dust of the road still upon him. He spent days in thanksgiving and distributed gold. The gold led to squabbles, which the emperor settled by putting a new person in charge of the Ajmer shrine.

Jahangir believed that the saint's blessings had helped him navigate the toxic swamps of the ascent to power and survival. He had been emperor for a dozen years when he told a story about his 'divine' connection to Salim Chishti. On 29 December 1618, he camped on a lakeside near Fatehpur Sikri after a four-month journey from Ahmedabad, since astrologers would not let him enter the city before the auspicious day of 9 January 1619. After offering prayers at Salim Chishti's shrine, Jahangir narrated an event from his early childhood.

Akbar had once asked Salim Chishti how old he was, only to hear that life and death were in God's hands. Akbar was persistent. Shaikh Salim's answer was mysterious: he would die when the prince (Jahangir) was able to recite something from memory. Akbar gave instructions that the child should not be allowed to memorise any lines, whether prose or verse. But when Jahangir was two years and seven months old, a woman who had come to the palace to ward off the 'evil eye' (*nazar*) from children found the prince alone and taught him a couplet written by the 15th-century Persian scholar-poet Jami:

> O God, open the rosebud of hope
> Display a flower from the everlasting garden.

Jahangir, obviously unaware of the implications, repeated this verse to Salim Chishti. That night, the venerable mystic developed a fever. He had a last wish—to hear the renowned musician in the galaxy of Akbar's court, Tansen Kalawant, 'who was unequalled as a singer'. His wish was granted. When the music was over, Salim Chishti asked for the emperor. Akbar came to his bedside. Shaikh Salim placed his own turban on Jahangir's head, saying, 'We have made Sultan Salim our successor [to the throne], and have made him over to God, the protector and preserver.' Shaikh Salim Chishti died on 15 February 1572.[8]

As promised by Salim Chishti, Akbar had three sons. Shah Murad, a 'pearl of the necklace of fortune', was born on 7 June 1570 'under the sign of Capricorn according to the Greeks but Sagittarius according to the Indians, a lucky-starred child from whose brow shone signs of great fortune ... in the quarters of Shaikh Salim in Fatehpur'. Murad was named 'at an auspicious hour', and banquets 'beyond any imagination', at which all 'laps were made heavy with coins', were given to the general populace. Prayers of gratitude were offered at holy places. As a young man, Murad showed great promise. The Jesuit priests who were his tutors thought that he was exceptional, perhaps a genius. Neither priests nor astrologers foresaw that he would drink himself to oblivion. Murad died an alcoholic at twenty-eight.

Akbar's third son, Danyal, was born in the household of Khwaja Muinuddin's descendants on 11 September 1572 under 'the sign of Aries by the calculation of the Greek metaphysicians and under the sign of Aquarius according to the sages of India, at Ajmer.' In flying rhetoric, Fazl asserts that God had 'placed all souls in the world under obligation for the rising of this luminous star'. A magnificent celebration was duly given, and the people loyally rejoiced.[9]

Jahangir remembers Danyal as a person of pleasing appearance but of acquisitive temperament, seizing elephants and horses, animals he loved, from others. He composed verse and 'was fond of Hindi songs' but 'took to improper ways'. Not all the luck in his destiny could preserve him from self-destructive alcoholism. When Akbar prohibited drink in his household, Danyal began to plead with servants to smuggle in wine. A musketeer brought some in the barrel of a gun. Rust dissolved in the strong liquor, turning it poisonous. Danyal could not survive the first sip. He 'wore himself out with drinking', dead at the age of thirty-two in 1604, seven months before his father.[10] Jahangir adds that their father doted upon his daughters, overlooking any childish impudence on the part of his 'darlings', and told his heir to take care of his sisters Shakarunnissa Begum and Aram Banu Begum as he would his mother.[11]

Jahangir had as much faith in astrologers as his father did. Akbar consulted them even for routine travel. It was they who decided the precise time of his return to Agra after a hunt in 1569 or when to leave for a banquet at the home of Shajaat Khan in May 1570.[12] Jahangir's education began in 1573 at a precise age, when he was four years, four months and four days old.

The emperor entrusted his 'darling son' to a tutor with 'spiritual excellence'. A 'murmur of prayer arose from young and old alike' as a Quran was placed in the boy's lap. He was lifted by nobles onto the shoulders of his teacher Maulana Mir Kalan Harawi. Instructions began with the alphabet, 'the foundation of learning and centre of things visible', guiding the student to the 'highness of wisdom'. A celebratory feast was held on 17 November.[13]

Those who believe 16th-century education was limited might want to look at the curriculum for 'every boy' mentioned in the *Ain-i-Akbari*: morals, arithmetic, surveying, geometry, astronomy, physiognomy, household matters, rules of government, logic, natural sciences, music, astronomy, mechanics, theology, history and more.

Jahangir was an educated prince. He wrote poetry, preferred the classical forms of *ghazal* and *rubai*, and disliked laments like *marsiya*. He loved the work of Amir Khusrau and Hafez, sponsored verse competitions and patronised poets.

A parallel education in the hard school of warfare began early. In 1576, when he was seven, Jahangir was given the rank of commander of 10,000 and the technical command of imperial forces, as he had, in his father's estimation, displayed obedience, endurance, prudence and good disposition. A hierarchy was set: Murad was assigned 7,000 and Danyal 6,000. At the age of twelve, Jahangir was sent to welcome his grandaunt Gulbadan Begum on her return to India from Hajj. In the same year, he went on his first military campaign to Kabul against his uncle Muhammad Hakim. It was a lesson he would absorb: sentiment was superfluous in defence of the realm. Jahangir led the Mughal forces that brought Kuch Behar in the east into the domain, and at the age of sixteen, he was raised to the rank of 12,000.

A Mughal prince was assigned an *ateke,* a mentor, to negotiate the difficult early years from child to man. Jahangir's first guardians were Shaikh Ahmad, Shaikh Salim Chishti's son, and Qutbuddin Khan, who were appointed on 3 September 1579.[14] When Jahangir turned thirteen, Akbar decided that he needed 'a confidential companion to keep him from bad company and to encourage his good habits'. Teenage princes required great surveillance: 'Things that rob men of their senses are too numerous to be reported, and those who are intoxicated by this unpalatable wine are too many to be counted.' This responsibility was given to Bairam Khan's son, the polymath-warrior-poet Abdur Rahim, who possessed both 'foresighted wisdom and devotion'. Akbar joined the celebratory banquet for this appointment on 8 September.[15]

Jahangir's first marriage, on 13 February 1585, to his maternal cousin, the daughter of Raja Bhagwant Das of Amber and Man Singh's sister, was a dazzling event: the dowry was 20,000,000 rupees *(tankas),* 100 elephants, Persian horses, rare jewellery, gold utensils and 700 sets of dresses. Akbar threw 101 handfuls of gold and jewels over the bridal litter for distribution among the poor. Hamida Banu gave her daughter-in-law 101 gold roses with stems of emeralds, rubies and diamonds. Their first child, a daughter named Sultan an-Nisa, was born in 1586. Khusrau, born on 6 August 1587, was their second child, after which his mother was given the title of Shah Begum. Jahangir's second son, Parvez, was born in 1589 from his wife Karamsi, the daughter of Raja Keshu Das Rathore. Khurram, later Shahjahan, was born in 1592 to Jagat Gosain Manmati, the daughter of Raja Udai Singh, or Mota Raja, of Marwar. The mother of Jahangir's youngest son, Shahryar, born in 1592, is unknown and undescribed. Shahjahan's bloodlines were more Rajput than Timurid.

Astrologers determined the date of Jahangir's formal coronation: 20 March 1606, Thursday, on Nauruz. Emissaries bearing gifts arrived from India's southern kingdoms and from the proximate Persian and Ottoman empires. There were military parades, musical concerts and fireworks. The *khutba* (sermon) was read in the new king's name. Rewards were doled out to loyalists.

Among the beneficiaries was Raja Bir Singh Deo, who had killed the 'poisonous' Abul Fazl in 1602 on Jahangir's orders. 'I promoted Raja Bir Singh Deo, a Bandela Rajput, who had obtained my favour, and who excels his equals and relatives in valour, personal goodness, and simple heartedness, to the rank of 3,000.' The new monarch was unrepentant about having Abul Fazl killed. He blamed the historian for creating friction between father and son.[16] Abul Fazl had accused the truculent Salim of being evil, not a comment designed to please an heir. Jahangir, now secure on the throne, added some praise for his bête noire as excelling the 'Shaikhzadas of Hindustan in wisdom and learning'.[17]

He soon changed his name from Salim to Nuruddin. His father, he explains, rarely used Salim 'either drunk or sober',[18] preferring the affectionate 'Shaikhu Baba'. Curiously, he asserted that he did not want to be confused with the two famous Ottoman Salims who had been emperors between 1470 and 1574. Nuruddin ('Light of Faith') reflected his veneration for the Sun: 'My sitting on the throne coincided with the rising and shining on the earth of the great light.'[19] His regnal appellation Jahangir meant 'one who seizes the world'.

His inherited treasury was certainly worthy of a great power. It was laden with gold and silver coins, diamonds, rubies, sapphires, pearls, emeralds and the finest cloths from Gujarat, Persia and Turkey, along with arrow-proof coats and personal artillery. The estimated value, recorded in ledgers, was a phenomenal 34.8 crore rupees.

Wisdom was the more valuable legacy. Jahangir lauds Akbar's philosophy of amity between all classes and creeds in a dominion limited on the east and west only by the 'salt sea'. His father had closed the road to altercation between religions. Sunnis and Shias met in one mosque, Franks and Jews in one church, and all observed their own forms of worship. Akbar had associated with the good of every race and creed and persuasion, and was gracious to all in accordance with their condition and understanding. He passed his nights in wakefulness and slept little in the day. He counted his wakefulness at night as so much added to his life.[20]

The message was unambiguous. The Akbar doctrine would prevail.

The Astrologer Is Always Right

Jahangir did not see his grandchild, Khusrau's daughter, for three years because his astrologers advised him to wait for the right time to do so. This child, they said, would be auspicious for Jahangir but detrimental to her father's interests. Jahangir remarks that the prediction was accurate. Jahangir saw her in 1608:

> On Tuesday, the 13th, I sent for Khusrau's daughter, and saw a child so like her father as no one can remember to have seen. The astrologers used to say that her advent would not be auspicious to her father, but would be auspicious to me. At last it became known that they had augured rightly. They said that I should see her after three years. I saw her when she had passed this age.[21]

The stars were much in evidence in the names given for currency denominations. A 'propitious hour' was chosen for minting new coins in 'gold and silver of different weights'. The 100-tola *kaukab-i-tali* was the star of the horoscope, the 50-tola *kaukab-i-iqbal* was the star of fortune, the 20-tola *kaukab-i-murad* the star of desire, the 10-tola *kaukab-i-bakht* the star of good luck and the 5-tola *kaukab-i-saad* the star of auspiciousness.[22] From 1618, Mughal coins began to feature images of the zodiac rather than their date of issue: 'In the month of Farwardin [first month of the Persian solar calendar] the figure of a ram, and in Urdibihisht [second month] the figure of a bull ... This usage is my own, and has never been practised until now.'[23]

Astrologers continued to determine the exact time for the onset of any royal journey or the arrival into a city, as they had for Akbar. Astrology remained a leitmotif in the Jahangir era too. In 1613, to cite one of innumerable examples, 'the hour for entering Ajmer was fixed' by seers. When 'Baba Khurram' (Shahjahan) led his army out of Ajmer soon after, it was also 'at an hour fixed upon' by astrologers.[24] They determined the exact time of the emperor's biannual weighing ceremony.

Kesava Sarma, a Brahmin, was Jahangir's Jotik Rai. His son Isvaradasa later lobbied Aurangzeb for the continuation of patronage, without success.[25] Jotik Rai was 'repeatedly proved correct' in his predictions, says Jahangir, leaving him amazed.

With the transit of the Sun on 10 March 1620, Jahangir celebrated the onset of the fifteenth year of his reign in his beloved Kashmir, the soul-enchanting 'garden of eternal spring' whose flowers ('garden nymphs') shone like lamps and nightingales and whetted the desire for wine. For a lover of nature, there was no better holiday. He travelled via Bakkar, along the river Bihat, through the snow and rain of Baramulla (literally, the place of *varaha* or boars), stopping when he could to smell the flowers, watch a waterfall and learn about falcons and hawks caught in

Kishtwar, where the finest saffron of Kashmir was grown and sold for 4 rupees a maund.

The only niggle as the royal cortege alighted 'auspiciously' on the banks of Dal Lake was a forecast. Jahangir's Jotik Rai, 'one of the most skilled of the class in astrology', had told him the previous winter that the life of his four-year-old grandson Shah Shuja was in danger: 'It was predicted from the Prince's horoscope that these three or four months were unpropitious to him, and it was possible he might fall down from some high place, but that the dust of calamity would not settle on the skirt of his life'.[26]

Jahangir took utmost care to keep his grandson protected. Shah Shuja was kept under constant watch during the journey through difficult mountain passes. But the closest supervision could not avert what was written in the stars. A calamity did occur:

> [On] Sunday, the 17th . . . [Shah Shuja was playing near] a window with a screen in front of it looking towards the river. They had put a screen in front, but had not fastened the door, and the prince in play went towards the window to look out. As soon as he arrived there he fell headlong.[27]

He dropped a distance of seven yards.

By sheer chance, a *farrash* (servant) was seated beside a carpet below this window. 'The child's head fell on this carpet, and his feet on the back and shoulders of the *farrash*.' The child fainted. God's compassion, writes Jahangir, saved Shah Shuja. Jahangir ran out of his chamber in bewilderment ('my senses forsook me'). He held his grandson in a long embrace until the boy recovered and immediately prostrated in a prayer of gratitude. Alms were distributed, and means of livelihood arranged for the poor.[28]

Jotik Rai was not wrong; he had foreseen that 'the dust of calamity would not settle on the skirt of life'. A portrait of Shah Shuja, now in the Sackler Gallery at the Smithsonian in Washington, shows a confident boy, dressed in royal finery, holding a rose.

Jahangir was still in Kashmir when a second augury came true. Jotik Rai, on checking Jahangir's horoscope, had warned two months before the event that a queen would die, or, to use the florid original sentence, 'one [of] the chief sitters in the harem of chastity would hasten to the hidden abode of non-existence'. Padishah Banu Begum passed away during this royal trip to Kashmir. A grieving emperor wrote that 'the heart-rending event laid a heavy load on my mind'. Jotik Rai had 'discovered this from the horoscope of my destiny, and it fell out accordingly'.[29]

The third 'strange' incident occurred in 1621. Jahangir was in Agra, home of the 'throne of success'. On 10 March 1621, 'the sun that bestows bounty on the world lit up the abode of fortune of Aries with his world-illuminating light and gladdened the world and its inhabitants'.[30] The emperor celebrated the wedding of his son Shahryar with a feast at the traditional ceremony of consummation of the marriage. He gifted the groom a jewelled coat (*charqab*), a turban, a waistband and two horses, one with a gold saddle and the other with an embroidered one.

The bad news was that his beloved Shah Shuja was once again in danger. He 'had an eruption so violent that water would not go down his throat, and his life was despaired of'. The astrologers were almost 'unanimous' in their prediction that Shah Shuja would die, for Shahjahan's horoscope said that he would lose a child that year. Jotik Rai, however, was certain that Shuja would live, for Jahangir's horoscope said that 'no distress or trouble would find its way to the royal mind from any road'. Ergo, someone other than Shuja would die. Shahjahan's child from a wife living in Burhanpur passed away.

Jahangir pays handsome tribute to the *munajjim* Jotik Rai: 'Besides this, many of Jotik Rai's judgements [*ahkam*] turned out correct. This is not without strangeness, and it is therefore recorded in these memoirs.' The emperor measured his praise in more than words. Jotik Rai was weighed against money, which meant a reward of 6,500 rupees.[31]

When Jahangir fell seriously ill in 1621, Jotik Rai foresaw full recovery. The 'continuous pain and trouble' did indeed go away. A grateful Jahangir had Jotik Rai 'weighed against *muhars* and rupees' on 2 September 1621; this time, Jotik Rai got 500 muhars and 7,000 rupees. There were collateral benefits to putting on weight.[32]

There were women among the astrologers. In 1622, a pearl valued at between 14,000 and 15,000 rupees was lost in the harem. Jotik Rai announced that it would be found in two or three days. A second astrologer named Sadiq added that the pearl would be discovered in a clean and pure place, 'such as the place of worship or oratory'. A female soothsayer predicted that a fair-skinned woman would bring the pearl in a state of ecstasy and give it into the hand of Hazrat ('the king'). Everyone was right. Jahangir records:

> It happened that on the third day one of the Turkish girls found it in the oratory, and all in smiles and in a happy frame of mind gave it to me. As the word of all three came true each one was favoured with an acceptable reward. This is written because it is not devoid of strangeness.[33]

Like Father, Like Son

Jahangir's insurrection of 1599 was stopped at the gates of Agra by his grandmother.

The tremors began when Akbar fell ill in 1591. Malevolent whispers accused Jahangir, frequently insubordinate, of being part of a conspiracy to kill his father. Camps began to mobilise until Akbar's recovery calmed tensions. The emperor decided it was time to separate the siblings. Jahangir was kept in Agra. Twenty-one-year-old Murad was sent to Malwa in 1591 and then further south to Gujarat and the Deccan. In 1594, Akbar implicitly expanded the succession stakes by giving his grandson Khusrau, then only seven years old, a *mansab* of 5,000.[34] Three years later, the third son, Danyal, was sent to Allahabad.

When the troubled and troublesome Murad drank himself to death in 1599, Jahangir was ordered to take his place in the Deccan, with Man Singh sent alongside to keep an eye. Abul Fazl writes that Jahangir, misguided by 'evil-minded persons', refused to go. Danyal was sent instead. Jahangir would go only as far as Ajmer, where drink and bad advice encouraged a mood of open rebellion. When Man Singh was suddenly ordered to leave for Bengal to deal with rebellion, Jahangir saw his chance. He ordered his 30,000-strong army to march towards Agra.

The tactful commander of Agra, Qulich Khan, welcomed the prince with gifts and ceremony but prevented him from seizing the fort. As Jahangir pondered his next move, he heard that his grandmother was coming out to confront him. That made up his mind. He fled. The angry dowager pursued her grandson.

> Evading her brief pursuit, he travelled eastward by riverboat. Eventually the rebel prince and his troops reached Allahabad, at the confluence of the rivers Ganges and Yamuna, where Salim took the fortress, seizing both the territory and the rich treasury of Bihar, and established himself as ruler.[35]

It was a fortuitous pause in a potential catastrophe. Jahangir created an autonomous base in Allahabad, but, encouraged again by poor advice he marched towards Agra a second time in 1601. Akbar issued an ultimatum, and he retreated. Akbar tried to heal the rift by making de facto de jure. Jahangir was appointed the governor of Bengal and Orissa. Jahangir, always unwilling to shift too far from the capital, remained in Allahabad, took the title of sultan and ordered the Friday sermon to be read in his name. Among his more interesting supporters were members of the Chishti family, who saw him as one of their own. In 1602, he compounded his father's distress with the murder of Abul Fazl. The most sparkling 'jewels' of Akbar's court were now dead: Birbal in 1586, Tansen around the same time, Raja Todar Mal in 1589, and Abul Fazl's brother Faizi in 1595.

In early 1603, the powerful women in the palace decided to intervene. Salima Begum, Akbar's second wife, offered to effect a reconciliation between Akbar and Jahangir. Akbar agreed. Salima Begum brought Jahangir back from Allahabad. As they neared Agra, they were joined by the ageing Hamida Banu. The two grand ladies took the chastised Jahangir to face his father. As the prodigal approached in humility, the two women threw Jahangir at his father's feet. Akbar, moved, embraced his son and placed his turban upon Jahangir's head.

An emotional reunion did not quite erase the root cause of angst. Jahangir refused to lead a campaign against Mewar, apprehensive about being distant from Agra in the fifth decade of his father's reign. In November 1603, he returned to Allahabad. Akbar's tolerance snapped. In August 1604, he set out to chastise Jahangir. Fortune favoured the son. Akbar was forced to turn back when news arrived that his mother, Hamida Begum, who had combined a mother's love with sage advice, was dying. She passed away within a few hours of his return. Akbar shaved his head and served as her pallbearer. Hamida Begum was buried beside her husband at Humayun's Tomb in Delhi. Grief initiated reconciliation.

Jahangir reached Agra on 9 November 1604 in sorrow and penitence. But as soon as the rituals were completed, Akbar ordered his son's arrest. Jahangir was imprisoned for ten days, not for insubordination but for being a drunk. He was denied wine and treated by doctors. Jahangir would remain in Agra for the remaining year of his father's life.

Just when his succession seemed assured, a conspiracy to deny Jahangir the throne surfaced. A formidable alliance of Raja Man Singh and Aziz Koka renewed efforts to persuade the emperor to anoint Khusrau as his successor. The acrimony became so bitter that Khusrau's mother, torn between husband and son, committed suicide on 6 May 1605 by ingesting a lethal dose of *tiryaq* (opium) while Jahangir had gone hunting.

It was, says Jahangir, as if she had foreseen the rebellion of 'her unworthy son'. He asserts that 'she could not endure the bad conduct of her son and brother [Man Singh]' and was so devoted that 'she would have sacrificed a thousand sons and brothers for one hair of mine'. Disgusted with life, she committed suicide, driven by 'the indignation and high spirit which are inherent in the Rajput character' when her pleas to Khusrau failed. Jahangir adds, 'no evil fortune is greater than when a son ... causes the death of his mother and becomes contumacious and rebellious to his father'. He did not eat or drink for four days. Akbar consoled his son with a robe and his personal turban.[36]

On his coronation in March 1606, Jahangir offered a distracted and sullen Khusrau a 'lakh of rupees' for a new house, with the condition that it should be built outside the fort.³⁷ Khusrau was interested in power, not in a palace. On the night of the eighth of Zi-l-Hijja (Saturday–Sunday, 6 April 1606), swept away by 'the pride of youth' and the advice of 'worthless companions', Khusrau rode out of Agra Fort with 350 horsemen after two *gharis* had passed, on the thin pretext that he was going to visit his grandfather's tomb. A lamp attendant informed the amir al-umra (commander), who rushed to the emperor's private quarters and asked a eunuch to convey his request for an immediate meeting.

Jahangir initially thought that there was some urgent news from Gujarat or the Deccan. When informed about what had happened, he asked the amir, 'What must be done? Shall I mount myself, or shall I send Khurram?' The commander offered to lead the chase but wanted clarity: 'If he [Khusrau] will not turn back on my advice, and takes up arms, what must be done?'

A battle meant casualties. Khusrau could be among them. Jahangir's reply was a lesson in power: 'If he will go in no way on the right road, do not consider a crime anything that results from your action. Kingship regards neither son nor son-in-law. No one is a relation to the king.'³⁸

After the order, Jahangir remembered that Khusrau and the amir had a history of hostility between them. The amir might make it a personal feud rather than an imperial duty. Fresh orders were issued. Shaikh Farid Bukhari was placed in command and Khurram given charge of the treasury. Jahangir marched out himself in the early morning.

This was the one time that he forgot to 'ascertain the hour, etc.' from an astrologer before leaving but was soon relieved to learn that the moment of departure augured well:

> It is a strange thing that after I had started I asked Hakim Ali, who is learned in mathematics, how the hour of my departure had been (i.e., whether propitious or not),

and he replied that in order to obtain my object if I had wished to select an hour, there could not have been for years one selected better than that in which I mounted.³⁹

The stars were on his side.

Jahangir prayed at his father's mausoleum in Agra 'for aid to my courage from the spirit of that honoured one'. A co-conspirator of Khusrau, Mirza Hasan, was brought before him at the graveside, which he interpreted as an answered prayer: 'This was the first good omen manifested through the kindness and blessing of that venerable one.' Hasan's hands were tied, and he was mounted on an elephant before being condemned to the 'claws of death'.⁴⁰

Jahangir was so distraught that he forgot to consume his 'regular allowance of opium' in the morning, as he realised while resting under the shade of a tree at noon on that exceedingly hot day. He adds, with a touch of black humour, that Khusrau was probably in a worse state, having been denied his intake of opium.

He stopped in Delhi to pray at his grandfather's tomb and the nearby shrine of Nizamuddin Auliya. He distributed money to the poor, pious dervishes and Brahmins before he headed towards Panipat, the site of the second birth of the empire.

Khusrau was expected to go east, where his uncle Raja Man Singh was governor, but took the road to Lahore, where he hoped for assistance from disaffected Afghans, Uzbeks and Persians. The Afghans were a perennial source of challenge for the Mughals, not least because they felt that their dynasties had been displaced. Fourteen years later, in 1619, Jahangir praised a general, Amanullah, the son of Mahabat Khan, for defeating Ahdad or, to use the colourful phrases of the emperor, made the 'black-faced and black-hearted' Afghans 'the harvest of his blood-drinking sword'.⁴¹

Khusrau plundered merchants and cities to finance his uprising. Jahangir used more conventional methods to bolster allies, paying off a tribal chief of Badakhshan, Jamil Beg, to keep him on side. A loyal general, Dilawar Khan, based in Panipat, took the initiative and raced ahead to reinforce Lahore Fort with cannon and swivel guns. He was in time. Two days later, Khusrau laid siege to the citadel. At one point, a gate was breached, but the defenders held on. Dilawar Khan was promoted to vizier after hostilities ended.

Khusrau was defeated by Shaikh Farid's imperial force. Jahangir was in Sultanpur, about to eat a dish of roast meat, when he heard that the battle had begun. He left the food and mounted, even though his wadded coat could not be found, armed only with a sword and spear, at the head of some 50 horsemen, which grew to around 500. He was crossing a bridge at Gobindwal when a wardrobe man named Shamsi brought news of victory. Shamsi was promptly renamed Khushkhabar Khan ('bearer of good news').

Raja Baso was sent after the fleeing Khusrau, who was captured while trying to cross the Chenab. Tearful and trembling, Khusrau was brought before the emperor, now camped at Mirza Kamran's garden in Lahore, on Thursday, the third of Muharram, with 'chains on his legs from the left side [from left hand to left foot] after the manner and custom of Genghis Khan'. On either side were two associates, Abdur Rehman and Husain Beg, speaking wildly. An ox and an ass were slaughtered on the spot. The two were wrapped in their skins and paraded around the city. Beg died of suffocation. At least 300 rebel troops were impaled or hanged on wooden posts.[42]

Jahangir waited five days for the auspicious moment for entering Lahore: 'Monday, the last day of Zi-I-Hijja until the 9th of Muharram of the aforesaid year, I remained in Mirza Kamran's garden because the time was unpropitious.'⁴³

His stepmother Sultan Begum's intervention had saved Mirza Aziz Koka's life but not his lands or his titles. Koka, treated as family as the son of Akbar's wet nurse Jiji Anaka, spent two years in prison but could not be cured of vaulting ambition.⁴⁴ In 1614, he was back in confinement, caught fomenting another plot on behalf of Khusrau. His second reprieve was unusual. Jahangir writes: 'I dreamt that the late king [Akbar] said to me: "Baba, forgive for my sake the fault of Aziz Khan, who is Khan Azam." After this dream, I decided to summon him from the [Gwalior Fort].'⁴⁵ Along with a reprieve, Koka received a purse of 1,00,000 rupees.

Victory led to rumination. Jahangir tries to assuage the guilt of his own rebellion against his father by blaming 'short-sighted men in Allahabad' and forgives himself by saying that he eventually acted 'according to the dictates of reason and knowledge' and 'waited on my father, my guide, my *qibla,* and my visible God'.⁴⁶ He had waited until the last year of his father's life to bow before his temporal *qibla.*

Fathers, however aggrieved, did not order the death of sons in the Mughal dynasty. Their elimination was left to brothers. In 1616, Jahangir was bewildered when he heard that Persia's Shah Abbas had ordered the death of his son Safi Mirza and raised the episode with the Persian ambassador. The ambassador's response was succinct: the son would have killed the father if he had been left alive.⁴⁷ Shah Abbas killed or blinded three of his five adult sons.

Shaikh Farid Bukhari, who had saved Jahangir twice in two years, was raised to the rank of 5,000 horse, honoured with the title 'Master of Sword and Pen' and sent to Gujarat. Gratitude, however, could not prevail against governance; he was shifted to Punjab after reports that his men were misbehaving with the people. The Shaikh's own reputation remained impeccable. He was famous for distributing coins, clothes, shoes and blankets to the poor and looked after the children of his staff as his own. Charity began at home.[48] Jahangir described him as 'one of the ancients of this State' when he died in 1616.

Jahangir's priority after Khusrau's defeat was mending relations with the Afghan chiefs. He headed towards Kabul: 'On 30 March 1607, at the auspicious hour determined by court astrologers, Jahangir left Lahore fortress, crossing the Ravi river to spend the first night encamped in the suburban Dilamez Garden,' writes Lisa Balabanlilar.[49] The king had the protection of twenty-three guard posts. The relaxed journey took seventy-two days.

Sheer joy breathes through the prose as Jahangir celebrates nature in one of the most rugged and scenic regions of the world. At one point, the emperor ordered all his servants to wear flowers in their turbans. Stopping at a lake for three days, he learnt how to fish with a local net, caught twelve fish, and then, with royal panache, ringed their noses with pearls before they were returned to the lake.

The emperor rode either an elephant or a horse or was carried in a litter of gold and silver enamelled with precious stones. He crossed the Khyber Pass on 20 May and entered Kabul on 4 June, once again at an hour determined by his astrologers. He lived in a garden, walked through the green of Shahr Ara (so delicate that wearing shoes would be a travesty), Mahtab Bagh ('Moonlight Garden'), Orta Bagh and Chahar Bagh. He picnicked with scholars of a local madrassah, participated in cooking contests and spent evenings conversing with companions or the ladies of his household. He ordered the creation of another garden named Jahan Ara. Government travelled with him. A fiscal liberal, he reduced taxes. Inherently generous, he spent a 1,000 rupees in alms each day of his stay in the Afghan capital.

In a burst of 'fatherly affection', he ordered that Khusrau's chains be removed. Some of this euphoria diminished when Khurram informed him about a plot in which some 500 supporters of Khusrau would assassinate the emperor while he was hunting in Surkhab near Kabul. One of the ringleaders, Sultan-Shah Afghani, was publicly shot in Lahore. Khusrau was back in fetters.

Jahangir was enraged:

> Although Khusrau had repeatedly done evil actions and deserved a thousand kinds of punishment, my fatherly affection did not permit me to take his life. Although in the laws of government and the ways of empire one should take notice of such disapproved deeds, I averted my eyes from his faults, and kept him in excessive comfort and ease.[50]

The comfort ended. Khusrau was blinded in 1607. It was a political punishment, for Mughals believed that the blind could not rule.

A subterranean romanticism around Khusrau came to Jahangir's notice in 1609 through 'a strange affair at Patna', then as now the capital of Bihar. A routine change of governors was taking place when an unknown man named Qutb, dressed as a dervish and beggar, attracted attention by claiming that he was Khusrau and that he had survived the effort to blind him and escaped. He displayed scars and marks around his eyes as evidence and promised ministerial rewards to those who joined him. Such was his appeal that he seized Patna Fort and the treasury. He was eventually overcome by an imperial force sent from Gorakhpur. The Mughal officials who had lost Patna Fort, Shaikh Banarsi and Ghiyas Zain Khani, had their beards cut off. They were dressed in women's clothes, 'seated on asses, and paraded round the city of Agra and in the bazars, as a warning and example to others'.[51]

Between 1610 and 1616, Khusrau was held by Ani Singh Rai Dalan, after which he was placed in the custody of Asaf Khan, Shahjahan's father-in-law. In 1620, he was handed over to Shahjahan, who ordered his death in 1622.[52]

'Never Darken Your Years With Sectarian Quarrels'

The first book that Jahangir read after becoming king in 1605 was a translation of the Ramayana. The Sanskrit had been interpreted by Deva Mishra and then rendered into Persian by Naqib Khan of Qazwin. The book was from Akbar's library. It was evidence of more than intellectual curiosity. Jahangir, like his father, believed in shared power, sometimes described as 'benevolent neutrality'. This was how he had ruled as sultan in Allahabad, and this was how he reigned when emperor.

From the very beginning of his memoirs, Jahangir emphasises his empathy with his father's philosophy: do not confuse or darken your years with sectarian quarrels; believe in the universal peace promised by all religions; never kill any living creature with your own hands or flay anything except in battle or during a hunt; honour the luminaries, the Sun, the Moon, etc., which are manifestations of God's light; recognise the power and existence of Almighty God.[53]

He contrasts, with some pride, his liberalism with the supremacism of his contemporaries, like the Safavids, the Ottomans and the Uzbeks. Persia was Shia, Turkey was Sunni, while his empire had 'room for all classes and followers of all creeds'. So:

> On the principle that the Shadow must have the same properties as the Light, in his dominions, which on all

sides were limited only by the salt sea, there was room for the professors of opposite religions, and for beliefs good and bad, and the road to altercation was closed. Sunnis and Shias met in one mosque, and Franks and Jews in one church, and observed their own forms of worship.[54]

He pointedly tells the new chief justice, Shaikh Ahmad Lahori, that imperial policy rejected enmity and banished sectarian discord. Father Fernao Guerreiro, a Jesuit at his court, believed that Jahangir deserved the appellation of 'Just King'. Father Jerome Xavier, a grandnephew of St Francis Xavier, who was in Agra in 1595, praised Jahangir, then prince, as a patron helping Jesuits construct a church. Two decades later, the first English envoy to the Mughal court, Sir Thomas Roe, held that all religions enjoyed 'good esteem' in Jahangir's time.

But the foundational alliance with the Amber clan seemed under threat after Raja Man Singh's flagrant support for Khusrau. Man Singh had been his *ateke*. After a few months, Jahangir rebalanced the relationship with impressive acumen. Raja Man Singh, 'one of the greatest and most trusted noblemen of my father [who] had obtained alliances with this illustrious family', and 'had no expectation of favour' because of 'certain acts', was rehabilitated. Jahangir praised the Kachhwaha Rajput family for sincerity of friendship and quality of valour, and sent a *charqab* (robe of honour), a jewelled sword and a horse from his personal stable.[55]

In 1608, Jahangir gifted Man Singh his best horse, which had come from Persia's Shah Abbas. He comments that the raja was so delighted 'that if I had given him a kingdom I do not think he would have shown such joy'.[56] Bhao Singh, the 'most capable' of Man Singh's sons, was raised to a *mansab* of 1,500, and Raja Jagannath, the head of the Amber family, to one of 5,000, with a special robe of honour. When Man Singh died in July 1614, Bhao Singh was named heir, and Maha Singh, a claimant, was compensated with the territory of Garha and an increase of *mansab* by 500. Man Singh's sixty wives allegedly committed sati.[57] Man Singh's death was the last sigh of the Akbar generation.[58]

Those who had dithered in 1606 were brought into the fold:

> Ray Ray Singh, one of the most considerable of Rajput Amirs, ashamed on account of the fault he had committed in the matter of Khusrau, and who was living at his home, came, and under the patronage of the Amir-ul-umara obtained the good fortune of waiting on me; his offences were pardoned.[59]

Abul Fazl's son Shaikh Abdur Rahman was given the title 'Afzal Khan' and promoted to 1,500 horse. In 1608, he was sent to Bihar as governor.[60]

Jahangir expanded his marital alliances to include the ruling families of Bikaner, Khandesh, Jaisalmer, Marwar, Little Tibet and Kashmir,[61] and enhanced goodwill through continual transactional diplomacy. In 1612, Raja Tekchand of Kumaon was honoured with dresses, a jewelled dagger and a hundred horses, while his territory was reaffirmed.[62] In March 1618, at the start of the thirteenth year of his reign, Jahangir sent a jewelled sword, a rosary, four rings (diamond, ruby, emerald and sapphire) and two hawks to the Jam of Kutch on the western coast of the empire. He sent another four (ruby, cat's eye, emerald and sapphire) to Raja Lachmi Narayan of Kuch Behar in the east.[63] Gifts were also sent that year to 'my brother', Shah Abbas of Persia, but Jahangir sniffed at Persia's offerings, which arrived with merchandise from Iran when Jahangir was in Gujarat, as 'trifling'.

The comfort levels of stability are noticeable in the minutiae of palace life. The emperor is happy to report that on the thirteenth anniversary of his coronation, his 'domestic servants celebrated the day with brimming cups'. Some things did not change. When Jahangir left for Gujarat despite heavy rain on 'Thursday, the 7th ... the astrologers and astronomers had already fixed the auspicious hour for the march'. Their permission was a 'necessity'.[64]

Jahangir's inclusive policies were anchored in beliefs confirmed by experience. He drew inspiration and knowledge from both Hindu and Muslim hermits. Between 1617 and 1620, he went six times to meet the reclusive Gosain Jadrup of Ujjain, learned in the 'science of Vedanta, which is the science of Sufism', who had become an ascetic at the age of twenty-two, in the Brahmin's cave-abode. The world bowed before emperors, and emperors bowed before hermits.

Jahangir describes two meetings with Jadrup. In 1618, he met the ascetic, now sixty, on a Saturday afternoon in 'the retirement of his cell'. He was enraptured by 'sublime words' on divine knowledge, religious duties and doctrines of 'wholesome Sufism'.[65] In 1619, the king 'hastened' to the hermit's hut 'without ceremony' in Mathura, where Jadrup had settled. He describes the meeting:

> I enjoyed his society. Sublime words were spoken between us. God Almighty has granted him an unusual grace, a lofty understanding, an exalted nature, and sharp intellectual powers, with a God-given knowledge and a heart free from the attachments of the world, so that, putting behind his back the world and what is in it, he sits content in the corner of solitude and without wants.[66]

The hermit's dress was half a yard of cotton cloth, his sole possession an earthenware piece for water, and his bed a hole in the ground. Jahangir admires the recluse in verse:

Luqman had a narrow hut,
Like the hollow of the flute or the bosom of a harp.
A noodle put the question to him—
'What is this house—two feet and a span?'
Hotly and with tears the sage replied—
'Ample for him who has to die.'[67]

Jadrup persuaded Jahangir to convert one of the weight measures used in the kingdom to Vedic norms and to forgive his belligerent son. Khusrau was released in 1619 and survived until 26 January 1622.[68] Paintings depicting Jadrup with both Akbar and Jahangir are at the Fogg Museum in Harvard University, the Musee National des Arts Asiatiques in Paris, and the Victoria and Albert Museum in London.[69]

Jahangir was similarly reverential to Miyan Shaikh Muhammad Mir, a Sindhi dervish who lived in Lahore. Mir was 'very eloquent, virtuous, austere, of auspicious temperament, a lord of ecstasy, [who] had seated himself in the corner of reliance upon God and retirement, and was rich in his poverty and independent of the world'. Jahangir, unable to visit Lahore, invited the man of god to Agra as his 'truth-seeking' mind would not rest. The dervish came despite his age and frailty, spoke to the king for as long as he desired and left for Lahore as soon as the meeting was over. The only gift he accepted was a white antelope skin to serve as a prayer rug.[70]

Faith became a healer. In 1614, Jahangir kept his illness a secret even from his physicians lest 'some injury might occur to the country'. Clearly, he feared the instability that might follow if it became known. His only confidant was Nurjahan, whom he had married in May 1611, for, in his words, no one was fonder of him. For three days, he maintained a normal routine, showing himself to the people at the *jharoka* in the morning or drinking wine in the evening, until signs appeared on his skin. He went to pray for his health at the shrine of Khwaja Muinuddin Chishti and vowed to pierce his earlobes in the style of slaves if he recovered, to indicate that he was now a servant of the saint. He kept his vow. Being Jahangir, he started to wear a luminous pearl in each ear. Friends and officials quickly imitated their king.[71]

The humility inherent in shrine reverence as an intermediary to God was intrinsic to the Mughals' inherited faith. This is how Jahangir describes his father:

> Despite his wealth, beyond the scope of counting, and his armies, he considered himself the lowest of creatures before God, the beloved ... Notwithstanding his kingship and his treasures and the buried wealth, which were beyond the scope of counting and imagination, his fighting elephants and Arab horses, he never by a hair's breadth placed his foot beyond the base of humility before the throne of God, but considered himself the lowest of created beings, and never for one moment forgot God. *Always, everywhere with everyone, and in every circumstance/Keep the eye of thy heart secretly fixed on the Beloved.*[72]

The people were reassured by the emperor's public participation in popular Hindu festivals such as Diwali and Dussehra. During Dussehra, elephants and horses of the royal stable were decorated and paraded.[73] Jahangir revived the practice of wearing the rakhi (a wristband of affection presented by a sister to a brother), which Akbar had stopped when sycophants began to string them with jewels. Jahangir ordered that they could only be in cotton and silk 'after the ancient manner'. In 1617, he christened the day of his accession 'Mubarak-shamba' because it coincided with the Muslim festival of Shab-i-Barat and Rakhi.[74] Rakhi is the Hindu festival celebrating the love between sisters and brothers; Shab-i-Barat is the blessed Islamic night of salvation when Allah forgives the faithful and grants them their wishes.

Veneration of the Sun struck a popular chord. Humayun had begun the jharoka at sunrise. Akbar recited litanies to the sun, and so did Jahangir. The solar and lunar years were honoured with the weighing of the emperor against gold, silver and precious items, whose equivalent value was distributed among the poor.[75]

Court language was expanded to include more words from Sanskrit and Hindi. Jahangir was given the ancient Sanskrit titles of *Chakravartin* ('ruler who turned the wheel'), *Vishwajit* ('world conqueror') and *Digvijay* ('overlord'). His near-continuous travels became *vijayyatra*.[76]

The third dimension of his reign was engagement with intellectuals and religious scholars. As a prince, Jahangir had sponsored translations of Sanskrit texts into Persian. As a king, he was the patron of Jain and Brahmin scholars. As an individual, he read translations of Sanskrit texts, and one even has an annotation by him. Akbar was impressed by Jain monks who had achieved mental feats like *avadhana*, in which the mind focuses on multiple things simultaneously. There is a record of Akbar and Jahangir visiting a Jain temple in 1594.

Truschke notes that the Mughals were invested in Sanskrit astrological calculations, as the following incident illustrates: 'One time a daughter bound by the curse of the *Mula* constellation was born in the house of glorious Sultan Salim [Jahangir] ... [Akbar] called upon wise men such as Shaykh [Abu al-Fazl] to counteract that curse.'[77] The ruling planet of *Mula* is Ketu, and it is presided over by Nriti, the goddess of dissolution. When the wise men failed, Akbar asked a Jain monk

Karmacandra to perform 'whatever is the purifying rite in Jain philosophy'.

Karmacandra prepared the purification water 'with pots made of silver and gold with perfect injunctions. At the time of lighting the auspicious lamp, Shaykhu ji [Jahangir], the son of the Shah, came and was hospitably received after giving ten thousand silver gifts'. Using the purified water, the Jain minister bathed the eyes of Akbar, who was surrounded by women from the palace. The curse was alleviated.[78]

Jahangir engaged with Jain monks until a disagreement ended the relationship between the 1610s and 1620s: 'His court attracted intellectuals who sought to rework Sanskrit-based stories in Persian, and a few retellings of the Ramayana epic are dedicated to Jahangir.'[79]

Akbar's copy of the Ramayana had 176 illustrations by masters of Mughal art; Hamida Banu's had 55 paintings. Both copies were preserved in Jahangir's library. Abdur Rahim Khan-i-Khanan, who had the third copy with 135 illustrations, describes the deity Ramchandra as one of the great kings of India whose 'external and spiritual graces were exemplary, being manifestations of divine attributes … pleasing virtues, great victories, and conduct, which show his magnificence'. Jahangir lauds the Ramayana as 'one of the celebrated books of the ancients of India' and commends its use as a guide to kingship.[80]

He rewarded Hindi poets, and they reciprocated with adulatory praise for him. When Raja Suraj Singh, Man Singh's brother, visited the court, he brought the poet Keshavdas in his entourage. Keshavdas describes Jahangir as 'a capable ruler in every respect', presiding over a court with poets, generals, skilled painters, deserving scholars, warriors, masterminds, stable masters and artistes who sang 'beautiful songs, haunting to the soul'. He received an elephant as a reward.[81]

The *jharoka darshan* was at seven in the morning. The use of Indian words in formal language kept increasing. In 1616, Jahangir praised Shauqi, a mandolin player, as a wonder of the age and 'delighted him' with the title of Anand Khan for providing such pleasure.[82]

The head of Jahangir's atelier in Allahabad, Aqa Reza Herati, included a woman, Nadira Banu, in his elite group of painters. Jahangir encouraged assimilation of European techniques and icons. Prof. Mujeeb writes:

> He was a connoisseur of painting, which his father had introduced to court, and a good judge of poetry; his memoirs are a classic of their genre ... no one among the rulers, and very few among the poets and writers of India, have had as keen an eye as Jahangir for the beauty of nature, for birds and flowers and gardens, and as sensitive a mind for the effects of environment and atmosphere. Akbar had initiated the art of painting; Jahangir became a connoisseur.[83]

Akbar sat for portraits. Abdul Samad portrayed the emperor painting. Akbar snubbed the orthodox who sniffed at portraiture as quasi-idolatry; he disliked those who disliked painting. Jahangir's master artists Basawan and Manohar depicted Madonna and the Child. Jesus, while not considered a god in Islam, is a major prophet of virgin birth. Jahangir's palace in Agra included, along with pictures of the king and queen of England, a portrait of Sir Thomas Smythe, the ruler of an incipient power, the East India Company, of which he was governor.

After the Nauruz festivities of 1613 ended with the usual open house, Jahangir despatched Muhammad Hussain Chelebi to Iraq and Constantinople to purchase rarities and curiosities on behalf of the crown. The Mughals had diplomatic relations with the Ottomans. Jahangir writes that although he grew up in Hindustan, he was not ignorant of Turkish. His memoirs were translated into Ottoman Turkish during the reign of Sultan Mustafa III.[84]

The King and the Gardener

One hot day, a thirsty sultan wandering incognito came to a garden and asked the old gardener if there were any pomegranates so he could have some juice. The gardener's beautiful daughter brought him a cupful of pomegranate with leaves floating on top. The king wondered about the leaves. It was not advisable, she replied, to drink all at once; the leaves would ensure that he sipped the juice rather than swallowed it. The sultan asked how much profit the gardener made. Three hundred dinars. How much did he give to the king? There was no tax on trees, although there was a tenth on cultivated crops.

The king's thoughts shifted. A similar levy on garden produce would enhance his treasury without hurting gardeners too much. The king asked for a second cup of juice. The girl brought it, but the quantity was less. 'The first time,' she explained, 'I filled the cup with the juice of one pomegranate and brought it; this time I pressed out five or six and did not get as much juice.'

The gardener told the king, 'The blessing of produce depends on the goodwill of the king. It occurs to me that you must be a king. Your disposition has changed since you asked about the income from the garden. Consequently, the blessing passed away from the fruit.'

The sultan understood. He asked for a third cup of juice, and it was full to the brim.

Jahangir called this story, which he narrates in detail, a 'memento on the page of time'.[85] He notes with satisfaction that not a single *dam* (a basic unit of currency) or *habba* (grain) was collected as agricultural tax in his state.

Jahangir set a brisk pace in decision-making from the outset of his rule. He did not like the capital, Agra; the air was too warm and dry. Physicians agreed that it depressed the spirits, induced weakness and was conducive only to the phlegmatic and melancholy. He did not shift the capital but was continually on the move. On the positive side, the fruit was splendid; he loved mangoes above all. Agra's inhabitants were excellent craftsmen, and it had become an abode of scholars from every faith. An early decision embellished the political topography of the city. A thirty-yard 'chain of justice' linked the fort to a stone post so that anyone with a grievance could ring its sixty bells to complain against delay or deceit by officials. The bells, weighing 'four Indian *maunds*', were made of 'pure gold'. Sceptical European missionaries thought they were made of gold-plated silver.

A twelve-point *dasturu-i-amal* ('rules of conduct') became the manual of administration. Cess on commerce (*tamgha*) was abolished, along with river tolls and 'other burdens' imposed by landlords. Officials were ordered not to harass traders; the inspection of merchandise required their cooperation. Rest houses and mosques (also an alternative accommodation for travellers) were built, and wells dug on lonely roads. Inheritance of property was sacrosanct, irrespective of the faith of the deceased, and if a death was intestate, the property of the dead was sold to pay for public works like the repair of bridges, tanks and wells. Prohibition of wine or rice spirits (*darbahra*) was imposed, at which point Jahangir ruefully mentions that he started drinking at the age of eighteen. A trifle sheepishly, he admits that he still drank, but only because it helped digestion. It was a fragile excuse.

Strict action was ordered against any forcible usurpation of private property or a peasant's land. Corporal punishment, such as the cutting off of a person's nose or ears, was stopped. Abduction of women by landlords under the ruse of marriage became illegal; a marriage would require evidence of free will on both sides. Public hospitals with physicians were opened. Checks on animal slaughter for food began. There were two meatless days every week, Thursday to mark the day of Jahangir's accession and Sunday in honour of the Sun. (In the last decade of his life, Akbar ate only what was described by his son as 'Sufi food'.) Large numbers of prisoners serving long sentences were released, with 7,000 in Gwalior alone. The government framework was appeased: *jagir*dars were retained with higher ranks, officers' emoluments were raised by 20 per cent to 300 per cent and the allowances of ladies in the palace were increased by a range of 20 per cent to 100 per cent.[86] Jahangir had learnt from his father's experience on taxation. Abul Fazl ruefully admits that it took twenty-five years for Akbar's decision to abolish tolls and import duties to be fully implemented, attributing the delay to the emperor's nonchalance and the avarice of profiteers.[87]

Jahangir expanded the chain of food kitchens initiated by his father:

> In the whole of the hereditary dominions, both the crown lands and *jagirs*, I ordered the preparation of *bulghur-khanas* [free eating houses], where cooked food might be provided for the poor according to their condition and so that residents and travellers both might reap the benefit.[88]

A dozen years later, the emperor was still fervent in his desire to help the poor. Describing a march through Gujarat in 1618, he wrote:

> [I] ordered the macebearers and *tawachiyan* to collect the widows and poor people from the villages on the

road and near it, and bring them before me, so that I might bestow charity on them with my own hand, which would be an occupation and the helpless ones might also find grace. What better occupation could there be than this?[89]

Welfare was justice. Reform was continuous. In 1620, while camping in Rajaur, Jahangir learnt that a Muslim sect practised infanticide of unwanted newborn girls and had buried alive a girl of ten or twelve. He ordered the death sentence for such crimes.[90] Above all, Jahangir wanted to be remembered as a just monarch who had established *adalat* (God's justice).

He had the confidence to tell a story against himself when he had no reason to remind anyone of his mistakes. Jahangir records the occasion when he checked whether a crocodile was a man-eater by throwing a sheep and then a servant into the lake in which it lived while travelling between Lahore and Kabul. Both survived. In an inexcusable act, and despite his reverence for hermits, Jahangir had alcohol forced down the throat of an ascetic who was in a state of rigidity from meditation to find out if wine would dilute his *tapasya*. It did not. This was cruelty, not levity. Jahangir was, however, ready to regret any miscarriage of justice; he delayed the implementation of any death sentence until sundown to give time for an appeal.

At noon, there could be spectacular entertainment featuring dancers, musicians or animal fights. The public audience at 4 pm was formal. Nobles stood obedient and quiet, according to rank, for the Diwan-i-am, where the 'harassed and the oppressed', in the words of Abul Fazl, got their chance to complain directly to the dispenser of justice, a central tenet of legitimacy in Mughal feudalism. There was unrest if the emperor was absent for more than a day or two. One incident in 1621 was so unusual that Jahangir recorded his misjudgement. A Kashmiri blacksmith named Kalyan fell desperately in love with a widow, 'a woman of his own caste', but his ardour was rejected. The emperor summoned both and advised the woman to reciprocate the man's love, but she refused. Kalyan said that if the emperor gave her to him, he would show his love by throwing himself from the '*shah-burj* [king's tower] of the fort'. Forget the shah burj, replied Jahangir all too casually, if he jumped from the roof, he would order their marriage. Kalyan 'ran like lightning and threw himself down'. Blood began to flow from his mouth and eyes. The emperor was deeply grieved, but repentance could not save the passionate lover. Kalyan died.[91]

Despite his flaws, Jahangir's interest in good governance, supplemented by his shrewd assessment of people and his eclectic nature, would have placed him on the pedestal of unusual rulers but for the addictions that aged him by fifty and killed him at fifty-nine.

Opium, Wine and High Jinks

Mughal kings from Babur to Shahjahan shared a relaxed attitude towards intoxicants. Opium and liquor were part of conventional elite relaxation, while serious drinking was inseparable from their favourite pastime, hunting.

Ancient cultural traditions elided inhibitions imposed by faith. During Genghis Khan's age of glory, it was disrespectful to refuse kumis, the traditional beverage of fermented mare's milk. A royal feast in their ancestor Taimur's time in the 14th century began with alcohol; abstinence was not deemed praiseworthy. Another forefather, Sultan Said Khan, otherwise obedient to the Islamic sharia, said, when drinking a bowl of kumis, that he had expanded Islam to accommodate social obligations. Paradise, after all, was blessed with Tasnim, the river of wine. *Masti tafih* (being totally drunk) was part of male culture.

Many women in the Taimur family drank, as they did in the Mughal palace. 'Nurjahan arranged mixed gatherings, where alcohol was served, on her properties,' writes Lisa Balabanlilar.[92] In 1617, Jahangir attended a party hosted by Nurjahan, where wine was served to nobles and friends. Wine was the luxury, and more often the ruin, of the elite. A wine cup even became a metaphor for relations with Persia during this time. The Persian ruler Shah Abbas sent an unusual request to the Mughal court after being shown an Iraqi crystal cup purchased by Jahangir's agent on his way back to India. If the Mughal could send the cup as a gift after drinking some wine from it, said the Persian monarch, he would treat the gesture as a mark of affection. Jahangir took a few sips in the presence of Muhammad Riza, the Persian ambassador, ordered his craftsmen to make a matching lid and saucer, and sent the crystal set to Abbas.

Three years later, Jahangir spent two days as Nurjahan's guest at Nursarai, her new garden palace, where 'great pains' had been taken to produce 'delicate and rare things'. In March 1621, he was at the Nurafshan next to a lake to celebrate the sixteenth year of his rule.[93]

Babur is quite unabashed about a long drinking session on a boat, which culminated in retching. Humayun famously told his sister Gulbadan: 'I am an opium-eater [*man afyumi*] ... do not be angry with me.' Akbar had to be forcibly prevented from driving a sword into his own body in a fit of drunken courage. He mourned the death of Abul Fazl by shaving his head and giving up opium. Jahangir saw the lives of three brothers and an uncle, Muhammad Hakim, consumed by wine. His autobiography is testimony to his own copious drinking. He employed a wine and opium steward and pays fond tribute to Kamal Khan, his head of kitchens, in service since Humayun's time, who, at the age of ninety, was 'quicker than lads of 14' despite being always 'intoxicated with wine'.[94] On another occasion, in 1608, Jahangir was told about the death of a servant who used to drink even during Ramadan, the month of fasting, but had stopped the double blasphemy. His death, quipped the king, was due to a fatal mistake, which was the servant's decision to stop drinking alcohol after years of indulging in it even during the holy month. The king gave up alcohol during Ramadan out of respect for the month of fasting.[95]

A forty-year-old Jahangir describes an evening of revelry in Kabul. He and drunken guests tried to jump across a stream in the middle of a garden on a Thursday night and drank wine from a reservoir cut into rocks.[96]

He was happy to experiment. In Punjab, he discovered *buza* and *sar*, a beverage made from bread and rice, which became more potent when aged for two or three years. He felt awed by a certain Sultan Mahmud, who could drink a jar of it. It also served as an aphrodisiac.[97]

As a matter of routine Jahangir met a select few for drinking and discourse at 8 pm. The potency of the double-distilled liquor served was such that it made Sir Thomas Roe, the English ambassador to the Mughal court between 1616 and 1619, sneeze, to the amusement of the court. Six cups, wrote Sir Thomas, improved the emperor's good temper. He praised the 'drinking and commanding' Jahangir as one of the finest men he had met. When the monarch could no longer hold his head up, the evening ended in a muddled whisper.[98]

Jahangir writes:

> When I first took a liking to drinking I sometimes took as much as twenty cups of double-distilled spirit;

when by degrees it acquired a great influence over me, I endeavoured to lessen the quantity, and in the period of seven years I have brought myself from 15 cups to five or six. My times for drinking were varied; sometimes when three or four sidereal hours of the day remained, I would begin to drink, and sometimes at night and partly by day. This went on until I was 30 years old. After that I took to drinking always at night. Now I drink only to digest my food.[99]

As an excuse, it was elastic, but Jahangir's chronicle of the first eighteen years of his reign, is a punctilious memoir with a range of detail across a living canvas. He presented a copy of the first part, in the twelfth year of his reign, to his favoured son, Shahjahan. The autobiography stops in early 1624. The account of the rest of his reign, submerged in ill health and melancholy, was transcribed in bureaucratese by Mirza Muhammad Hadi.

Jahangir begins to fade after the lunar eclipse of 1621, interpreted by astrologers as an ill omen for him. Fate could not be averted or deflected by alms and prayers.[100] He fell ill that year and started to cede greater authority to Nurjahan. In early 1622, he 'gave the establishment and everything belonging to the government' to Nurjahan and 'ordered that her drums and orchestra should be sounded after those of the king'.[101]

News arrived that Khusrau had died of colic pains, a sanitised euphemism for parricide. As one chapter closed, another opened. Shahjahan, upset by the growing power of a stepmother clearly planning to shift the succession to her favourite, his youngest brother Shahryar, decided that he had no option except war.

Jahangir, ridden with uncharacteristic self-pity, decided to punish 'that one of dark fortune'. Shahjahan, he proclaimed, would henceforth be called *bidaulat* (wretch):

> Wherever in this record of fortune *bidaulat* is mentioned it will refer to him. From the kindnesses and favours bestowed upon him I can say that up until the present time no king has conferred such on his son. What my reverend father did for my brothers I have done for his servants, giving them titles, standards, and drums, as has been recorded in the preceding pages ... My pen's tongue fails in ability to set them forth. What shall I say of my own sufferings? In pain and weakness, in a warm atmosphere that is extremely unsuited to my health, I must ride and still be active, and in this state must proceed against such an undutiful son.[102]

Jahangir's last entry for 1623 describes his taking delight in fish. The best, he says, was *rohu*.[103] His account of 1624 struggles through a mere six pages as he loses interest in events and events lose interest in him. His *firman* that Shahjahan be turned into a 'wanderer in the desert of disappointment' did not unite the nobles, who remained split. The last sentences of Jahangir's autobiography hint at some accommodation with the *bidaulat*, but by this time he was not fully in charge.

The highlights of Jahangir's later life were visits to his beloved Kashmir. Nature and verse dominate his descriptions of the leisurely working holiday of 1620. He is a naturalist with the eye of an anthropologist and the temperament of a poet. Jahangir encouraged poetry as an elegant virtue. The following exchange is an example of refined riposte. Jahangir recites:

> Turn not thy cheek, without thee I cannot live a moment
> For thee to break one heart is equal to a hundred murders.

Mulla Ali Ahmed responds:

O censor, fear the weeping of the old vintner;
Thy breaking one jar is equal to a hundred murders.

The emperor writes that the merchants of Kashmir, the 'flower-garden' of eternal beauty, were Sunni Muslims, the soldiers Shia. Its Hindu Rishis were simple, gentle, celibate, unpretentious and vegetarian; they restrained the 'tongue of desire' and the 'foot of seeking'. Kashmiri culture diminished differences; the Brahmins of Kashmir were indistinguishable from the Mussalmans, except that the former worshipped in 'lofty idol temples' and wrote books in Sanskrit.

He drank wine at the Sukh Nag waterfall, ate three or four *shah-alu* cherries and apricots from Kabul and delighted in the sweet music of the *papiha* (hawk-cuckoo) and the lament of the *koyal* (cuckoo). He lists thirty birds he had not seen in Kashmir before.

Government travelled with the monarch. Jahangir accepted an offering of two yaks from the 'zamindar of Tibet' and gave the *pargana* of Jammu to Raja Sangram. He pardoned the repentant Shaikh Ahmad of Sirhind, a religious hardliner who had been in prison for two years, ordered a punitive raid on the tribes of Afghanistan, promoted officials like Amurdad Bahadur of Qandahar and Man Singh (the son of Rawat Shankar) and rejoiced in the conquest of Kangra.

Dussehra was celebrated by decorating the horses, but autumn brought pangs of mortality:

There's no exhilaration in decay, but to the eye
The glory of autumn is more brilliant than the spring.

Among his favourite quatrains was an 'amazing' verse he discovered by chance at Mandu:[104]

My congenial friends have left me,
One by one they've fallen into the hands of death.
They were poor drinkers at the banquet of life.
A moment sooner than us they became drunken.

When it was time to leave Kashmir, astrologers, as always, determined the 'auspicious hour and favourable time'. The imperial force stopped for four days at the Raja Todar Mal tank near Lahore on the journey back to Agra.[105]

When robust, Jahangir used to smile at his doctors, quoting a line of Persian poetry: 'We have a pleasant physician; come, let us all be ill.' By 1618, Hakim Masihuzzaman and Hakim Ruhallah were telling their king some facts of life and death. He had to cut down on opium and alcohol. Now fifty, the emperor, famous for hosting *majlis-i-sharab-i tertib* (wine parties), decided to 'decrease somewhat my usual number of cups'. He had his wine diluted with water and lived another nine years.[106] Jahangir censures himself with delicacy, quoting a couplet by his court poet Talib Amuli, who was enrolled in 1620:

Two lips have I, one for drinking,
And one to apologize for drunkenness.

The last years were a struggle. Lisa Balabanlilar has compared Jahangir with Babur: 'charming and drunken, highly sensitive, occasionally cruel, loyal, proud of a charismatic lineage and completely confident in his right to rule—acknowledging his personal failings even as he made the case for power and kingship'.[107] A few months before his death, the emperor admitted the obvious: he had become an addict because 'no one had the power to forbid me' since he began taking opium at nineteen.

In his last days, he was too ill to walk or even to consume opium. He died in Lahore at the age of fifty-nine.

5

Second Lord of the Auspicious Conjunction

SHAHJAHAN BELIEVED THAT HIS destiny was written in the conjunction of Jupiter and Venus at his birth. Equally, he took pride in having been born in the millennium year of the Islamic calendar. His coins proclaimed Sahib Qiran-i-Sani ('second lord of the auspicious conjunction of Jupiter and Venus'). Sani means second. The first lord was his great ancestor Amir Timur, born under the same stars. Astrology, trusted as a science, played a significant part in royal decisions, mundane or critical, whether they related to the appointments of the day, or the feasibility of a military expedition. In 1586, there was indecision among Akbar's advisers when the emperor decided to punish the ruler of Kashmir for breaking an agreement. Abul Fazl, in the pro-war camp, concedes that he was not sufficiently persuasive against a strong view among counsellors that it would be difficult for the army to negotiate the mountains.

Akbar summoned his astrologers. They looked into the ascendant of the year and the situation of the stars. They concluded that if some effort were made, Kashmir would soon be conquered. When this was reported to the emperor, he ordered the expedition.

The astrologers were vindicated. Kashmir was conquered. In 1591, when Akbar summoned astrologers from both the Greek and Indian traditions to determine an auspicious hour for the foundation ceremony of a new city on the banks of the Chenab, the project was postponed when they could not find a good hour. Astrologers were in constant attendance in court and on travel.

On 17 July 1592, Akbar and his son Danyal turned back while on their way to Kashmir on the advice of an astrologer after an ominous 300 meteors flashed across the skies from east to west. One of Shahjahan's more famous astrologers was the Brahmin Vamsidhara Misra, a scholar of many talents and also renowned as a Sanskrit poet.

Shahjahan was born in Lahore Fort on 5 January 1592, four years after the marriage of his mother Manmati (1577–1619) to Jahangir. Manmati, also known as Jodh Bai, was the daughter of Raja Udai Singh of Marwar, nicknamed Mota ('fat') Raja for self-evident reasons. She was graced with titles such as Jagat Gosain ('saint of the world') and Bilqis Makani ('pure lady of the house'). Her brother Maharaja Kishan Singh founded the city of Kishangarh. Jahangir's eldest son, Khusrau, born on 16 August 1587 in Lahore, also had a Rajput mother, Rajkumari Man Baisa (1570–1604), daughter of Raja Bhagwant Singh.

Three days after the birth of Shahjahan, Akbar went to see the 'world-adorning beauty' (hyperbole being a fundamental right of every grandfather) and named him Khurram, meaning joyful, because astrologers had advised that the name should begin with 'k' or 'kh'. 'The kingdom's most respected and influential astrologers, both Hindu and Muslim, fell to work on drawing up the new prince's horoscope,' writes Fergus Nicoll. The Shia cleric Mulla Mahmud of Indjan promised in Shahjahan a 'star of the constellation of the caliphate'.[1]

Akbar shared a deep bond with this grandson. Jahangir writes in his memoirs that Khurram (later Shahjahan) was more attentive to Akbar than all his other children. Akbar described Khurram as his 'real child' and gave charge of his upbringing to his childless first wife, Ruqaiyya Sultan Begum, who 'loved him a thousand times more than if he had been her own'.[2] An unnamed astrologer had told Ruqaiyya Sultan before Khurram was born that he was destined for imperial greatness. Khurram stayed with her until he was thirteen. A Mughal prince got a personal residence after puberty. Both grandfather and father addressed Khurram affectionately as 'Baba' Khurram. Whoever does not have a son is not happy, declared Jahangir. A daughter was cherished, but it was understood that her primary loyalty would shift to her husband and her children. A son's birth was an occasion for expensive celebrations. Even as a rebel prince, Shahjahan put on a magnificent pageant in 1624 when his son Murad was born in Rohtas Fort. The feasting continued for three days; there was poetry, music and more egalitarian entertainment. The consumption was impressive: 30 kg of ambergris, a perfume from the intestine of the sperm whale; 74 kg of poppy seeds; 2,000 pods of musk; 185 kg of amber resin; 2,000 bottles of Egyptian willow scent; 10,000 bottles of rose water imported from Yazd in Persia; 1,850 kg of saffron from Kashmir. The loyalty of nobles was reinforced with lavish gifts.[3] Even the allegedly abstemious Aurangzeb hosted a splendid feast, with dancing, music and fireworks, in addition to the usual distribution of gifts, on the birth of his first grandson, Muizzuddin, in 1661. Jahangir had set the benchmark for royal revelry with a dazzling signature display in March 1606 during his 'auspicious accession'.

The celebrations were lavish.

> [The] people gave themselves over to enjoyment and happiness. Players and singers of all bands and cases were gathered together. Dancing lulis [sic] and charmers of India whose caresses would captivate the hearts of

angels kept up the excitement of the assemblies. I gave orders that whoever might wish intoxicating drinks and exhilarating drugs should not be debarred from using them.[4]

It was an open house. The first marriage of a prince was a highlight of his life, a memorable occasion for family and clan, and a spectacle for the people. Months of preparation preceded the wedding of Shahjahan's eldest son, Dara Shukoh, to his cousin Nadira Begum. The festivities spread across days of music, dance, fireworks and public display of gifts, and were topped off by a spectacular wedding procession for the nuptials at the bride's home.

The first occasion for festivity in a prince's life was his circumcision, almost always done at the age of four. A painting in the *Akbarnama* folio of the British Library portrays the dancing, music and joy on the occasion of Akbar's circumcision in the presence of his parents after three traumatic years of their separation. Kabul's streets were decorated. Separate tent halls for men and women were lit with lamps. There was food and drink for the citizens. While the proud father exchanged gifts with nobles, alms were distributed to the poor.

The prince's studies began after this rite of passage. With every prince a potential ruler, elaborate care was taken over his education. The bookends of the curriculum were designed around *ahl-i qalam* and *ahl-i saif*, the pen and the sword. Humayun, whose veneration of the Sun appealed to indigenous Indian sentiment, added instructions in *ahl-i Hind*, or the customs and manners of Hindustan, for Akbar. Shahjahan had eight tutors. He learnt, in addition to Islamic studies, Indian music, Indian sciences, Hindawi, rhetoric, poetry, prosody, calligraphy, art appreciation, dance, military strategy and the use of weapons, sword, dagger, pike and musket. Abul Fazl, also a tutor to Akbar's son Murad—whose studies were delayed until eight by ill health—insisted that a prince also needed to understand the value of obedience. But he clearly failed to teach the prince the merits of moderation. Murad died at the age of twenty-eight from alcoholism. It was never too early for a prince to learn. Humayun was eleven when he rode into Badakhshan in 1519, and Akbar nine when given charge of Ghazni in 1551. Aurangzeb berated his youngest son, Kam Baksh, for his indifference to studies with a stern rebuke: 'A person without knowledge is a beast.' A prince was taught to be independent, brave, sophisticated, ruthless, benevolent (*jud*) and generous (*sakhawat*), according to the *Mauizah-i Jahangiri* ('Advice on Governance'), written by Muhammad Baqir and dedicated to the emperor. Generosity, wrote Baqir, was the virtue that concealed all defects and created bonds of loyalty and affection, enabling fame, prosperity and success.[5]

The standing of a prince was measured by the paternal gestures extended to him. The emperor's visit was proof of the highest favour. On 30 July 1607, Jahangir celebrated Khurram's sixteenth lunar birthday at his son's home in Kabul's Urta Garden, which he found 'delightful and well-proportioned'. The prince sat on a floor-cushion, its sides plated with gold. A special pavilion between cypress trees was erected for Jahangir. The only shadow over the day was cast by astrologers, who discovered a warning in the special horoscope for the occasion. Jahangir records their alarm: 'A most important epoch according to his horoscope would occur, as the prince's health had not been good'; in the language of the court, his disposition would change from equability. To ward off potential disaster, the emperor ordered that Shahjahan should be weighed 'against gold, silver and other metals, which should be divided among faqirs and the needy'.[6]

The weighing ceremony derived from *tuladaan*, an ancient Indian ritual adopted and adapted by the Mughals. In Hindu practice, the money was given to priests for the maintenance of temples. Akbar widened the scope of his largesse. On solar occasions, Akbar was weighed against gold coins and other stones twelve times; on lunar ceremonies, eight times in silver. A visitor from Samarkand described such an occasion: 'When the Emperor sat on the scales, I said "The Sun of the World is in the house of Libra."' Astrologers joined a prince's entourage when he became old enough to take decisions. The prince's day began before sunrise when he emerged from the *khalwatgah, khwabgah, shabkhana* or *shabistan-I Iqbal* (all synonyms for bedroom; *khalwat* means seclusion, *shab* means night, *khwab* dream and *gah* room), leaving behind his companion of the night, if any. After the morning prayers, he was briefed on overnight news and intelligence while he got dressed. The historian Munis Faruqui writes:

> [The prince] would also most certainly have set aside a little time to meet with his personal astrologers. With fully prepared charts at their disposal, these astrologers would be expected to answer any question the prince might throw at them: what activities might meet with success or failure this day, what time to commence an activity, what foods to consume or avoid, whether to issue a particular order or wait. Such guidance, privately delivered in the context of his household, always had the potential to cause last-minute changes in a prince's schedule, such as cancellation of imperial functions or putting off administrative or political decisions.

Propriety and protocol were strict at breakfast. About an hour after sunrise came the *jharoka darshan*, the public appearance, followed by the *diwan-i-am*, the interaction with select nobility (*ashraf*), officers and distinguished guests. The three hours following lunch were reserved for personal affairs and family. The working day ended at sunset after a second round of business. The evening was spent in music, dance, poetry, magic shows, alcohol and good food. Aurangzeb banned alcohol, but edicts are seldom effective against generational habits. Those who wanted to drink continued to do so. There is a record of an altercation between Aurangzeb's son Azam and a musician, Ajab Singh Raja, and his sister, the two sides accusing the other of being drunk.[7]

It is difficult to conceive of a more fortunate life than Shahjahan's. His invaluable inheritance was the policy of inter-faith harmony nurtured so effectively by his grandfather despite the challenge from a powerful orthodox alliance, which found a leader in Akbar's younger brother Muhammad Hakim, who held the appanage of Kabul ('appanage' derives from the French term for bread, meaning 'equip with bread'). Hakim positioned himself as the non-Indian, used the *Chaghatai shahrukhi* as the currency in his realm, and appealed to Central Asians in the imperial army to defect and destroy the 'natives of Hindustan'. In 1581, Akbar sent an integrated army of Uzbeks, Rajputs, Shias and Sunni Muslims under the effective command of Raja Man Singh. Hakim was driven out of Kabul. Akbar ended the system of appanage. The political faith of the empire until the time of Shahjahan is best described in the famous inscription authored by Abul Fazl for a temple in Kashmir, which has been mentioned earlier in this book. He found in every temple people who saw God and heard praise of God in every language spoken. For Akbar all religions were different paths to God.

Shahjahan's seventy-four years between 5 January 1592 and 22 January 1666 spanned the high plateau of Mughal glory. He lived through the last thirteen years of his grandfather Akbar's reign and twenty-two years of his father's. His rise began in 1606, when his impetuous brother Khusrau rebelled. Khusrau paid a heavy price when he was blinded at the age of nineteen. Jahangir's second son, Parvez, was given the usual sequence of responsibilities, but the emperor made no secret of his preference for his third son, Khurram.

Shahjahan's stipend in 1607 was 1,00,000 rupees per month, which climbed to 80,00,000 rupees by 1617.[8] In 1609, he was given charge of the treasury, with Raja Rai Singh as the designated guardian. He received the care of a virtual crown prince. Hakim Misri, an Egyptian doctor, was honoured with the title Jalinas Zamani ('Galen of the Age') when he cured Shahjahan of a serious illness (Galen was an iconic Greek physician).

Shahjahan's first military assignment was a triumph. After a quick campaign in 1614, he brought Mewar to submission. Within another five years, he had subdued the Deccan and taken the hill kingdom of Kangra. In 1613, Jahangir sent a large cauldron to the shrine of the family saint, Khwaja Muinuddin Chishti, at Ajmer, still on display there, for the preparation of food for pilgrims at the shrine. He needed the saint's blessings.

Shahjahan seemed equally blessed in his personal life. His marriage on 10 May 1612 to Arjumand Banu, or Mumtaz Mahal, daughter of Asaf Khan and niece of Nurjahan, became a love story for the ages.

He was twenty, she nineteen. She died in June 1631 during the birth of their fourteenth child, a daughter. Shahjahan had only one child outside of this marriage, in 1619, but that child did not survive infancy. Shahjahan was thirty-nine when he conceived a fairytale mausoleum for Mumtaz, an immortal adoration of love, the Taj Mahal, which was completed by 1648. Shahjahan took care to display consistent filial obedience until forced to rebel by his stepmother Nurjahan's hostility. Little was considered more contemptuous than disloyalty; you had to remain true to your salt. Jahangir applauds the sacrifice of a soldier in Shahjahan's service whose head was displayed on a pike by the enemy. The noble who conveyed the news said, in lofty tones, that there was no greater deed than laying down one's life for his master: the head on the pike was higher than that of others. In another incident, Shahjahan punished the treachery of Rustam Khan, whom he had earlier raised from cavalryman to agent in Gujarat, by stripping him of all possessions. In the Mughal code, Rustam Khan did not know right from wrong.

Baba Khurram Wins His Spurs

Emperor Jahangir became a father as Shahjahan prepared for the difficult Mewar campaign in 1614. Mewar, as Jahangir noted, had never bowed before any king of Hindustan. The emperor warned dissidents, ordering a noble, Khan Azam, to show loyalty to 'Baba Khurram', from whom he had never parted until then. He raised Shahjahan's rank to a *mansab* of 12,000.

Shahjahan's first military campaign was a triumph. Deploying his own men alongside the imperial army, the prince achieved success in Mewar after a mere few months of fighting. His principal generals were Muhammad Taqi, who was accused of using scorched-earth tactics, and Rai Sundar Das. The terms of settlement were negotiated by Mulla Shukrullah, the *mir-i adl* (principal judicial officer). Rai Sundar Das was promoted and given the title of Raja Bikramjit, and Shukrullah made Afzal Khan; both were sent to the emperor's court. A painting in London's Victoria and Albert Museum shows Mewar acceding to Shahjahan.[9] Rana Amar Singh, excusing his own presence because of old age, sent his son Karan Singh to the Mughal court. In an astute display of statesmanship, Jahangir awarded the Rajput prince a robe of honour and a jewelled sword. Shahjahan waited on his mothers before he went to court to receive gifts of exalted status like a valuable pearl rosary, a jewelled charqab (sleeveless vest), a gold brocade coat and an Iraqi horse with a jewelled saddle.

In 1616, Jahangir further elevated his favoured son, who would thereafter be styled Shah Sultan Khurram. The accompanying gifts, aside from the familiar jewelled saddle, horse and elephant, included a carriage built in the English fashion. Jahangir had received such a carriage from the first English ambassador to the Mughal courts, Sir Thomas Roe, and wondered if the king of England was so poor that he could afford nothing more than such a contraption. Shahjahan, one presumes, did not need to complain about the furnishings of his carriage.

Shahjahan's influence was rising faster than his titles. In 1616, the offences of Raja Bikramjit of Bandhu, whose ancestors were considerable zamindars, were pardoned through the patronage of 'my fortunate son Baba Khurram', wrote Jahangir. In the same year, Shahjahan's father-in-law Asaf Khan got custody of Khusrau, another decision that would have pleased the prince.

The empire was confident, rich and resurgent. The alliance with the Amber Rajputs had survived the hiccup of Man Singh's support to Khusrau. Ram Das Kachhwaha became the raja when Man Singh's grandson Maha Singh died of drink in 1617. The great imperial project was the Deccan campaign of 1616–1617. The tried, tested and trusted Shahjahan was given charge of reducing the independent sultanates of Ahmednagar, Bijapur and Golconda to submission. As Jahangir waited anxiously for news of the campaign in 1617, he sought an omen. Following a Persian tradition, which held that the poetry

Prince Khurram, later Shahjahan, being weighed against gold, silver and precious metals in a ceremony known as *tuladaan*, in the presence of his father Jahangir on his 15th birthday, recorded as 31 July 1607. The equivalent of the weight in coin was distributed among the poor. A Mughal prince's education began a little after the age of four, and he was often sent to the battlefield by the age of ten; Akbar was given command of troops when he was twelve. By fourteen or fifteen, he was sent as governor of an appanage. Painting, circa 1615.

Source: Wikimedia Commons/Public Domain

A mid-17th century astrologer reads a horoscope while an assistant pores over papers; the anxiety on the face of the man whose stars are being interpreted is palpable. A person, wearing little more than a loincloth, seems natural company for the soothsayer.
A page from the Late Shah Jahan Album, circa 1650.
Source: Wikimedia Commons/Public Domain

The court chronicler Abul Fazl, an outstanding intellectual whose knowledge extended to astronomy and astrology, presents a copy of his epic, *Akbarnama*, to Emperor Akbar. Abul Fazl was killed during the strife-ridden politics of succession because Jahangir believed that he had poisoned the monarch's mind against the natural heir.
This Mughal painting is dated between 1603 and 1605.
Source: Wikimedia Commons/Public Domain

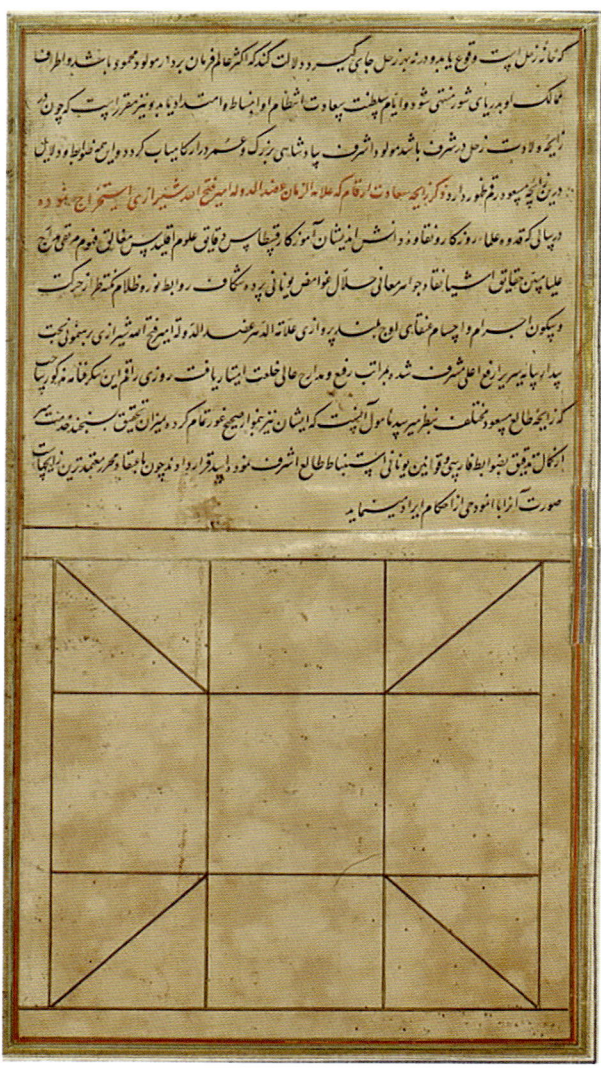

A page from the *Akbarnama* depicting the birth horoscope of Emperor Akbar drawn by the astrologer Fathullah Shirazi.
The Mughals consulted three schools of astrology: Indian, Persian and Greek. Akbar formalised their role in court with the creation of an official position, that of Jotik Rai, or Lord of Astrologers. For more than a century, Jyotik Rai was a Brahmin scholar from Banares. Although the diagram has been left blank, the details are supplied in the Persian text.
Source: Wikimedia Commons/Public Domain

```
                    AKBAR'S HOROSCOPE.
                           E.
     |          II.       |       I.        | Tail of Dragon. |
     |       Mercury.     |                 |                 |
     |         Jupiter.   |     Venus.      |                 |
     |  III.              |                 |     LEO.        |
     | Sun.      LIBRA.   |    VIRGO.       |     XII.        |
     | Saturn.            |                 |         CANCER. |
     | SCORPIO.           |                 |             XI. |
     |        IV.         |     Natus.      |       X.        |
     |                    | Sunday, 5 Rajab, 949             |
     |                    | A.H. = 15th October,              |
     | S.| SAGITTARIUS.   | 1542, O.S., Circa 2 A.M. | GEMINI. | N
     |                    |                 |                 |
     | Mars.    V.        |      VII.       |      IX.        |
     | CAPRICOR-          |                 |                 |
     |   NUS.             |                 |    TAURUS.      |
     | Moon.     VI.      |    PISCES.      | VIII.           |
     |      AQUARIUS.     |                 |    ARIES.       |
     |    Head of Dragon. |                 |                 |
                           W.
```

¹ Ulugh Beg Mīrzā was a grandson of Tīmūr and son of Shāhrukh. For information about his Tables see the works of Hyde, Greaves and Sédillot. He was born in 1393 and put to death by his own son in 1449. His Tables were first published in 1437. See Jarrett II. 5n., and an interesting paragraph and note in Erskine's *Bābar* (51.)

² I have added the numbers of the Houses to the diagram, and have inserted the date of birth. It will be seen that there is a difference of form between the horoscope as here given and the more elaborate dia-

This horoscope was drawn by Maulana Chand, who had been ordered by Humayun to record the exact moment of Akbar's birth at the Fort of Umarkot in Sind. Humayun, then in desperate exile, was away on an expedition. Maulana Chand predicted that the child, born in virtual destitution, would create one of the great empires of history because the birth had occurred at an astrological moment which comes but once in a thousand years.

Source: Abul Fazl, *The Akbarnama of Abul Fazl*, vol. 1, trans. H. Beveridge (Calcutta: The Asiatic Society, 1907), 70

Akbar presides over a religious discourse with representatives of all faiths at the Ibadat Khana, or House of Worship.
The two men in black dress and hat are Jesuit missionaries Rodolfo Acquaviva and Francisco Henriques. The Portuguese had ruled Goa for a little more than a century when this painting was done in 1605.
Source: Wikimedia Commons/Public Domain

Shahjahan with his favourite son, Dara Shukoh, the eldest of four brothers and designated heir who lost the crown to Aurangzeb in the wars of succession. Aurangzeb claimed that Dara had become a Hindu because of his affinity to Indian philosophy. Shahjahan believed that Dara, with his inclusive vision, was most suited to rule India. Painting, circa 1638.
Source: Wikimedia Commons/Public Domain

The aesthete Shahjahan holds a ruby during the Diwan-i-Am, or Public Durbar, while an attendant brings a tray of jewels, the preferred gift to Mughal monarchs. Aurangzeb, then Prince Alamgir, stands below the throne. By the time this painting was done, 1650, a halo around the king's head had become routine suggesting a quasi-divine status. Aurangzeb, despite his claims to a puritan simplicity in behaviour and strict adherence to sharia in personal life, never abandoned the halo in his portraits although it was akin to heresy.
Source: Wikimedia Commons/Public Domain

Jahangir in court, with a halo, circa 1620, just before he fell seriously ill. The variety of skin colour is evidence of a multi-ethnic nobility. As Jahangir's health deteriorated, power shifted to his favourite queen, Nurjahan, who nursed him as fervently as she nursed her ambitions for her son-in-law Shahryar. Once more ambition led to bitter war, in which Shahjahan prevailed. Painting, circa 1620.
Source: Wikimedia Commons/Public Domain

Mughal faith in astrology reflected the dynasty's pre-Islamic cultural roots. The Mughals were descended from Genghis Khan on the mother's side, and the other fabled conqueror from Central Asia, Amir Taimur, from the paternal bloodline. This painting, showing astrologers drawing Taimur's horoscope at his birth, was included in the imperial copy of *Akbarnama* produced around 1602.

Source: Wikimedia Commons/Public Domain

Humayun, defeated by Sher Shah Suri, was able to retake the throne of Delhi because of the vital assistance he received from Persia's Shah Tahmasp I. This is a painting of a banquet hosted in 1544 by the Shah in honour of his guest: there is wine in the goblet placed before each guest, music and dance. Every Mughal ruler before Aurangzeb enjoyed wine; Babur and Jahangir often in excess, the others in moderation although there is a famous episode of a suicidal Akbar's life being saved by Raja Man Singh during a drunken evening. Shahjahan, having watched his father's health being destroyed by alcohol, wanted to remain abstemious but was persuaded to take his first sip of wine by Jahangir because kings always drank.

Source: Wikimedia Commons/Public Domain

A portrait of three emperors, with Akbar in the centre, his heir Jahangir to his right, and grandson Shahjahan to his left with whom he is conversing, done by Bichitr, circa 1630, in the early years of Shahjahan's reign. All three were firm believers in astrology. Their period marked the apex of empire, sustained by inter-faith understanding, which was decimated by Aurangzeb leading to chaos and collapse. Shahjahan built the Taj Mahal at Agra in memory of his wife Mumtaz Mahal.

Source: Wikimedia Commons/Public Domain

This portrait of Humayun was done during the reign of Shahjahan, circa 1650. The Mughal's eyes are narrow and slanted reflecting their Mongol ancestry. By the time of Shahjahan the bloodlines had changed, and along with it the shape of the eyes and the colour of the skin, which became more wheatish. The painting is from the Late Shah Jahan Album.

Source: Wikimedia Commons/Public Domain

Jahangir, a firm believer in astrology, was the first Mughal to issue coins with images of the zodiac on one side. The astrologer determined all aspects of life, from the mundane to the vital. They selected the day's visitors, the moments when it was auspicious to travel, the schedule of a military campaign, and the auspicious moment for a coronation.

Source: Wikimedia Commons/Public Domain

Even Aurangzeb set aside Islamist religiosity when it came to astrology. His astrologers made him wait weeks for his two coronations. He believed that he had become emperor against all odds only because such glory was written in his horoscope. Equally remarkably, he told his son Bahadur Shah that while the Mughal Empire looked impregnable in his lifetime, it would crumble within a few quick years after he died. That too came true.

Source: Wikimedia Commons/Public Domain

of Hafiz had mystical powers, he dipped into the diwan of the poet and found this couplet:

The day of absence and night of parting from the friend are over.
I took this augury, the star passed and fulfilment came.

Twenty-five days later, news of victory arrived.

Shahjahan's emissary Sayyid Abdullah Barha presented a letter reporting that all the enemy chiefs and sultans, 'laying the head of duty in the noose of obedience, had consented to service and humility'. Shahjahan's favourite commanders had delivered again. Raja Bikramjit stormed Ahmednagar. He and Afzal Khan settled the terms of tribute with Bijapur. Mirza Makki Koka and Rai Jadu Das finalised a settlement with Golconda. Barha presented the keys of Ahmednagar Fort and other strongholds to Jahangir, along with multiple jewels, including the historic Chamkora diamond, whose name, according to Jahangir, was derived from a plant called sag-i-chamkora, because it was found in the vegetable by one of the ladies in the household of Murtaza Nizam ul mulk after the conquest of Berar.

Jahangir sent his son a ruby from his turban 'by way of good augury'. The true reward among his gifts was power. He bestowed upon him the title of 'Shahjahan' with a *mansab* of 30,000 personnel and 20,000 horse in recognition of his 'distinguished service'.[10] A special chair was ordered for him to sit beside his father in court. Khurram kept 'Shahjahan' as his regnal title; it is the name he is known by today.

When a querulous Ottoman emperor protested that a Mughal prince could at best be called Shah al-Hind ('King of India'), the court poet Abu Talib Kalim responded with a chronogram. Since the numbers of 'Hind' (5+50+4) in the Persian alphabet were equivalent to the numbers of 'Jahan' (3+5+1+50) in the Persian alphabet, the claim was justified: a king of India was king of the world. Babur became Padshah from Mirza after his victory over the Lodi kingdom in 1526. Akbar rose to Shahenshah ('king of kings'). Jahangir meant 'world conqueror'. Aurangzeb styled himself Alamgir ('conqueror of the universe').

Nurjahan, whose revenues had been raised by 2,00,000 rupees through the grant of extra lands, welcomed the hero of 1617 with a dazzling 'feast of victory' on Thursday, the 14th of Shaban. The event was crafted to be memorable, for it honoured several special events: the anniversary of Jahangir's ascension; Rakhi, the Indian festival celebrating the love between sisters and brothers; and Shab-i-Barat, the blessed Islamic night of salvation when Allah forgives the faithful and grants their wishes. The venue was Nurjahan's home, situated amidst water tanks. The reflection of lanterns and lamps seemed to set the water on fire, wrote the emperor. Nurjahan presented Shahjahan with a *nadiri* coat (a dress reserved for Mughal royalty) embroidered with flowers and adorned with rare pearls, a *sarpich* (an ornament for the turban) with rare gems, a turban with a fringe of pearls, a waistbelt with pearls, a sword with a jewelled *pardala* (belt), two horses (one with a jewelled saddle) and a special elephant with two females. The ladies and children of Shahjahan's household were given fine cloth and gold ornaments. His officials each got a horse or a dress. The guests were served intoxicating drinks according to every desire. Nobles got drunk. Supper was a variety of roast meats and fruits. The emperor spent time with the ladies of the palace after the men had left. The cost of this single evening was calculated at a phenomenal 3,00,000 rupees.

High life in the Jahangir era was heady.

The Teetotal Prince in a Palace of Wine

The licence to drink had ancestry. Babur's father, Umar Shaykh, loved his cup. Babur refrained until he had conquered Kabul and then made up for it. *Masti-tafih* (alcoholic blackout) was a princely privilege. Babur's memoirs turn, in passages, into a poetic party where wine and drugs become masculine preening. One illustration in the *Baburnama*, created during Akbar's reign, depicts a drunken frolic. Humayun was a drug addict. Akbar nearly killed himself once during a drunken depression. He also enjoyed opium. Jahangir expected courtiers to partake of *sharab-i-marhamat* (wine of loyalty), and he quoted Hafiz's command to the cupbearer to brighten the goblet with the light of wine and to the minstrel to sing, since the world was working as desired.

Jahangir is remarkably candid about his alcoholism. His first taste of liquor, while a child, was in the form of a cough remedy administered by his mother and wet nurses, a spoonful of it mixed with water and rosewater. He became a serious imbiber at fifteen during a campaign along the Nilab ('Blue Water' or Indus) when an attendant said alcohol would relieve his weariness.

His addiction reached a level where wine was insufficient; his daily consumption rose to twenty cups of arrack, fourteen in the daytime. His hands trembled. Hakim Humam had the physician's right to honesty: 'Lord of the world, by the way in which you drink spirits, God forbid it, but in six months matters will come to such a pass that there will be no remedy for it.' The king became moderate but not abstinent. He diluted the arrack, diminished his intake and, in seven years, brought it down to six cups with Thursday and Friday dry. He became vegetarian on Thursdays and Sundays. When he was forty-six, his doctor imposed a limit of 'eight surkhs [a red berry used as a weight] of opium when five *gharis* of day have passed, and six surkhs after one watch of the night'.[11]

The empire flourished not because Jahangir drank every evening from his teenage years but because he disciplined himself, when emperor, to remain largely sober during the day. Any mention of the previous evening's revelries by a careless emir was punished.

Shahjahan evolved into an ideal Mughal prince, with one difference: he was a teetotaller. Jahangir tried affectionate persuasion on his son's twenty-fourth birthday, a Friday, to get him to drink. Acknowledging that Shahjahan had never defiled himself with wine, the father offered endearing advice by quoting the Uzbek philosopher-doctor Ibn Sina:

> Baba, thou hast become the father of children, and kings and kings' sons have drunk wine. Today, which is the day of thy being weighed, I will give thee wine to drink, and give thee leave to drink it on feast days and at the time of the New Year, and at all great festivals. But thou must observe the path of moderation, for wise men do not consider it right to drink to such an extent as to destroy the understanding, and it is necessary that from drinking only profit should be derived.[12]

He also cited a quatrain attributed to the wise Bu Ali or Ibn Sina or Avicenna:

> Wine is a raging enemy, a prudent friend;
> A little is an antidote, but much a snake's poison.
> In much there is no little injury,
> In a little there is much profit.

An emperor's wish is a prince's command. Jahangir complained that persuasion had required persistence. No persistence was needed with his second son, Parvez, who had degenerated into an embarrassing sot by the time Sir Thomas went to call on him in Burhanpur. The Englishman maintains a poker pen but cannot hide his amazement when Parvez gets drunk on the wine that the English dignitary has brought as a gift, having opened the case immediately.

Shahjahan was abstemious for good reason. He had seen the havoc drink had wrought in his family. Few deaths were more pitiable than that of his handsome, pleasant and poetic uncle Danyal, who died from drinking contaminated wine at the age of thirty-three.

During a visit to Kabul in 1607, Jahangir revels in the memory of Babur. He describes the stone terrace where 'Firdaus-makani [heaven-dweller] used to sit and drink wine. In one corner of this rock they have excavated a round basin which could contain about two Hindustani maunds of wine'. Jahangir had a similar basin made by its side, engraved with his name 'together with that of Sahib-qirani [Taimur]. Every day that I sat on that throne I ordered them to fill both of the basins with wine and give it to the servants who were present there'.[13] The consumption was copious.

Nurjahan: Father's Love, Son's Nemesis

On Friday, 30 March 1619, court astrologers were summoned to determine the time for funeral rituals after Shahjahan's mother, Jagat Gosain Manwati Jodha Bai, 'attained the mercy of God'. Jahangir went to mourn at his son's home on Saturday. Both returned to Agra Fort on Sunday, the 1st of Urdibihisht, at the auspicious hour chosen by astrologers. The emperor scattered money in the streets and bazaars to obtain God's blessings for the deceased.

Queens, partners to kings in the seesaw of life, had a place of honour in the palace. They did not hold office but exerted influence as elders during bitter family disputes. They travelled with their consorts when a prince rebelled. Shahjahan had nearly lost his wife and his son Murad when a cannonball hit their tent during the Battle of Thatta. Akbar's love for his foster mothers, the carefully chosen wet nurses who had protected their foster son with fierce devotion, is a motif in the *Akbarnama* until its narratives of the 1560s. Jiji Anaka, from the Afghan clan of Atga, saved the child Akbar from physical harm in the midst of battle. The equally beloved Maham Anaka was instrumental in the ouster of Akbar's grasping guardian Bairam Khan. Women from the spiritual leader Salim Chishti's family were selected as foster mothers for the child Salim. When his wet nurse, who had been kinder than his own mother, died in March 1607, Jahangir placed the feet of her corpse on his shoulders for the last journey. The mourning emperor neither ate nor changed his clothes for a few days.

Jahangir wore a ruby in his turban valued at a 1,00,000 silver rupees, gifted at his birth by his grandmother Hamida Banu. A mother's blessing was a seal of approval. Jahangir's first decision after defeating Khusrau in 1606 was to send for his mother, Maryam Zamani. Shahjahan brought her from Agra to Lahore. Jahangir prostrated before his mother, obeisance that was due from the young to the old according to the custom of Genghis Khan, and re-entered the fort of Lahore only after obtaining her permission. Maryam Zamani lived to the age of eighty.

Nurjahan (1577–1645) was the most powerful queen of the Mughal era. Her story begins as attraction at first sight before it matures into an epic of empire. Jahangir's diary for 1611 starts, as always, at Nauruz, the new year, in March, with a predictable paean to the greatest star, the Sun, in the constellation of Aries. As page after page over the next two months is filled with the routine, such as ritual offerings from nobles like Miran Sadr Jahan, Jahangir Quli Khan or Raja Kalyan of Bengal, an impending marriage is not considered important enough for mention.

Her name was Mehrunnissa. She was a Shia lady in a male-dominated Sunni dispensation and a widow of Sher Afghan Khan, a Persian who had migrated to India, obtained a *jagir* in Burdwan and died in a skirmish in 1607. Jahangir saw her during the Nauruz festivities on 11 March 1611. She became his twentieth and last wife on 20 May. Her first title was Nurmahal, her second Nurjahan, from 'Light of the Palace' to 'Light of the World'. While still in the shadows, in 1612, her niece Arjumand Banu, daughter of her brother Asaf Khan, was married to Shahjahan.

We must wait until 1614 for Nurjahan to enter the emperor's memoirs. Jahangir records the care and love he received from Nurjahan when he fell seriously ill. Jahangir was seized with such a fever and headache that he became apprehensive about death and kept his illness secret for 'fear that some injury might occur to the country'. His only confidant was Nurjahan Begum, '[more] than whom I did not think anyone was fonder of me'.[14]

Nurjahan broke convention with audacity and confidence, setting aside the veil, hunting, serving alcohol at her parties, ruling the empire during the last seven years of her husband's life and, during one crisis, briefly leading troops in battle. Her feat at a hunting expedition in 1617 became legendary. When four tigers came in sight, Nurjahan, atop an elephant, requested permission to go for the kill. Jahangir could hardly believe what he next witnessed: she shot two tigers with one shot each and knocked over the two others with four shots. In the twinkling of an eye, she deprived the bodies of these four tigers of life. Until now, such shooting was never seen: that from the top of an elephant and inside a howdah, six shots and not one miss. An adoring Jahangir gave his wife a pair of diamond bracelets worth 1,00,000 rupees and scattered a thousand gold coins, or *ashrafis*, over her.

A famous painting dated 1619 shows Nurjahan hunting tigers, although by this time Jahangir had vowed that he would not injure any living thing with his own hand. Even a conventional pastime like hunting required the intervention of astrologers. Jahangir records in 1610:

> As the desire to hunt overcame me, at a propitious hour determined by the astrologers, when a watch and six *gharis* had passed on the night of Friday, the 15th Ramzan, corresponding with the 10th Azar in the 5th year of my reign, I started to hunt.[15]

Nurjahan's wealth kept pace with her power. She became a multinational merchant who owned trading ships. This was not rare. Mughal princesses became businesswomen, writes Lisa Balabanlilar, as sea trade with Europe grew from the Portuguese base in Goa and from Daman and Diu on the lucrative Gujarat coast. Nurjahan's agents collected duties on ships plying the river Yamuna carrying cotton produce from Bengal, raw silk from Patna and thousands of drugs and spices. She employed between two and three thousand people and maintained five hundred horses at Sikandra.[16]

Shahjahan augmented the business done by his merchant fleet with forceful persuasion. Faruqui writes:

> Khurram was actively involved in buying and selling goods, and he could get rough when thwarted. He demanded that Europeans offer his representatives the right of first refusal on anything that landed in Surat, Mughal India's most important port city and part of Khurram's *jagir* through the 1610s and 1620s.[17]

Before he left India in 1619, Sir Thomas Roe had noted that while Jahangir was the titular head, Shahjahan had become the real ruler. Jahangir was full of admiration for his son after his conquest of Kangra: 'A drop from the cloud of his sword is a tempest.' Nurjahan set out to prove that this sword could be blunted.

Shahjahan had become too powerful to accept any dilution in his authority or any challenge to the succession. Nurjahan concluded that Shahjahan would not share power if he became emperor. In 1620, Nurjahan was forty-three and Shahjahan twenty-eight, both in the prime of their lives. They began to position themselves for the future during another crisis triggered by the emperor's health.

In 1618, Jahangir caught fever in the unbearable heat of a summer visit to Gujarat. He also showed signs of asthma. But his principal doctors were unable to reduce his wine intake. In early 1619, he needed eye surgery to open a vein and remove blood congestion. Kashmir, where he spent seven months in 1620 between March and October, may have been a paradise but was not a hospital. The asthma returned. Nurjahan's care seemed the only saving grace. Her role in the administration of the kingdom increased. Her writ was accepted as the emperor's will.

In a provocative gambit, Nurjahan made a move designed to finesse Shahjahan out of the succession stakes. She arranged the marriage of her only daughter, Ladli Begum, from her previous marriage, with fifteen-year-old Shahryar, Jahangir's youngest son, which took place in December 1620. She began raising Shahryar's profile in court, for popular opinion dismissed him as a *nashudani* (worthless). The Indian people are remarkably accurate in their assessment of their masters.

In the winter of 1619–1620, Jahangir visited the home of his 'auspicious son' Shahjahan to celebrate the birth of Izad Baksh, who died early. Shahjahan gifted the emperor a 'short, broadsword [*yak-awiz*]' of Venetian workmanship, beautifully with its hilt and sapphire fastenings cut in Europe. It was the last phase of bonhomie between the two.

Shahjahan had proved himself. By 1617, he had brought the southern Sultanates to heel and deflated the remarkable Malik Ambar (1548–1626), an Ethiopian from Harar named Chapu who had risen from being a slave in Ahmednagar to independent commander with a force of around 50,000 (Malik was a title, meaning 'owner'). After Shahjahan returned north, Malik Ambar began to reverse the Mughal gains. By 1620, with the help of allies like Shahaji Bhosale, father of the Maratha hero Shivaji, he had displaced the Mughals as the effective power in the region.

Jahangir decided to send Shahjahan back to the Deccan. Neither knew it then, but when son took leave of his father in Lahore, it would be their last meeting. With the emperor's health in question, Shahjahan suspected a conspiracy by Nurjahan to keep him physically distant from the throne. To protect his interests, he asked for and received custody of his elder brother, Khusrau.

In 1621, between August and September, during the Dussehra festival, Jahangir felt short of breath. This was attributed to excessive rains and damp air. When he came down from the hills, where he was at the time, his health became worse. Hakim Rukna was summoned from Agra. His remedies failed. The emperor's pain increased, as did the weakness. Hakim Mirza Muhammad, who had migrated from Persia during Akbar's reign and was known as a masih-uz-zaman ('messiah of the age'), could not diagnose the problem and refused to suggest a cure. Hakim Abul

Qasim became vexed and terrified. Jahangir says he gave himself up to the 'Supreme Physician' and began drinking excessively to alleviate the pain. Nurjahan used her persuasive skills to reduce the alcohol consumption and change his diet. The astrologers, however, were optimistic.

Jotik Rai gave Jahangir 'the glad news of his 'recovery and restoration to health'. The king's weight came down from over 3 maunds to 2 maunds and 27 sers (1 maund, the old Indian weight, is equivalent to 37.32 kilograms).[18] He recovered. Jyotik Rai was rewarded handsomely. Nurjahan gave another expensive feast to celebrate, at a cost of 2,00,000 rupees.

As expenses for the Deccan army, Shahjahan had been sent 20,00,000 rupees from the imperial treasury, but the 'viral' news was his father's near-death experience. Shahjahan decided to eliminate one possible challenge; he ordered the death of Khusrau. Most contemporary accounts say that Khusrau was strangled. Shahjahan put it out that Khusrau had died of colic. Jahangir accepted this dubious explanation in 1621, but his subsequent actions prove that he was no longer neutral in the succession politics that followed.

In early 1622, Jahangir ordered that Nurjahan's drums and orchestra should be sounded after those of the king. Edicts were signed by Nurjahan Padshah Begum or the empress. She joined the emperor at *jharoka darshan*. Her name was added to coins in exalted terms: 'By order of the King Jahangir, gold has a hundred splendours added to it by receiving the impression of the name of Nurjahan, the Queen Begum.' Jahangir encouraged speculation by saying that he would be happy to retreat to a life of quiet devotion while his talented wife reigned, but he was never so deluded as to surrender his throne. Shahryar got command of the imperial forces and the *jagir* of Hissar, the traditional fiefdom of a preferred heir. As late as 1626, Jahangir issued a proclamation ordering Khusrau's son Dawar Baksh to avenge his father's murder by killing Shahjahan.

Qandahar became the flashpoint. In March 1622, Jahangir recorded frequent reports that Persia's Shah Abbas had left Khurasan with an army towards the long-disputed province of Qandahar. Jahangir sent a 'gracious *firman* to Khurram to come and wait on me with all possible speed with a victorious host, and elephants of mountain hugeness, and the numerous artillery that were assigned for his support'. He promised Shahjahan an army of innumerable soldiers financed by countless treasures to teach the Persian king what it meant to break faith with the Mughals. A *firman* was not a request. Shahjahan, now convinced that Nurjahan was using the invasion as an opportunity to move him from his secure base in the Deccan, tried to buy time with a feint. When time ran out, he declared war on his father.

Family wars were a perennial feature of Mughal history. Babur was defeated and driven out from Uzbekistan to Kabul by relatives. Humayun fought his brothers longer than he did his declared enemies. His death was kept secret in 1556 to enable thirteen-year-old Akbar to reach Delhi from Punjab without challenge. Akbar's brother Mirza Hakim supported, fomented and led rebellions for two decades, culminating in his comprehensive defeat by 1585. Hakim's young sons Kaikobad and Afrasiyab were taken into custody. In 1594, Akbar undermined twenty-five-year-old Salim (Jahangir) by granting his seven-year-old grandson Khusrau a high rank of 5,000, sparking ambitions that led to Khusrau's uprising against Jahangir. Jahangir scotched the potential aspirations of his nephews, Danyal's three minor sons, by ordering their conversion to Christianity. It is incidental that

Jahangir was a patron of Christian art, with pictures and statues of the Virgin Mary in his palaces, misleading the Jesuits who felt he was ready for conversion. Jahangir once claimed to have seen Jesus, a revered prophet in the Quran, in a dream.

Jahangir, without a trace of irony given his past, quoted the Persian poet Sadi in 1623 to describe his anger at Shahjahan, the *bidaulat*:

> In the end a wolfs cub becomes a wolf
> Although he grew up with man.

One great poet was insufficient for the embittered father. He recalled Firdausi's satire on Mahmud of Ghazni.

> The tree that is bitter in its nature
> If you plant it in the garden of Paradise,
> And water it from the eternal stream thereof,
> If you pour on its root pure honey,
> In the end it shows its natural quality
> And it bears the same bitter fruit.

The narrative of the next seven years, until the end of Jahangir's reign, is one of relentless fratricide. Factions fought against a fluctuating centre and between themselves; provinces protected themselves as best they could; the pre-eminent general Mahabat Khan usurped power for a hundred days. There were no victors. But the principal Rajput powers, including Amber, stood by the emperor. In March 1623, Raja Jai Singh, grandson of Man Singh, reaffirmed his allegiance to the crown. Jahangir promoted the son of Maharaja Bir Singh Deo, describing him as the greatest of Rajputs.

Shahjahan found support among those who did not want the Mughal dynasty to become a Nurjahan dynasty, most notably Abdur Rahim, the warrior-poet son of Bairam Khan. But in 1623, Shahjahan was thwarted at Agra by the ageing Itibar Khan, appointed governor of the fort and treasury a year earlier, and then defeated by imperial forces led by his bibulous brothers Parvez and Mahabat Khan, arrayed like the 'waves of the sea'. Shahjahan's ranks included the Brahmin general Sundar, 'his guide in the desert of error'; Darab, son of the Khan-i-Khanan; and amirs like Himmat Khan, Sharza Khan, Jado Rai, Uday Ram, Atash Khan and Mansur Khan from the Deccan, Gujarat and Malwa.

Fate, as mercurial as its reputation, determined the outcome. An imperial commander, Abdullah Khan, deserted with 10,000 men in the midst of fighting, but the logistics of the switch caused so much confusion that it became counterproductive. The course of battle changed from near-disaster for Jahangir to victory. Sundar was killed by a gunshot: 'At his fall the pillars of courage of the rebels shook.' Jahangir knelt in prayer when he heard that his troops had prevailed. The next day, Sundar's head was brought to him, the ears cut off by the soldier who had stolen the pearls in the lobes.[19]

Since defeat is an orphan, Abdur Rahim negotiated his way back to the royal court. Jahangir raised Parvez to the rank of 40,000 and sent him in pursuit of his brother, who retreated through Ajmer. By 10 September 1623, Shahjahan had fled across the river Tapti towards the Deccan. Parvez, always a reluctant warrior, lingered in Burhanpur. Shahjahan reached Orissa through Golconda with just 7,000 troops, but that was sufficient for him to seize Burdwan and Dhaka, and take Bengal from the Mughal governor Ibrahim Khan. His commander, Raja Bhim, captured Rohtas and Patna. That year Jahangir's health and rule faltered. In 1624, he handed over the continuation of his memoirs to a scribe, Mutamid Khan. His most powerful general, Mahabat Khan, disobeyed an order to go to Bengal. In 1626, with a force of 4,000 Rajputs and 2,000 Afghans, Mahabat Khan turned against the emperor, driving the royal couple out of Lahore. Nurjahan maintained her sangfroid. She moved calmly with her husband towards Kabul, drinking wine and marvelling at the wonders of nature along the way. Her rage at Mahabat Khan is aptly captured in *Fathnama-i Nurjahan*: she calls him deceitful, unfaithful, disloyal, evil, a villain, ignoble, malicious, unlucky, a beast, dishonourable, a tyrant, a monster, irreligious, arrogant, a leper and a non-Muslim citizen of Satan's community—an impressive thesaurus of vituperative terms.

Shahjahan recalibrated his options as it became clear that the emperor's life was ebbing. He returned to the Deccan in 1626, from where he sought pardon from his father. The response came from Nurjahan. Shahjahan would have to surrender the forts of Rohtas and Asir, and send his eldest sons, Dara, ten, and Aurangzeb, eight, to Lahore as hostages.

Parvez died on 28 October 1626 of alcoholism. Mahabat Khan, abandoned by frustrated troops, fled towards the Deccan with a rump band of 2,000 men. Shahjahan, then in Nasik, had to do no more than stay still. In October 1627, a Rajput messenger brought him news of Jahangir's death.

Those nearest the throne made the first bid for power. Khusrau's son Dawar Baksh, in alliance with Asaf Khan, defeated Nurjahan and Shahryar. Nurjahan retired to her home in Lahore, where she died in 1645 and was buried alongside her husband. Dawar Baksh became king for two months while Asaf Khan kept in touch with his son-in-law Shahjahan, who marched up from the Deccan. In December 1627, Shahjahan told Asaf Khan to seize the hapless Dawar Baksh, his younger brother Gurshashp, and Danyal's sons Tahmurs and Hoshang. They were 'sent out of the world' on 23 January 1628. Shahjahan shed more family blood on his way to the crown than any of his predecessors. He knew a fact of Mughal life: the dead cannot take revenge.

Shahjahan waited outside Agra for twelve days from Thursday, 28 January 1628, because his astrologers would not allow him to enter the capital. A coronation had to await their clearance.

He was crowned on Monday, 4 February. The astrologers received their due rewards along with the nobility. Mumtaz Mahal, steadfast through the seven years of peril for Shahjahan, was allotted 2,00,000 *ashrafi*, 6,00,000 rupees and an annual allowance of 10,00,000 rupees. Shahjahan's daughter Jahanara Begum got 1,00,000 *ashrafi*, 4,00,000 rupees and 6,00,000 rupees per year in cash or land revenue. Shahjahan's sons Dara, Shuja and Aurangzeb got 1,50,000 rupees each, while 3,50,000 rupees was distributed between Murad, the youngest son, and the other princes. Asaf Khan was raised to a *mansab* of 8,000 and appointed the governor of Punjab. Mahabat Khan was named Khan-i-Khanan.

The new emperor instructed his craftsmen to set the Ulugh Beg ruby in a jewel-encrusted seat, which became the Peacock Throne. A second ruby, inscribed with the name of Timur, and sent by Shah Abbas to Jahangir, was added to the majestic throne. Shahjahan would be an effective monarch for thirty years, re-annexing Ahmednagar and turning Bijapur and Golconda into tributaries by 1636. Shahjahan's version of the wars was written into the histories of his period. Chronicles like the *Maasir-i Jahangiri*, *Iqbalnama-i Jahangiri*, *Shahjahannama* and *Ahwal-i Shahzadagi* blame Nurjahan for driving a wedge between father and son.

Sanskrit, Sufis and Sanyasis

Akbar's policy of integration moved on parallel tracks—those of politics and culture. Akbar, Jahangir and Shahjahan added the Sanskrit inheritance of India to their philosophy of power, with Brahmins and Jains as their intellectual spearhead. Astrology was already part of the belief system, raised to a formal position at the court in the institution of a Jyotik Rai, held by a Brahmin.

Six major works of scholarship sponsored by Mughal emperors between 1589 and 1652 are extant: *Jagadgurukavya* by Padmasagara (1589), *Mantrikarmacandravamsavaliprabhanda* by Jayasoma (1594), *Hirasa Ubhagaya* by Devavimala (undated, estimated to be early 16th century), *Bhanucandraganicarita* by Siddicandra (circa 1620), *Vijayaprasastimahakavya* by Hemacijaya (1624–1632) and *Vijayadevamahatmya* by Vallabha Pathaka (1652). This intellectual stream nourished amity through intellectual understanding.

Cultural bridges had been built before. Zaynal Abedin, ruler of Kashmir between 1420 and 1470, had ordered the translation of Kalhana's *Rajataringini* ('River of Kings'), the Mahabharata and other Sanskrit literature into Persian and Arabic, and Persian texts into Sanskrit. He was an inspiration for Abul Fazl, who praises him for abolishing communal taxes on Hindus and forbidding cow slaughter. At least two sultans of Gujarat, Qutb al-din Ahmad and Mahmud Begada, encouraged Sanskrit in their courts, as did Sher Shah Suri during his brief rule and the Qutubshahi dynasty in Golconda. Raja Man Singh brought Pundarikavitthala to Akbar's court. Akbar honoured Govinda Bhatta of Rewa with the title of *Akbariyakalidasa* ('Akbar's Kalidas'). The Rajputs were successful in protecting cows and temples in Mathura and Vrindavan through edicts, and introduced the *dhrupad* and *pakhawaj* to court music.

Padmasundara from Jodhpur was the first Jain intellectual to enter the charmed circle. By 1569, he had produced, at the emperor's request, a transliteration of Sanskrit poetics called *Akbarasahisrngaradarpana* ('Mirror of erotic passion for Shah Akbar'). He was joined in 1582 by Hiravijaya, a leader of the Jain Tapa Gaccha sect, who was honoured with the title *Jagadguru* ('teacher to the world').

Akbar, known as *Sarvabhauma* ('world ruler'), gave the title of *Jyotivitsarasa* ('the elegant astronomer') to the intellectual courtier Narasimha. Abul Fazl was elevated towards the end of his life *Dalasthambana* ('pillar of the army'). Manasima and Bhanucandra were *Acharya* or *Upadhyay*. The Jain monk Jinacandra was *Yugapradhana* ('great man of the age'). Jahangir gave the same title to Jinasimha.

Two Jains, Nandivijaya and Siddhicandra, were honoured with the Persian title of *Khushfahm* ('the wise'). The presence of Jain seers at the Mughal court increased after the conquest of Gujarat in 1573. They helped persuade the emperor to restrict animal slaughter and to change his own dietary habits. Karamcandra is remembered for restoring Jain idols looted during pre-Mughal campaigns in Rajasthan. Hiravijaya started a Jain library that was described as a home to Saraswati. After his death in 1596, Vijaysena became the leader of the Jains in court. In 1610, Jahangir banned animal slaughter during Paryushan, the holy days of the year for Jains. Francois Bernier suggests that the credit for this goes to the Brahmins, but the Frenchman may have been a trifle careless about the difference between Brahmins and Jains. The important fact is that it happened.

Akbar added Jains, Brahmins and Christians to his multi-faith house of worship, or *ibadatkhana*, while the *maktabkhana* (translation bureau) did extensive work in creating greater understanding between Hindus and Muslims. Abul Fazl wrote the preface for a Persian Mahabharata; the Ramayana was also translated into Persian. All eighteen books of the Mahabharata, along with the genealogies and names of the sages and gods, are in the Persian *Razmnamah,* with illustrations that depict both the main events and burnished side-stories, reflecting Persian literature's addiction to marvels. A painting of ten animated Hindu and Muslim scholars, fanned by two servants in the background, is now exhibited in the Free Library of Philadelphia.

The Jain monk Santicandra got orders favourable to his Tapa Gaccha sect during the 1580s after writing 128 laudatory verses in praise of the king and his ancestors, compiled under the title of *Krparasakosa,* in which Akbar's mother Hamida Begum is said to possess divine energy comparable to Lakshmi. He praises the emperor as *Digvijaya* ('conqueror of four directions') for abolishing taxes on Hindus—'*hindubhyah sakalebhya eva*'—and offers a unique interpretation of Akbar's name: 'A' stands for supreme lord, 'K' for Brahmin, the second 'A' for the soul (*atma*), while 'vara' means best.

Krisnadasa composed the first Persian grammar in Sanskrit in the 1580s. Akbar added a recitation of Sanskrit names for the Sun, which he venerated. Faizi translated the *Kathasaritsagara* ('Ocean of stories'), an anthology of folklore. His brother Abul Fazl's detailed examination of Indian philosophy in *Ain-i-Akbari* is familiar. Siddhicandra says that Fazl's knowledge extended to all the *astras,* including astrology, omens, yoga, Mimamsa, Buddhism, Jainism, Sankhya, Vaisheshika, Carvaka, Vedanta, poetry, music, drama, lexicography, mythology, erotica, political science, mathematics and veterinary knowledge.

Jahangir sponsored translations of Sanskrit texts when he was in Allahabad. Copies of the Ramayana were dedicated to him. Karnapura, a poet, wrote a Sanskrit grammar in Persian for Jahangir. Between 1623 and 1624, Giridharidas dedicated his *Namah-i-Ram* (Book of Ram), written as an epic about an Indian hero in a kingdom of equity and justice, to him. The other translation of the time, Saadallah Masih Panapati's *Dastan-i-Ram-o-Sita*, is a classic romance of enduring love and sacrifice, written as history and not legend.

Vijayadeva Suri was known as *Jahangirmahatapa* ('Jahangir's great ascetic'), while Siddhicandra was described as *Nadirahzaman* and *Jahangirpasand* ('wonder of the age' and 'Jahangir's favourite'). Rudrakavi, who authored the *Jahangircarita* and the *Kirtisamullasa* for the emperor, acclaims the treasure house of Jahangir's empire, the beautiful women of his palace and the reverence offered to dervishes (*phakirsa*) in Agra. Jahangir is compared to great ancient kings.

Shahjahan was a patron of Kavindracarya Sarasvati, a *Vidhyanidhana* ('inexhaustible treasure-house of knowledge'). The venerable Kavindracarya, leader of the Benares Brahmins, was lauded by sixty-nine pundits, named or anonymous, in a festschrift of more than 300 verses and prose passages in Sanskrit, Prakrit and Marathi, for persuading Shahjahan to cancel a tax on pilgrims to Benares and to the confluence of the holy rivers at Prayag. The festschrift is titled *Kavindracandrodaya* (Moonrise of Kavindra).[20]

Brahmins who served as royal astrologers acknowledged that the poet had performed an immense service, calling him an avatar of Vishnu. Purnanda Brahmacharin mentions that 'Kavindra, lord of the three worlds', gave daily lessons to the lord of Delhi, Shahjahan, and his son Dara Shukoh in the Vedas, philosophy, sacred texts, Sastras, commentary (*bhasya*) and poetry (*subhasita*). More than half the verses of the *Kavindrakalpalata* are dedicated to Shahjahan. Kavindra's *dhrupad* included laudatory references to the monarch. His work in Hindi reflects the rise of Indian languages in the imperial culture, particularly after Abdur Rahim Khan-i-Khanan's immensely popular Hindi poetry.

In 1609, Rudrakavi celebrated Abdur Rahim in *Khanakhanacarita* to help his patron Pratap Shah's diplomatic efforts to resolve, amicably, a siege of his kingdom by imperial forces. Had poetry been enough, Pratap Singh would have succeeded:

From seeds that are pearls sliding down
The bursting temples of elephants
Abandoned on battlefields soaked with enemies' blood
And torn up by beasts,
The lovely creeper of the khan's fame is blooming,
Its roots strangle Shesha, it gives rise to stars,
And bears the fruit of the moon as it oozes Ganges nectar.

Jagannatha Panditraja, a renowned vocalist who wrote verse and dissertations on music in Sanskrit, spent the prime of his life in the Mughal court. In *Rasagangadhara*, he praises the '"black thread" of Jahangir', the *nurudina*, asking whether it became black from the collyrium shed in the tears of the queens of Jahangir's enemies. The *Badshahnama*, an official history of Shahjahan's reign, lauds Jagannatha as *kabirai* and *mahakabirai* ('king of poets' and 'great king of poets'), who sang bhajan and *dhrupad* in a voice filled with pleasure and decorated with joy. His talent was rewarded; on one occasion, he received 4,500 rupees.

Jagannatha sang in '*zaban-i-Karnatak*'; he was an exponent of Carnatic music, the oldest style of classical music in India. He was also a *kalavant* in *dhrupad* (a conjunction of *dhruva* and *pada* or 'constant with composition'). He praised Shahjahan as 'the sun that pierces the darkness of destitution' and likened another patron, Asaf Khan, to the waves of the Ganges and the snow-capped peaks of the Himalayas.

Dara Shukoh oversaw numerous literary projects, including a translation of the Upanishads into Persian and a treatise on the unity of Hindu and Muslim ideas, *Majma al-Bahrayn* ('Confluence of Two Oceans'). Imperial authority sought integration into Indian aesthetics, as evident from dozens of surviving 17th-century texts like the *Krpasakosa, Danasahacarita, Khanakhanacarita, Jahangircarita, Jahangirduvalli* and *Kirtisamullasa*.[21]

Reverence for dervishes and ascetics, Hindu or Muslim, inspired religious integration, for implicit in it was the conviction that there was more than one route to God. In 1618, as noted earlier, travelled from Ahmedabad in twenty-eight marches and forty-one halts over two months and nine days to meet the revered Jadrup Gosain, 'who is one of the austere ones of the Hindu religion', adding that 'association with him is a great privilege'.[22]

He was intrigued by reports of unbelievable feats performed by ascetics. Jahangir was in Kashmir in 1621 when he heard of a 'Sannyasi Moti' ('Pearl of Ascetics') from the sect known as sarva-basi (all-abiding), who had complete control over his self. The emperor witnessed the phenomenon:

> For instance, they never speak. If for ten days and nights they stand in one place, they do not move their feet forwards or backwards; in fact, make no movement at all, and remain like fossils. When he came into my

presence I examined him, and found a wonderful state of persistence.²³

The ascetic was impervious to any inducement. Italian traveller Niccolao Manucci, a medic-freebooter who settled down in India, narrates a story about Shahjahan that indicates the emperor's high respect for Brahmins. During a hunt, Shahjahan rode far ahead of his men, stopped and sought water to quench his thirst from a villager, who turned out to be a Brahmin. Unaware of the royal personage, he threw a little grass into the vessel of water. When the king asked why, he replied, 'It is what I do to my asses when they are tired, so that they may not get colic pains.'

Shahjahan said nothing. His men arrived. The villager was terrified. The king rewarded the man who had slaked his thirst with the gift of that hamlet. It became known as Brahmin's Village.

Popular stories can be as indicative of their time as any official document. A tale about a Persian monarch of the period and his drunken gardener indicates how people believed in astrology but were often bemused by astrologers, since the science was so easy to fake.

Shah Abbas ordered a new garden in his seraglio. The master gardener decided he would begin to plant fruit trees according to his design in a few days. But nothing could be done without reference to the court astrologer, who took out his instruments and books and declared that planting had to begin within the hour, for the trees would not thrive otherwise. Shah Abbas planted the first tree.

The gardener was shocked when, fortified by Shiraz wine, he returned in the evening to the garden. His pattern had been messed up: an apricot tree had been placed where he had wanted an apple, and a pear tree planted instead of an almond. He replanted the whole lot.

The astrologer complained to the king. Shah Abbas summoned the gardener. How was it, said the indignant monarch, that trees planted by his own hands had been dug up? The gardener cursed the astrologer and pointed out that his predictions had already come to a sorry end, for the trees he had planted at noon had been torn up by their roots by evening. Shah Abbas laughed heartily and turned his back on the astrologer, who walked away in silence.[24]

European visitors, predictably, had little sympathy for astrologers. In the first week of July 1663, Francois Bernier complained in a letter to Francois de la Mothe Vayer about the preponderance of degrading impostors fooling superstitious Indians in Shahjahanabad, the Mughal capital built adjacent to the old city of Delhi:

> Hither ... the astrologers resort, both Mahomet and Gentile. These wise doctors remain seated in the sun, on a dusty piece of carpet, handling some old mathematical instruments, and having open before them a large book which represents the signs of the zodiac. In this way they attract the attention of the passengers, and impose upon the people, by whom they are considered as so many infallible oracles. They tell a poor person his fortune for a payssa ... and after examining the hand and face of the applicant, turning over the leaves of the large book, and pretending to make certain calculations, these impostors decide upon the Sahet or propitious moment of commencing the business he may have in hand. Silly women, wrapping themselves in a white cloth from head to foot, flock to the astrologers, whisper to them all the transactions of their lives, and disclose every secret with no more reserve than is practiced by a scrupulous penitent in the presence of her confessor ... I am speaking only of the

poor bazar-astrologers. Those who frequent the court of the grandees are considered by them eminent doctors, and become wealthy. The whole of Asia is degraded by the same superstition. Kings and nobles grant large salaries to these crafty diviners and never engage in the most trifling transaction without consulting them.[25]

Astrologers were consulted for trifling as well as epochal events. The stars were not kind to the Mughal capital of Fatehpur Sikri, built by Akbar in the 1560s. He left his new city in 1585 and returned just once, in 1601. The centre of power reverted to Agra. On 29 December 1618, Jahangir did not enter Agra after five and a half years of travel because of an outbreak of bubonic plague. He did not camp at nearby Fatehpur Sikri either until 6 January, when astrologers gave him permission to do so.

In Mughal cosmology, saints and seers had the power to shape destiny. Astrologers were interpreters of fate. They were right when they predicted that Jahangir's third son, Khurram, rather than the eldest, Khusrau, was destined for greatness. The intrepid French merchant-traveller Jean Baptiste Tavernier (who was born in 1605 in Paris and died, aged eighty-four, in Moscow), Baron of Aubonne, who visited India six times between 1630 and 1668 in search of gems, says that Shahjahan presided over his empire like a father over his family. He was impressed by the security on the roads, the probity in finance and justice in administration (the English version of his *Travels in India*, first published in 1676, was brought out by Macmillan in 1885). The more famous French physician Francois Bernier praises Shahjahan's benevolence and patronage of the fine arts and artists, the beauty and delicacy of their paintings and miniatures, and the excellence of muskets. Akbar had rejected the orthodox Islamic resistance to portraiture, saying that he disliked men who hated painting. Even

Aurangzeb's ideological revanchism stopped short of banning portraits; his own portrait is dated 1661 and bears the seal of Ashraf Khan. 'No other Mughal emperor,' asserts Stanley Lane-Poole, the British orientalist-archaeologist, 'was ever so beloved as Shah-Jahan.'[26]

British historians of that generation did not waste compliments. Shahjahan's reign was notable chiefly, writes Lane-Poole, for its tranquil prosperity. Shahjahan was convinced that this tranquillity would be preserved best by his eldest son, Dara Shukoh. But fortunes were decided by battle, not good intentions. His third son, Aurangzeb, won the war in 1658, and Shahjahan spent his last years in royal incarceration. From this isolation, he often railed at the nobles, demanding loyalty and seeking punishment for the usurper, reminding anyone who would listen that he was lord of the conjunction, Sahib-i-Qiran Sani.[27]

It was said of Dara Shukoh that he could only be a Sahib-i-Qiran of the heart, not of destiny.

6

The Last Prediction: After Me, Chaos!

G OD KNOWS!' EXCLAIMED JAHANGIR. He was in Ramgarh when a comet shaped like a *harba* (spear) appeared in the sky on 20 October 1618. His astrologers said it indicated weakness for kings and success for enemies.

Jahangir saw the comet three *gharis* before sunrise, a luminous vapour in the form of a pillar:

> When it assumed its full form, it took the shape of a spear, thin at two ends and thick in the middle. It was curved like a sickle, and had its back to the south, and its face to the north … Astronomers took its shape and size by the astrolabe, and ascertained that with differences of appearance it extended over 24 degrees. It moved in high heaven, but it had a movement of its own, differing from that of high heaven, for it was first in Scorpio and afterwards in Libra. Its declination was mainly southerly. Sixteen nights after this phenomenon, a star showed itself in the same quarter. Its head was luminous, and its tail was two or three yards long, but the tail was not luminous. It has now appeared for eight nights; when it disappears, the fact will be noticed, as well as the results of it.[1]

Shortly after, news arrived of the birth of a grandson:

> On the eve of Sunday the 12th of the Ilahi month of Aban, in the thirteenth year of my accession, corresponding with the 15th Zi-l-Qada of the Hijri year 1027, in the 19th degree of Libra, the Giver of blessing gave my prosperous son Shahjahan a precious son by the daughter of Asaf Khan [Mumtaz Mahal]. I hope that his advent may be auspicious and blessed to this everlasting State.[2]

This grandson was Aurangzeb.

Shahjahan arranged for a birthday 'entertainment' at Ujjain. The 'day was passed in enjoyment at his quarters,' writes the emperor. His private servants who had '*entrée* into this kind of parties and assemblies were delighted with brimming cups'. Shahjahan brought that 'auspicious child', along with offerings of a tray of jewels, ornaments and fifty elephants, thirty male and twenty female, and asked the grandfather to name the baby. 'Please God, it will be given him in a favourable hour,' said Jahangir. The favourable hour would be determined by astrologers. Seven of the elephants were sent to his private stud; the rest were distributed among officers. The value of the offerings accepted was 2,00,000 rupees.[3]

The skies had not been silent when Dara Shukoh was born three years earlier. In March 1615, Jahangir was celebrating the tenth year of his accession with a feast and ceremonials in the 'usual manner'. Illustrious princes and high nobles offered their salutations and received appropriate gifts as a mark of royal appreciation and received *mansab* of Itimaduddaulah was raised. Kunwar Karan received a special horse, a jewelled sword and a rosary of emeralds and pearls called *smaran*, a Sanskrit term that Jahangir uses. Raja Bir Singh Deo got a special horse, Jahangir Quli Khan an elephant. Abdul Karim Mamuri was ordered to build a private palace for the emperor in Mandu. The emperor examined the gold, jewels and cloth brought by Asaf Khan.

On Sunday, 29 March, 'when twelve *gharis* of the day had passed, it began from the west, and four out of five parts of the sun were eclipsed in the knot of the dragon. From the commencement of the seizure until it became light eight *gharis* elapsed'. Alms of all kinds, in the shape of metals, animals and vegetables, were given to fakirs and the impoverished to thwart the ill effects, for an eclipse was a premonition of misfortune.[4]

On the night of 30 March 1615, Dara Shukoh was born 'in the ascension of Sagittarius'. Jahangir named the boy Dara Shukoh with the 'hope that his coming will be propitious to this State conjoined with eternity, and to his fortunate father'.[5]

Both astral events were considered ominous by Jahangir. In retrospect, they might serve as metaphors. Dara Shukoh was eclipsed, but the Aurangzeb meteor burnt out the empire.

Aurangzeb believed in his horoscope, written at his birth, with total conviction. This horoscope had not only predicted every event that occurred in his life but also the disaster that would overwhelm the Mughal Empire after he was gone.

In 1695, twelve years before his death, he told his heir, Mirza Muhammad Muazzam (1643–1712), who succeeded him as Bahadur Shah, '*Az mast hamah fasad-i-baqi!*'

That is, 'After me: chaos!'

The horoscope had been charted by Mulla Ala-ul-mulk Tuni, a scholar and official in Shahjahan's court who was raised to the title of Fazil Khan. The accuracy of his predictions is confirmed in a contemporary history, *Ahkam-i-Alamgiri* by Hamid-ud-din Khan Bahadur, later translated into English as *Anecdotes of Aurangzib* by Jadunath Sarkar.[6]

Aurangzeb trusted Fazil Khan. He was the intermediary during his tense negotiations with Shahjahan after he had usurped power in 1658. Fazil Khan was promoted to the august position of vizier a little before his death in 1663.[7] Aurangzeb had inherited a powerful tradition from his forefathers.

Christopher Minkowski writes:

> Evidence from contemporary Persian chronicles makes it clear that the Mughal rulers employed Hindu astrologers, giving them the title of Jotik Rai, or in Sanskrit, Jyotisraja, king among *jyotisas* ... Some evidence suggests that the Jotik [Rai] would travel with the emperor during military expeditions. It was the Jotik Rai's job to cast the birth chart of members of the royal family according to the *jyotisa* system, to answer questions according to the *prasna*, the *jyotisa* version of catarchic astrology, in which a chart is cast for the moment that the question was asked, and to choose favourable moments to undertake activities, according to the *jyotisa* system of *muhurta*. These experts in the 'astral sciences' produced divination texts and advised their royal clients on daily routine as well as plans for life and for action, both personal and political.8

Minkowski notes the 'period of about 85 years' from 1585, when the Viswanath temple was rebuilt, probably by Todar Mal, until it was demolished in the reign of Aurangzeb, has been long remembered for the learned Brahmans like Narayan Bhalta, Kavindhacarya Sarasvati and Jagamalta Panditraja. Narayan Bhalta's mentor was Todar Mal. Akbar conferred the title *Jagatguru* ('teacher of the world') upon him. Bhalta officiated at the installation of the lingam at the temple. Akbar's Jotik Rai has been identified as Nilakantha. Jahangir's was Kesava.

Shahjahan is believed to have had two, Paramananda and Malajit (or Srimalaji). Shah Shuja's astrologer in Bengal was Balabhadra. They were all Brahmins. Aurangzeb had his own entourage, but their names are not available because they were not identified when their predictions were recorded in various accounts of the time. We know of Fazil Khan from Aurangzeb's conversation with his son late in his life.

The Brahmin astrologers were scholars and academics. Nilakantha wrote the sections on astrology in the *Todarananda*, the 1572 text commissioned by Raja Todar Mal, and completed his work on a specific Persianate branch of astrology, *tajika*, by 1587. His son Govinda, born in 1569, wrote on the relationship of his family with the Mughal kings. His father was the leader of the pandits and a shining adornment in Akbar's circle. Govinda's son Chintamani describes himself as the leader of astronomers and astrologers in Jahangir's court.

Narsimha, a Chitpawan Brahmin from the Konkan who moved to Benares, was given the sobriquet of *Jyotirvitsarasa*, the most appealing of astrologers, by Akbar. In 1663, Isvaradasa, son of Kesava Sarma, says that his father was given the title of *Jyotisaraya* by Jahangir. Sarma has praised the Mughal lineage up to Aurangzeb in his Sanskrit work *Muhurtaratna* (*Jewel of Time*). Krisna, from Benares, recorded Akbar's polyglot general Abdur Rahim Khan-i-Khanan's birth chart in *Jatakapaddhaty-udaharana* and described him as skilled in every regional language and science taught by the goddess Saraswati.[9]

Francois Bernier (1620–1688), the French physician who entered India through Surat in July 1658 after a twenty-two-day journey aboard an Indian trading vessel from Jeddah and travelled across north and east India during the first decade of Aurangzeb's rule, was astonished by the widespread belief in astrology. Bernier had a sharp eye and an evocative pen.

Bernier was amazed by the command that astrologers exercised over the people and caustic more than once in his travelogue:

> The majority of Asiatics are so infatuated in favour of being guided by the signs of the heavens, that, according to their phraseology, no circumstance can happen below, which is not written above. In every enterprise they consult their astrologers. When two armies have completed every preparation for battle, no consideration can induce the general to commence the engagement until the *Sahet* [*saiet*, or propitious] be performed; that is, until the propitious moment for attack be ascertained. In like manner no commanding officer is nominated, no marriage takes place, and no journey is undertaken, without consulting Monsieur the Astrologer. Their advice is considered absolutely necessary even on the most trifling occasions; as the proposed purchase of a slave, or the first wearing of new clothes. This silly superstition is so general an annoyance, and attended with such important and disagreeable consequences, that I am astonished it has continued so long: the astrologer is necessarily made acquainted with every transaction public and private.[10]

Bernier, writing in 1663, refers to Aurangzeb's 'principal astrologer', if only to display sardonic delight at a paradox. The astrologer's accidental death by drowning caused a great sensation in court, since this man of 'extensive experience', who had made 'happy' predictions for the king and nobles over many years, was unable to foresee 'the sad catastrophe' of his own death. This inspired discussion on Frangistan (shorthand for 'westerners') where the sciences flourish, professors in astrology were considered little better than cheats and jugglers.¹¹

All sections of Indians believed in astrology. Bernier describes the scene at Shahjahanabad in Delhi where nobles, some on majestic elephants, others on palanquins, fanned by servants, came to the crowded square. He is impressed by a Portuguese Goan of mixed descent who told fortunes along with the best of the tribe in the egalitarian bazaar, 'a rendezvous for jugglers, mountebanks and fortune-tellers sitting on a dusty piece of carpet, with a large book of the zodiac'.¹² They made appropriate gestures and sounds, looked at the hand and face of their importunate and impoverished customer, turned over the leaves of a large book and told every fortune for a paisa (4 paisa made an anna; 16 annas made a rupee).

If Bernier had been more familiar with India, he would have been less surprised. Prof. Mujeeb describes Delhi of the early 14th century:

> There was also widespread belief in astrology. In the time of Alauddin Khilji, people talked as never before—and perhaps never after—of prayer and fasts and litanies; they read books on Sufism, and there was a *miswak* [twig from a neem tree that was used as toothbrush-cum-toothpaste] and a comb stuck in every turban. This was entirely due to the influence of Shaikh Nizamuddin Auliya [the venerated Sufi saint of Delhi].¹³

Mujeeb adds:

> Astrologers were in great demand too. Horoscopes seemed necessary for guidance through life. No ceremony would be performed in any respectable family, and no work of any importance undertaken by

any individual without consulting an astrologer. As a result, almost every street had its astrologer, who could be a Hindu or a Muslim, and in this profession were some who 'performed almost miraculous acts by way of discovering secret motives, interpreting the commands of the Unseen and finding things lost' [according to the Arab traveller Ibn Batuta]. Muhammad Tughluq had great faith in *yogis* who performed wonderful feats, such as levitation and breath control, and treated them with the utmost respect.[14]

Ya Takht, Ya Takhta!

A throne or a funeral plank.

The ideal ruler, said a Mughal axiom, was master of the pen and the sword, but every prince faced a moment when the sword stood between crown and grave. Hardened by campaigns from their teens, most princes lived a fabled life only to die an early death in a succession system without rights of primogeniture. The survivor took the throne.

Courage and nerve were rewarded. On 28 May 1633, Shahjahan and his three elder sons were watching from horseback a fight between two elephants named Sudhakar and Surat Sundar on the banks of the Jamuna near Agra. Suddenly, an enraged Sudhakar charged towards the fifteen-year-old Aurangzeb who, holding firmly to his frightened mount, struck back with a spear but was hurled to the ground. Shah Shuja and Raja Jai Singh rushed to help while guards distracted the beast with fireworks. The danger eased when Surat Sundar returned to the fight and drew its foe away. Shahjahan rewarded his son with 5,000 gold coins and 2,00,000 rupees.[15]

There were similar stories from other generations of the Mughals. Aurangzeb once ordered his son Muazzam to kill a lion which had descended from the mountains and was ravaging the villages without the use of nets. The prince overcame the beast with the loss of only two or three of his men and won a place in his father's affections.[16] As a young commander, Aurangzeb gained a reputation for steely piety during the campaign for Balkh and Badakhshan in the summer of 1647, when he dismounted to perform the afternoon *Zuhr* prayer amid battle, causing his foe Abdul Aziz to cry out that fighting such a man was to court one's ruin.

Aurangzeb and Dara Shukoh were alike in their fierce determination for the throne but had contrasting visions of what they would do once in power. Dara Shukoh stretched the tensile strength of assimilation with Hindus until he was accused by his brother of being an infidel. Aurangzeb took animosity towards Hindus so far as to order the destruction of historic temples, inflict the hated *jizya* tax and severely damage the critical Mughal alliance with Rajput royal houses.

A votary of the philosophy of *wahd-al wujud* (unity of all beings), Dara Shukoh built, with Shahjahan's approval, bridges with Hindu seers and savants. He helped Gosain Vithalrai, a religious leader of Gokul, obtain a land grant in 1643. His wide-ranging conversations with Baba Lal, the spiritual leader from Punjab, are recorded in painting and text. The range of the discussions he engaged in can be gauged from two examples. What is kingship for a fakir, asked Dara. Being aware of oneself, without a care, answered the mendicant.

Dara asked whether it was permissible to use drugs to reach a mystical state. Cannabis, advised the sage, damaged one's good name and character. Poppy was unworthy. Opium was repellent to those on the threshold of divine truth, to lovers and to the recluse. Dara persisted: hemp opium in sweetmeat? If it was free of cannabis and opium, it would be agreeable for the worldly but forbidden to the ascetic, said Baba Lal.[17]

Dara honoured Sanskrit as a source of knowledge. He was the patron of Banvali Das, who adapted *Prabodhacandradaya* (Moonrise of Enlightenment), an 11th-century Sanskrit play, into Persian. Dara also sponsored the Persian translation of Advaita Vedanta works like the *Astavakragita* (Song of Ashtavakra), the *Atmavilasa* (Play of the Soul) and Bhagavad Gita. At the end of 1656, he summoned a large group of Sanskrit scholars in Benares to provide a Persian translation of the Upanishads. They finished their work by July the following year. Dara gave the title and wrote the preface of *Sirr-i-Akbar* (*The Great Secret*), submitting that the Islamic concept of *tawheed* (the unity of God) was found in the Upanishads, which could serve as a virtual commentary on the 'noble Quran'. Aurangzeb described this as heresy, but the Mughal establishment of Shahjahan did not find the comparison controversial.

Dara's eclectic challenge to orthodoxy included association with the Persian-speaking Armenian mystic Shah Sarmad, who made India his home and preached that all faiths represented different routes to the God he loved. Sarmad claimed that he obeyed the Quran but was simultaneously a Hindu priest, a Christian monk, a Jewish rabbi and a Muslim. Bikram Jit Hasrat writes that Dara addressed Sarmad as his guide and philosopher in the single letter on the subject that has survived.[18] In 1661, the third year of Aurangzeb's reign, Sarmad was beheaded for apostasy. He is buried in Delhi.

On behalf of Shahjahan, Dara took a question on the status of Hindus in the empire to the learned cleric Shaikh Muhibullah (1587–1648) in Allahabad. The answer he received is a definition of secularism in the 17th century: 'It is impertinent of me to give counsel, but justice requires that the welfare of the people should be the concern of the administrative officers, whether the people be believers or unbelievers, for they have been created by God.' A government must treat all subjects equally. The Prophet of God had taken 'the lead in being merciful to the righteous and the evildoers, the believers and the unbelievers,' said the Shaikh.[19]

Dara Shukoh's strength became a weakness. He acquired the superiority of an intellectual along with the entitlement of a designated heir. Shahjahan is quoted in the *Ruqaat-i-Alamgiri* as saying of his sons that Dara had become the enemy of good men, Murad had set his heart on drinking, Shuja was too fond of the good life, while Aurangzeb possessed the resolution and intelligence needed for the difficult task of ruling India but suffered from sickness and infirmity.[20] Dara made the costly mistake of alienating many important elder nobles through either enmity or arrogance: some of them were Ali Mardan Khan, Sadullah Khan, Sayyid Miran of Barha and Fazil Khan.

Scholarly and sophisticated, Dara seemed to take his administrative and military capabilities for granted. Swayed by flattery, he succumbed to fancy during the one campaign he led, in Qandahar, trusting a group that claimed they could achieve victory through magic spells and secret flying objects. His sister Jahanara put it best: he became heir to both the esoteric and exoteric kingdoms.

Aurangzeb's early studies extended, as was normal, from Arabic and religion to Hindi (Brajbhasha) and Persian poets like Saadi and Hafiz. His interests later shifted to history, military strategy and statecraft. He often quoted from Plato. According to Munis Faruqi, his evenings were spent in conversation, reading or prayer. He ordered his son Azam to study the actions of kings, the behaviour of the wise and the lives of prophets and saints.[21] Unusually for a Mughal prince, he did not drink.

Dara was the declared favourite of the father, who kept him close at court and honoured him with a red-coloured tent, an emperor's privilege. Even when appointed to Allahabad and Punjab, Dara refused to leave Delhi, sending proxies to govern instead. His opulent marriage in 1633 to Nadira Begum, daughter of his uncle Parvez, was a flagrant example of favour. It was the most expensive wedding recorded in the dynasty's history, involving a bridal trousseau of 8,00,000 rupees and a total cost estimated at around 23,00,000 rupees in 17th-century coin. Dara's sons Sulaiman and Sipihr were also accorded a red tent, establishing a hierarchy.[22]

The other brothers, Shuja, Aurangzeb and Murad, were kept in distant commands. Starting at seventeen years old, Aurangzeb was sent to the Deccan (1636–1644; 1652–1658), Gujarat (1645–1647) and Multan (1648–1652). In addition, he led military campaigns to Bundelkhand in 1635, Balkh in 1647 and Qandahar in 1649 and 1652. He became convinced that he was being deliberately kept away from the centre of power. Aurangzeb wrote to Jahanara demanding to know why, after two decades of loyal service, he was not worthy of the same confidence as his elder brother. According to Faruqi, Shahjahan 'undertook a particularly vengeful campaign to destroy the political and military effectiveness of Prince Aurangzeb's household'.[23]

Turning disadvantage into practical gain, Aurangzeb used the provinces to create a network of allies. There was ideological outreach to clerics who feared dilution of the Muslim identity of Mughal rule. He gave them prominence, stipends and influence in Aurangabad, the city he built in the 1630s. While Dara dwelt on inter-faith dialogue, Aurangzeb concentrated on intra-faith consolidation. In 1636, he made an important ally: Sidi Miftah Habash Khan, whose daughter was the wife of the son of Malik

Ambar, the most effective warlord in the Deccan before his death in 1626. Habash Khan helped induct Arab Syeds into Aurangzeb's army who displayed their ability in the battles against Dara Shukoh.[24]

Shahjahan repeatedly rejected Aurangzeb's requests to come to court. When in 1644 Aurangzeb arrived without permission, using the accidental burn injuries of his sister Jahanara as a reason, the unsympathetic father stripped him of his titles and placed him under house arrest. Rehabilitation came a year later when he was sent to Gujarat, but the rancour between the two remained. Faruqi writes:

> Aurangzeb's private imperial correspondence, anecdotal records collected posthumously, and accounts written by visiting foreigners ever so infrequently offer a glimpse of the prince's hostility toward his father. Here we see Aurangzeb mocking Shahjahan's favouring of Dara Shukoh. There we read of Aurangzeb attacking the court as out-of-touch with the daily realities of the empire. In a privately recorded conversation with a Deccan-based Sufi master, he decried the court's irreligiosity. He also indirectly questioned Shahjahan's military skills.[25]

Aurangzeb could be indiscreet. In the summer of 1644, Dara had invited his father and three brothers to a new house he had built on the river, decorated with tall mirrors from Aleppo. He took them to an underground chamber that had only one door. Aurangzeb deliberately chose to sit near the entrance, below his rank, and left early without permission. Such insolence could not be ignored. He was forbidden from court. After seven months, Shahjahan sent Jahanara to find out the reason for his misbehaviour. Aurangzeb explained that he was afraid that if Dara shut the single door to the chamber, the rest of them would be trapped and 'all would be over'. When ordered to move, he preferred to leave. Shahjahan restored all the favours he had taken away from Aurangzeb and sent him back as governor of the Deccan.[26]

According to Bernier, Dara was courteous, gracious, generous, sensitive, quick at repartee and extremely liberal; but he was smug, 'entertained too exalted an opinion of himself' and believed that 'there existed no man from whose counsel he could derive benefit'.[27]

His bursts of anger, though momentary, alienated the high nobles. Shuja excelled Dara in conduct and acquired the deep friendship of rajas like Jaswant Singh. He was brave, discreet, subtle and smart enough to sympathise with Shiism when wooing Persian troops, but he was captive to drink and the harem. Aurangzeb had better judgement; he was reserved, skilful, subtle and 'a complete master in the art of dissimulation'. Murad was brave, frank and open but also a fickle sot who was recalled eleven times in fourteen years from various provinces for misbehaviour or misdemeanours. The eldest daughter, Jahanara or Begum Sahib, was beautiful and lively; her father's keeper, she was the trusted supervisor of his kitchen in a time when poison was a favourite weapon of assassins, and had enough influence to accumulate great wealth.

Rumour, wrote Bernier, alleged incest between father and daughter, 'which it is difficult to believe'. Gossip-hungry Delhi feasted on such stories. According to Bernier, Shahjahan despatched one lover of Jahanara, a handsome Persian, with a poisoned paan (betel leaf).[28]

A second suffered a scalding end. When the emperor once surprised Jahanara in her quarters while she was entertaining a lover, the only place where the young man could hide was a large cauldron. Shahjahan conversed with her in his usual fashion before suggesting that it was time for her bath. He ordered water to be heated in the cauldron, with unfortunate consequences for the gallant.[29] The three sisters, all unmarried since no prince was deemed worthy of their hand, chose to side with different brothers in the power games. Jahanara supported Dara. Roshanara, less beautiful but no less ambitious, favoured Aurangzeb, supplying him with the most precious asset from the court—information. The youngest, Gauharara, was with Murad.

By 1657, the last effective year of Shahjahan's rule, Dara Shukoh's rank was raised to 50,000/40,000, the first figure delineating his rank (*zat*) and the second the size of the cavalry (*sawar*) he was expected to maintain from his income. He was titled Shah Buland Iqbal ('lord of exalted fortune') with a couch seat below the throne. The combined rank of Shuja, Aurangzeb and Murad Baksh was 55,000/42,000.[30]

Such imbalance was an invitation to turmoil.

Plans, Plots and Wars

The wars began, inevitably, with reports of the king's ill health. Shahjahan was sixty-five when he fell severely ill on 6 September 1657, struck by a disease which, according to Bernier, was 'unbecoming' but diagnosed in less colourful terms as a bladder or bowel malfunction. Babur was dead at forty-seven, Humayun at forty-eight, Akbar at sixty-three and Jahangir at fifty-nine. So it was unsurprising that the princes unfurled their banners when Shahjahan remained absent from the morning public view, *jharoka darshan*. Forty-two-year-old Dara Shukoh's reassurances of amity were dismissed as self-serving, particularly after he cut communications between the princes and their agents in court. Shah Shuja, forty-one, was in Bengal; Aurangzeb, thirty-nine, in the Deccan; and Murad Baksh, thirty-four, in Gujarat. It was time for them to live up to their names. 'Dara' meant king, 'Shuja' valiant, 'Aurangzeb' royal ornament and 'Murad' wish-fulfilment. They were the sons of Mumtaz Mahal, who had died during the birth of her fifteenth child. Three of her daughters were now adults; four sons and three daughters had died in infancy.

There was 'agitation and alarm' as the princes gathered resources, mobilised forces, sought allies and claimed succession. Shuja declared that Dara had poisoned the emperor, crowned himself, struck coin, took a grandiose title that conflated Amir Taimur, Alexander the Great and holy war, and marched from Bengal, disregarding a conciliatory message from his father. In Gujarat, Murad ordered that the *khutba* be read in his name, a sign of sovereignty, and collected 6,00,000 rupees from the merchants of Surat to finance his ambitions.

An imperial army led by Dara's son Sulaiman Shukoh and Mirza Raja Jai Singh stopped Shuja on 14 February 1658 at Benares. Shuja escaped to his base in Malda, Bengal, without being pursued, as Shahjahan had decreed that a prince's life must not be taken.

Cool-headed Aurangzeb waited, even after his house in Delhi had been seized and his loyalists imprisoned. Picking up Shuja's allegation that Shahjahan had been poisoned, he wrote to Murad, saying that though their father was alive, it was their duty to 'punish the presumption and pride of the apostate' Dara. In May 1658, he offered Shuja Bengal in a future dispensation. Shuja refused.[31]

Murad was amenable. Aurangzeb deployed a Persian proverb ('two hearts united would cleave a mountain'), promised his younger brother a kingdom and cloaked his intentions with sanctimonious humbug: 'I have not the slightest liking for or wish to take any part in the government of this deceitful and unstable world; my only desire is that I may make a pilgrimage to the temple of God [Mecca].'[32]

Aurangzeb began his march from Aurangabad on 5 February 1658. He paced his advance, camping at Burhanpur for a month and reaching Mandu on 25 March. Najabat Khan, an officer of 'firm fidelity', suggested that this hesitant pace would embolden Dara to send a strong force. That, explained Aurangzeb, was the essence of his policy. If he marched too quickly, he would have to confront the whole of the enemy army; but if he delayed, he would only have to defeat the advance contingent. If Dara crossed the Narmada, his fate would be akin to this verse:

> The man who goes far from his asylum and home
> Becomes helpless, needy, and forsaken.
> In the water even the lion becomes a prey of fishes,
> On dry land the crocodile becomes the food of ants.

The delay was strategy, not laziness. Najabat Khan apparently kissed the prince's feet in admiration.[33]

Dara Shukoh recalled powerful commanders like Shaista Khan, a strong supporter of Aurangzeb, from Malwa, and Mir Jumla from Aurangabad to prevent them from joining his brothers. Aurangzeb absorbed Mir Jumla's cannon, European gunners and infantry, crossed the Narmada on 3 April 1658, and met up with Murad Baksh near Dipalpur Lake on 14 April. The brothers sealed their pact with an oath on the Quran. They camped at Dharmat, some 14 miles from Ujjain. Dara sent Maharaja Jaswant Singh and Qasim Khan to confront this threat. They reached Ujjain in February 1658 but failed in their first objective—to prevent the brothers from uniting.

Two hours after sunrise on 15 April 1658, the rivals, equally matched in troop strength at 35,000 men, met at Dharmat. The Rajput charge by Jaswant Singh's men took the initial honours, scattering Aurangzeb's gunners, albeit at a heavy cost, and pouncing upon his 8,000-strong vanguard in chainmail armour, led by officers on elephants. The vanguard held its ground, the charge exhausted itself and the guns reopened. Murad Baksh attacked Jaswant Singh's camp from the left, taking one of his commanders Devi Singh Bundela into captivity and scattering the rest.

Aurangzeb won more than a battle. He won prestige.

The bad news reached Dara Shukoh ten days later. He raised a second army, with himself in command. Niccolao Manucci, in Dara's service until 1659, claims that over 1,00,000 were assembled, with armoured elephants and gunners seated on 500 camels, but adds that it was a ragtag enlistment of 'butchers, barbers, blacksmiths, carpenters, tailors'. Dara put into the field a more compact force, without waiting for his son Sulaiman Shukoh to join him, although Shahjahan implored him to do so.

The brothers met in Samugarh, near Agra, on the morning of 29 May 1658. Dara's Rajputs, led by Ram Singh Rathor, smashed through Murad Baksh's lines, wounding him. Manucci, who was there, reports that Aurangzeb was at serious risk of being taken captive. Disregarding the danger, he summoned his cavalry, shouting, '*Mardana dilawar-i-bahadur! Waqt ast!* (Men of valour! The time has come!).' His hands raised in prayer, he cried that he would sooner die than surrender. He ordered the feet of his elephant to be chained so that it could not turn back.[34]

Dara shifted from the centre to join the assault against Murad, lost command of the field and wavered from exhaustion in the terrible heat. Aurangzeb's discipline prevailed. Dismounting from his majestic elephant, Dara fled by horse to Agra Fort, which he reached that night at nine. At three in the morning, he left the city with his family, carrying as much treasure as he could.[35]

On 30 May 1658, the day after the victory, Aurangzeb sent a letter to Shahjahan through Fazil Khan, according to Muhammad Kambu and Aqil Khan. The war, he asserted, had been forced upon him by Dara. Shahjahan invited him for an audience through an emissary, Syed Hidayatullah, writing that he longed to see his son. Aurangzeb agreed, then changed his mind after being warned that he was walking into a trap. Shahjahan tried to soften his son with gifts, including the famous sword known as Alamgir. Fazil Khan brought a second letter on 5 June, professing the emperor's deepest love and kindness, but to no avail. There was no trust left.

On the night of 5 June, Aurangzeb ordered his artillery to open fire on the fort and met resistance. He cut off the water supply to the citadel. Thirst was more effective than cannon. On 8 June, Shahjahan opened the gates. Aurangzeb seized the treasure left behind by Dara, amounting to 27,00,000 rupees, and sent his eldest son Muhammad Sultan to wait on Shahjahan. It was tokenism. The king of kings had become a prisoner.

Aurangzeb explained the rationale for his action in the letters he wrote. It was not rebellion but his duty to abort 'Dara's usurpation, his lapse from Islam, and his exaltation of idolatry throughout the empire'. He was compelled 'out of regard for the next world, to take up the perilous load of the crown, from sheer necessity and not from free choice, for restoring peace and the rules of Islam in the realm'.[36] Evidence of divine support for his cause lay in his victory. Shahjahan, unimpressed, called his son a thief and warned him that his own sons would treat him the way he had treated his father.[37] He had no effective argument, however, against the outcome of a battle.

On 10 June 1658, Princess Jahanara brought a proposal for a five-way partition of the empire. Dara would get Punjab, Shah Shuja Bengal and Murad Gujarat. Aurangzeb would reign over central India with the title of Buland-i-iqbal, previously given to Dara, and his son Muhammad Sultan would take the Deccan. Aurangzeb refused.

He made no attempt to disguise his hatred and contempt for his brother: 'Dara is an infidel to Islam and a friend of the Hindus. He must be extirpated for the sake of the true faith and the peace of the realm. I cannot visit the emperor before concluding this business.' According to Aqil Khan Razi's *Haalat-i-Alamgiri*, or *Aurangzebnama*, the last chance of reconciliation disappeared when Aurangzeb, on his way to meet the emperor after much persuasion, was informed that he would be murdered by Shahjahan's 'fierce Tartar slave women'.[38]

The overweening Murad had already become troublesome. His men tried to loot the city, forcing Aurangzeb to intervene. Lulled by flatterers into overestimation of his utility, Murad made a fatal mistake by trying to increase the size of his army. Aurangzeb sent him a gift of 233 horses and 20,00,000 rupees and invited him for a celebratory feast. On the evening of 25 June, Aurangzeb plied his brother with wine in a private chamber until he fell into a slumber. Murad woke up in chains. The next morning, the 20,000 men under his command were inducted into the main body of the army.

Dara raised yet another force in Punjab, with Manucci at the head of his artillery. He could have received vital help from Kabul, then governed by the veteran Mahabat Khan, who was inimical to Aurangzeb. 'But,' writes Bernier, 'it was generally the fate of the unhappy Dara to undervalue the opinions of the wisest counsellors; and upon this occasion, instead of throwing himself into Caboul [Kabul], he proceeded towards Scimdy [Sind].'[39]

Dara realised the impact of Aurangzeb's Islamist outreach when, after Samugarh, neither supplication nor cash could persuade Multan's clerics to help him.

Aurangzeb reached Delhi on 5 July 1658 on his way to Punjab, but he turned back from Multan on hearing that Shuja was again on the move. There was also a growing worry that the Rajput nobles, led by Raja Jai Singh, might instigate a coup d'état to release Shahjahan 'from the iniquitous thraldom under which he groaned' and punish the 'unfeeling' Aurangzeb for outrage and cruelty, in Bernier's words. Aurangzeb turned back.[40]

Near Lahore, he suddenly encountered Raja Jai Singh with 'four or five thousand well-appointed' Rajputs. Expressing delight at their chance meeting and betraying no agitation or alarm, he called out, '*Salamet bachiz Raja-ji! Salamet bachiz Baba-ji!* (Salutations, my lord Raja! Salutations, my lord father!).' The war had ended, he said, and Dara was ruined. He took off his pearl necklace, placed it around Jai Singh's neck and asked him to proceed to Lahore at once as governor with full powers.[41] Jai Singh remained with Aurangzeb for the rest of his life.

Aurangzeb dealt with the other Rajput power, Jaswant Singh Rathore of Jodhpur, with finesse. The episode began as a near-disaster. On the eve of his battle with Shah Shuja at Khajwa near Allahabad on 5 January 1659, Aurangzeb was informed, while at prayer, that Jaswant Singh, with 14,000 troops, had switched sides and joined Shuja. Aurangzeb told his general Mir Jumla that this was a sign of mercy from God, for if Jaswant had defected during battle, it would have been hard to remedy the damage. During the fighting, Aurangzeb ordered his mahout to spur his elephant towards Shuja 'by any means you can'. Murshid Quli Khan remarked, 'This kind of audacity is opposed to the practice of emperors.' Aurangzeb replied, 'Neither of us has yet become emperor. Men become emperors only after showing this sort of daring. And if after one has become emperor his courage decreases, his authority does not last.' He recited a verse:

> That man alone can clasp in his arms the bride of kingship,
> Who plants kisses on the keen sword's lip.

Aurangzeb won the day. Shuja was stopped a second time but not yet defeated. He returned to Bengal.[42]

Aurangzeb sent a force of 10,000 under Muhammad Amin Khan to Jodhpur, but instead of pursuing a punitive war, he asked Jai Singh to write a mollifying letter to the maharaja, pointing out the benefits of alliance and the folly of resistance. Jaswant Singh saw the merits of this advice. His title and *mansab* were restored, and he was given high office. Dara waited in vain for Jaswant Singh's assistance in what would prove to be the third and last encounter with Aurangzeb.

The battle of Deorai, 4 miles from Ajmer and spread over three days from 11 March 1659, ended in the final rout of Dara. Aurangzeb offered a prayer of gratitude at the shrine of Khwaja Muinuddin Chishti and left 5,000 rupees for the servants of the shrine. Jai Singh was sent in pursuit of Dara Shukoh.

Dara became destitute. Bernier met him on the road and was forced to join the hunted exile as a physician. He witnessed the tears and shrieks of women when the governor of Gujarat refused to provide them sanctuary. Dara was picked up in Dhandhar, Kutch, by a local Afghan chieftain and sent to Delhi.

Before death, there was humiliation. Dara, dressed in coarse cloth, was paraded atop a miserable, worn-out elephant covered with filth. People wept: 'From every quarter I heard piercing and distressing shrieks, for the

Indian people have a very tender heart; men, women, and children wailing as if some mighty calamity had happened to themselves.'[43]

Dara Shukoh was declared an apostate and a heretic on the evidence of his preface to the Upanishads. Early on the night of 30 August 1659, executioners separated Dara from his weeping son Sipihr and ended the life of the intellectual who could have been emperor.

Aurangzeb lost his cold stoicism when shown his elder brother's head. He began to weep and cried, '*Ai bed-bakht!* ... Ah, wretched me, let this shocking sight not offend my eyes anymore. Take away the head and let it be buried in Humayun's tomb.'[44]

Murad, in Gwalior Fort from January 1659, was killed, or, in an ironic phrase, released 'from the narrow cell of his prison' on 4 December 1661 for the crime of trying to escape. The last rites of bloodshed were performed when Dara's eldest son, Sulaiman Shukoh, was put to death in Gwalior Fort in May 1662 and buried next to his uncle Murad Baksh.

A severed head tells no tales.

Aurangzeb permitted his father, confined to Agra Fort, the luxuries of habit and the necessities of age. Bernier, who disliked Aurangzeb, praises his attitude as kind and respectful. Antelope fights were arranged for the ageing father's entertainment. The son sent presents and eventually received what he had always craved: recognition, benediction and pardon.[45]

Shahjahan took solace in God, spending his time in prayer and listening to tales of the past, cared for by his daughter Jahanara, who also made the daughters of Dara and Murad part of her family. On 7 January 1666, he caught a fever. The doctors gave up hope on 22 January. With women weeping by his bedside, the builder of the Taj Mahal, mankind's most glamorous grave, gave instructions for his funeral with perfect composure. He consoled his two surviving wives, Akbarbadi Mahal and Fatehpuri Mahal, charged Jahanara with the care of those who would become helpless with his death, ordered the Quran to be read, repeated the Muslim confession of faith and offered a last prayer: 'O God! Make my condition good in this world and the next, and save me from the torments of hellfire.' A moment later, at 7:15 in the evening, he died.

Aurangzeb hurried from Delhi to Agra to pay his respects.

The children who had kept out of the conflict were not punished for the sins of their fathers. Sipihr Shukoh was married to Aurangzeb's daughter Zubdatunnisa. Dara's daughter Mehrunnisa was betrothed to Izid Baksh, Murad's son.[46] Jahanara was permitted to keep her estate and lived until the age of sixty-seven.

Shuja, who spent forty-three years of his life in Bengal, was defeated by Mir Jumla on 5 April 1660. He fled to Dhaka from Malda by river boat, and thence to Arakan, Burma, on 12 May, from where he disappeared. Defeat, once again, spawned romantic rumours denied to the living. As late as 1699, a Shuja pretender appeared in Allahabad.[47] A Dutch merchant, Jan Tak, reported to Aurangzeb that Shuja had most probably been killed by the Arakanese, although talk persisted that he had received sanctuary in the kingdom of Tripura.

Astrologers Had the Last Word

Astrologers had the last word when Aurangzeb took the crown.

On 12 May 1659, Aurangzeb entered Delhi to the sound of drums, pipes and trumpets, followed by bejewelled, caparisoned elephants and cavalry, musketeers, rocket-men and his servants flinging coins to the populace on either side. He then waited for twenty-four days: 'The court astrologers were of opinion that Sunday 5th June 1659, was a most auspicious day, and all arrangements were made for Aurangzeb's enthronement on that day,' writes Jadunath Sarkar. They specified the time: three hours and fifteen minutes after sunrise.

Aurangzeb, with cool but calm eyes, arrived early in the morning on 5 June, seated on the loftiest elephant. All the treasures of the dynasty were on display inside the fort. The ceilings and the forty pillars of the Diwan-i-Am were draped in brocades from Gujarat, gold-and-silver cloth from Persia, embroidered velvet, European screens and gold tissue from China and Turkey. The court waited for a signal from the soothsayers.

> The astrologers had declared 3 hours and 15 minutes from sunrise as the auspicious moment. The whole court anxiously hung on the lips of the astrologers, who keenly watched their [water] clocks and sandglasses. At last they gave the signal; the precious moment had arrived; the Emperor, who had been sitting dressed and ready behind a screen, entered the Hall of Public Audience and mounted the throne.[48]

The ceremony was simple. The sovereign stepped onto the dazzling throne, in a space fenced in with a golden railing. He was dressed in regalia, a cloth turban on his head glittering with diamonds, gems and an aigrette. His legitimacy was confirmed by a sermon in the king's name, the *khutba*, and the issue of coins, *sikka*. A crier issued a public proclamation of the emperor's regnal name and titles, followed by those of his predecessors, each mention being rewarded with a robe and cash. Aurangzeb continued the practice inherited from Hindu kings of being weighed in gold and silver, the equivalent of which was distributed as alms. Jewels were showered over the courtiers, who picked them up as tokens of good luck.

The event ended with trays of paan being distributed. The air was heavy with the fragrance of musk, ambergris attar and incense. Aurangzeb retired to celebrate with his family for precisely forty-eight minutes. His favoured sister, Roshanara, received a gift of 5,00,000 rupees, while his four daughters got 4,00,000, 2,00,000, 1,60,000 and 1,50,000 rupees. Both banks of the Jamuna were illuminated that night; the river looked like a 'flower garden of light'. Coin was struck in the name of Abul Muzaffar Muhiuddin Muhammad Aurangzeb Bahadur Alamgir Padishah Ghazi.[49] Sarkar's Persian sources include the *Aml-i-Salih* by Muhammad Salih Kambu, who writes on the basis of the state papers of Shahjahan and continues until his death; Muhammad Saqi Mustaid Khan's *Maasir-i-Alamgiri*, a record of the first decade of Aurangzeb's rule based on official documents, a project which the emperor aborted; the *Tarikh-i-Shah-Shujai*, written in 1660 in Malda in Bengal by Mir Muhammad Masum, a retainer of Shuja; the *Nuskha-i-Dilkasha* by Bhimsen, a Kayasth official in the service of Dalpat Rao, the Bundela chief of Datia who fought alongside Aurangzeb's armies in the Deccan; Isardas's *Fatuhat-i-Alamgiri*, which covers the period between 1657 and 1698; and the three collections of letters by Aurangzeb that have survived. The new emperor adopted fish as his symbol.

This was, technically, Aurangzeb's second coronation. The first, in July 1658, a brief ceremony at Shalimar Bagh, was a necessary assertion of power in the vacuum left after Shahjahan had been dethroned. According to Muhammad Kambu, the astrologers had identified 21 July 1658 as the auspicious day.[50]

Astrologers determined the date and time for both crucial occasions. The emperor, who lived by the letter of Islamic law, often against the spirit of Islamic doctrine, in effect ignored the Quranic injunction in Surah Yunus, Verse 101: 'Behold all that is in the heavens and on earth, but neither signs nor warnings profit those who believe not.'[51] Faith has its variations.

In 1658, Aurangzeb was realistic enough to stop short of claiming full sovereignty. The *khutba* was not read in his name. A painting, dated circa 1660, now in the St Petersburg Album, shows a young, olive-coloured Aurangzeb bathed in a shaft of heavenly light, seated on a cushion and facing two princes. There is a small box and a *rudra veena* at his side.

The pomp and circumstance of the second coronation and his persona as emperor belie the cultivated image of Aurangzeb as an abstemious ruler who disdained the glamour of a king and lived on the earnings of pious activities like sewing prayer caps. The jewel merchant Jean-Baptiste Tavernier (1605–1689) saw Aurangzeb drink water from a rock crystal cup with a gold cover and saucer enriched with gems; the credulous were told that he never used vessels of gold and silver.

Fear of the unknown, however, made him an ascetic in 1665 when a 'very large' comet appeared for four weeks. Aurangzeb stopped eating meat, reduced his meals to a minimal amount of millet bread and water, and slept on the ground with only tiger skin as cover. A comet was a dangerous omen for kings.[52]

Aurangzeb's faith in astrology is confirmed by Bernier, who was part of the royal entourage the previous year. Aurangzeb set out from Delhi on 6 December 1664 'at three o'clock in the afternoon; a day and hour which, according to the astrologers of Delhi, cannot fail to prove propitious to long journeys'.[53]

The journey was a typical exhibition of grandeur and power. Aurangzeb travelled on horse, elephant or a seat carried on men's shoulders, with an armed contingent of 35,000 cavalry and 10,000 infantry, and between 100 and 120 brass guns. His sister Roshanara Begum travelled on an elephant ablaze with gold and azure coverlets, a well-dressed female slave brushing the dust off them with a peacock tail, or moved on silk-embroidered litters hung between camels or elephants. The royal tents were red with hand-painted chintz from Masulipatnam. Delhi's traders did business in a mobile market. Each evening, an *akash diya* (lamp of the skies), hung at a height of 40 yards, offered illumination.[54]

Aurangzeb was in 'magnificent attire': a white delicate satin shirt with silk and gold embroidery of the finest texture, an aigrette on his turban of gold cloth, diamonds of an extraordinary size, a topaz with the lustre of the sun and a necklace of immense pearls from neck to stomach. Nobles kept on the right side of the emperor with 'gifts of extraordinary magnificence sometimes for the sake of an ostentatious display, sometimes to divert the King from instituting an enquiry into the exactions committed in their official situations or governments, and sometimes to gain the favour of the King'. When Aurangzeb went to visit the new house of Jafar Khan, his vizier between 1662 and 1670, he received gifts of gold coins worth 'one hundred thousand crowns, some handsome pearls and a ruby'.[55]

Tavernier saw the peacock throne when invited to view the crown jewels. It resembled a bed, two feet above the ground, and was inlaid with rubies, emeralds and diamonds. It was protected by a canopy with twelve columns, decorated with pearls, from which hung the royal sword, mace, shield, bow and arrows. Above the canopy was a golden peacock, whose spread tail was covered with precious jewels. On either side of the bird were bouquets of golden flowers dressed in precious stones.[56]

Aurangzeb's official portraits showed a sacrilegious halo around his head and a shaft of divine light descending upon the ruler. Halos are an acquired taste in Aurangzeb's case, as they prevailed over his religiosity.

As a young man, Aurangzeb had youthful weaknesses. He was eighteen when he saw at the home of an aunt the beautiful Zainabadi in Burhanpur, reaching up to pluck a mango from a tree in a deer park and singing to herself. He swooned and did not recover from the faint for a while. His worried aunt diagnosed the malaise and found the medicine. She sent Zainabadi to his palace through some intelligent manipulation. According to the *Masir-ul-umra*, Dara Shukoh did not miss the chance to taunt his brother for such a lapse in the puritan ethic.[57]

Aurangzeb married three concubines: Zainabadi, who died young; Aurangabadi, who passed away in a plague in 1689; and Udaipuri, mother of his youngest son, Kam Baksh, and companion in his old age. Aurangzeb wrote to Kam Baksh that Udaipuri was with him in illness and would follow him in death. She passed away a few months after her husband, in the summer of 1707.

His relations with his sons were infused with tension before being fraught with it. Rebellion was always high-voltage drama, but patricide and filicide were unacceptable. Aurangzeb did seize his father's throne but never harmed him.

A story illustrates the implicit rules of behaviour among Mughal royals. In early 1616, Jahangir was in Mandu when he came upon the grave of Nasiruddin, son of the 13th-century Tughluq sultan Ghiyasuddin Balban. Nasiruddin had twice tried to poison his ageing father and failed. The third time, he gave the poisoned sherbet himself. Balban, aware of what was happening, raised his hands in prayer: he was old, he said, and had seen prosperity and happiness such as attained by no other king. He sent a prayer that God treat his death as something decreed and forgive his son. He drank the poisoned chalice in one gulp.

Jahangir kicked Nasiruddin's tomb, ordered his servants to do so too, unearthed his buried bones and threw them into a fire. It then occurred to him that fire was venerated and should not be polluted by this 'filthy body'. He ordered the bones to be thrown into the river Narmada.[58]

Aurangzeb, who justified his rebellion with the argument that matters would never have come to the sorry pass if Shahjahan had been equally fair to his sons, was watchful over his children. He gave sons high office, as was customary, but maintained an elaborate intelligence system through a corps of *nazir*s (newswriters) and spies, who reported directly to the father.

Hamida Banu, supervisor of Muazzam's private chamber during his term as governor of Multan, sent information that the prince very often took a pen case and a memorandum book into his bedroom, which she could not enter as etiquette did not permit it. The emperor wrote back to tell her that if she could not enter the bedroom, she could certainly ensure that there was no pen case available.[59]

When Muhammad Azam, then in Gujarat, applied for permission to come to Delhi upon hearing that the emperor had fallen ill, using the specious excuse that the air and water of his province were not congenial for his health, Aurangzeb replied, 'I too had sent a similar petition to my father Shahjahan during his illness, and he had replied to it by saying that the air of every place is agreeable to men except the wind of evil passions!'[60]

In December 1691, his youngest son, Kam Baksh, misbehaved during the siege of Jinji. Matters reached a point where the generals Asad Khan and Rao Dalpat Bundela took the prince into custody in 1692. Aurangzeb commented in a *firman*, 'Why should I quarrel with my friends for the sake of a son?' He quoted Plato: friends are those who share your meal, share your danger, and share your travels.[61]

Four of his five sons were imprisoned. The eldest, Muhammad Sultan, jailed for supporting his uncle Shuja in the wars of succession, died in Gwalior Fort on 5 December 1676. Aurangzeb was shaken when his fourth son, Muhammad Akbar, joined a Rajput rebellion and proclaimed himself emperor in 1681. In a letter written in 1683, Akbar accused his father of being foolhardy, power-hungry, a regicide and a filicide, an enabler of atrocities in the Deccan and a religious hypocrite whose doomed policies had undercut the Mughal Empire's reputation for justice and wisdom.[62] Akbar found shelter with the Marathas after the end of the Rajput rebellion before escaping to Khurasan in Persia. He died in November 1704.

In 1687, Muazzam was caught corresponding with the enemy. He spent the next eight years in jail. Aurangzeb warned his son:

The art of reigning is so delicate that a King's jealousy should be awakened by his very shadow. Be wise, or a fate similar to that which has befallen your brother [Sultan] awaits you. Indulge not the fatal delusion that Aurangzeb may be treated by his children as was Jehangir by his son Shahjahan; or that, like the latter, he will permit the sceptre to fall from his hand.[63]

Such clarity was chilling.

Jizya: Collapse of the Rajput Alliance

On 2 April 1679, Aurangzeb imposed *jizya* on 'unbelievers', according to *Maasir-i-Alamgiri*, reviving the iniquitous tax after 105 years. There was no attempt to camouflage its intent. Some Hindu state officials and religious leaders were exempt, but it was levied on all other non-Muslims in three categories of 12, 24 and 48 dirhams a year. As a percentage of income, it hit the poor the hardest. If it was intended to pressure Hindus into conversion, it boomeranged. It bred resistance.

The anger was instant. Hindus protested in huge numbers, blocking the emperor's way to the mosque for his Friday prayers. He was unmoved. Manucci, who had settled down in Tanjore after his adventures in the north, records serious disagreement at the highest levels of nobility:

> All the high-placed and important men at the court opposed themselves to this measure. They besought the king most humbly to refrain; they represented to him that it would be too heavy a burden upon the people ... But all was in vain.[64]

Not long afterwards, there was an earthquake, which some nobles claimed was caused by the affliction upon the people. Aurangzeb laughed.[65]

Jahanara criticised the decision as bad policy, using an evocative metaphor: Hindustan was like a vast ocean, the royal family were like ships on its waves. Who would want to load with taxes the sea on which the ships sailed? She warned against rebellion.

Within months of this imposition, Shivaji, king and founder of the first independent Maratha realm, admonished Aurangzeb from a moral pedestal and political perspective, as noted by Jadunath Sarkar in his history of Aurangzeb. He reminded Aurangzeb that his ancestor 'Akbar Padishah reigned for fifty-two lunar years' practising the 'admirable policy of universal harmony, *sulh-i-qul*', towards Hindus, Muslims, Jains, Christians,

Jews, *falakia* (sky-worshippers), atheists and heathen because the 'aim of his heart was to cherish and protect all the people'. So, he became famous under the title of Jagat Guru, the world's spiritual guide. Jahangir, for twenty-two years, and Shahjahan, for thirty-two, sought 'happy times on earth'. They, too, had the power to levy *jizya*, but there was no bigotry in their hearts.

Shivaji asked Aurangzeb to read the Quran where God is styled *Rabb-ul-aalamin* and not *Rabb-ul-muslimeen*: God of the universe, not just God of Muslims. Islam and Hinduism were diverse pigments of the divine painter. The call to prayer from the mosque was chanted in remembrance of Him; the bell in the temple was rung in yearning for Him. 'To show bigotry for any man's creed is equivalent to altering the pages of the Holy Book,' wrote Shivaji.[66]

A closed mind is impervious to light. Aurangzeb ignored such salutary advice. As late as October 1701, the ageing emperor bitterly chastised a Muslim officer, Firuz Khan Jang, commandant of the base camp in Islampuri on the river Bhima, because he wanted *jizya* to be abolished in his region to get cooperation from the Hindus for supplies. The emperor called him worthless, despicable and corrupt.[67]

The ultimate irony was that it failed as a revenue model too because corruption proved more powerful than prejudice. Truschke writes:

> In practice the *jizya* did not give Aurangzeb increased control over the powerful *ulema*. Numerous contemporaries railed against abuses in the *jizya's* collection, to the extent that a huge percentage of *jizya* money never found its way past the pockets of greedy tax collectors. Aurangzeb was impotent to halt such theft.[68]

Aurangzeb had given an indication of his proclivities in Gujarat where he demolished a newly constructed temple in Ahmedabad in 1644. As emperor, he increased the pressure in stages until the tenth year of his rule. In 1666, in an act of pettiness, he ordered that a railing gifted by Dara Shukoh to the Mathura temple of Keshav Rai be removed.

According to Mustaidd Khan's *Maasir-i-Alamgiri*, a more general order to demolish Hindu schools and temples in the east was sent out in April 1669. The *muhtasib*s (guardians of morality) were told to punish the Brahmins of Benares and other cities of learning for teaching their 'wicked sciences' to Muslims; 'pollution' through knowledge was the ultimate fear of the bigot. Jadunath Sarkar, who has produced a list of the temples destroyed, writes that Aurangzeb targeted temples venerated by Hindus: the second temple of Somnath, the Vishwanath temple in Benares and the Keshav Rai temple of Mathura built by the Bundela Raja Birsingh Dev, which was razed in 1670.[69] Celebration of Diwali and Holi was curtailed in 1668. In 1671, Aurangzeb tried and failed to make all rent collectors Muslims. Communalism does not work in administration.

In 1679, Aurangzeb ended *jharoka darshan*, in which he used to appear twice or thrice a day. It was stopped because of its Hindu origins. The practice of placing a tika (mark on the forehead), a familiar part of Mughal court ritual, ceased. Since orthodoxy included gender discrimination, women were banned from visiting the shrines of Muslim saints.[70] As late as March 1695, Aurangzeb issued an edict forbidding all Hindus except Rajputs to carry arms, ride elephants or sit on a palki.[71]

Aurangzeb was confident that his power was beyond challenge. The empire was courted by foreign powers. Europeans were doing a flourishing trade with India.

An amused Bernier mentions that some countries sent envoys with token offerings in the hope of taking back magnificent return gifts: the Sharif of Mecca sent a few Arabian horses and a brush used to sweep the Kaaba; the presents from Yemen and Basra are not recorded. Bernier is critical of the Christian king of Ethiopia for sending twenty-five 'choice slaves' with two merchants, a Muslim and an Armenian Christian, along with fifteen horses, a mule with beautiful skin and ivory of extraordinary size. In a twist in the tale, the Ethiopians were in Surat on their way back when the Marathas raided the port city and the Ethiopians lost their valuables.[72]

The difference between confidence and overconfidence can be just one bad decision.

The reaction was inevitable. In May 1669, Jat peasants, led by the zamindar of Tilpat, named Gokla, shot dead a *jizya* collector, Abdun Nabi. Order was not restored across Mathura and up to Agra until January 1670. In 1672, the Satnami sect based in Narnol, some 75 miles southwest of Delhi, rose in rebellion, their pent-up anger sparked by a blow from a foot soldier that broke the head of a villager. The uprising took a religious hue; a woman seer declared that she had a magic spell that would make the Satnamis invulnerable. They seized Narnol, denied the government taxes and cut off grain supplies to Delhi. Imperial troops heard reports that the prophetess could turn wooden horses into live ones. Aurangzeb had prayers and amulets sewn onto the banners of the imperial forces that were sent, with artillery, to subdue this rebellion.

Further west, the rising faith of the Sikhs had found a leader in Guru Tegh Bahadur, who defied Aurangzeb's attempts at coercion and forcible conversion. Tegh Bahadur's torture and execution on a warrant from Aurangzeb in December 1675 signalled the start of open war by the Sikhs against the empire under the leadership of

Guru Gobind Singh. The conflict continued until Bahadur Shah came to terms with him in 1707 after Aurangzeb's death.

A combination of decisions alienated the Rajputs. The festering wound of *jizya* was compounded by a threat to the aristocratic order. Jaswant Singh's death in 1678 poured acid on their existing heartburn when Aurangzeb ordered that his two minor sons and widows be sent to the court in Delhi, fomenting rumours that they might be converted. The order was never obeyed.

The strongest military challenge to Aurangzeb came from the now alienated Rajputs led by Marwar and Jodhpur. The war ended with a treaty in June 1681, but the resulting peace was sullen. When chaos began to descend after the death of Aurangzeb, the Rajput states were among the first to declare independence.[73]

It took just a decade for Aurangzeb to dissipate his syncretic inheritance. 'The empire had been governed by men of the world, and their government had been good. There was nothing but his own conscience to prevent Aurangzeb from adopting the eclectic splendid ease of Shahjahan. The Hindus would have preferred anything to a Muslim bigot,' writes Stanley Lane-Poole, with the orotundity of a late-19th-century scholar. In matters of religion, he adds, the emperor was 'obstinate to the point of fanaticism'.[74]

Any self-imposed moderation in policy towards Hindus disappeared with the death of a generation of vintage nobles, the 'men of the world' who had held the empire together with courage and sagacity in the 1660s. Shahjahan died in 1666, Raja Jai Singh in 1667, and Jafar Khan in 1670. The most influential Hindu in administration, Raja Raghunatha, died in 1663 in an accident. He had joined Aurangzeb after the defeat of Dara in Samugarh, was promoted to chief finance minister, equivalent to Todar Mal under Akbar, with the rank of raja and a *mansab* of 2,500. Bernier described him as the acting vizier of the empire.

The year 1663 also witnessed the death of the veteran Mir Jumla, who ruled Bengal after Shuja until his death on 31 March at Kuch Behar. It was said after Mir Jumla's death that it was only now that Aurangzeb had become king of Bengal. Aurangzeb called him one of the most powerful and most dangerous of his friends—'dangerous' because he did not always agree with the emperor.[75] Jaswant Singh lived longer. He died on 10 December 1678.

A vizier like Jafar Khan ran his office, and his private life, on the lines of previous generations of Mughal administrators. When reprimanded for drinking by Aurangzeb, he replied that it was only wine that gave him the strength to serve, evoking a smile instead of censure. Manucci records the story of a Kashmiri trader who tried to sell Aurangzeb a coat of very rich golden thread, embroidered with verses from the Quran. The king was pleased with the workmanship but refused to pay the high price being asked. His son Shah Alam refused to buy it too, not because of shortage of funds but because it was more prudent to emulate his father. Jafar Khan bought the coat at its now highly devalued price and wore it to court on the festival of sacrifice (*Id ul Azha*). Aurangzeb remarked acidly, 'You seem to be better off than I am.' Jafar Khan replied that he had clothed himself 'in such holy words' so that they may cleanse him of sins and strengthen his intelligence and capacity to serve His Majesty better.[76]

Audrey Truschke calls Aurangzeb's attempt to ban alcohol the most spectacular policy failure of his reign. According to Manucci, who clearly ernjoyed the gossip he heard, Aurangzeb sent the chief cleric, no less a figure than the Shaikh-ul-Islam, Abdul Wahab, a bottle a day so that he could tipple in secret. The puritan in Aurangzeb curbed grand celebrations during Eid, the Shia mourning during Muharram and the revelry at Holi and Diwali.

At the start of his rule, Aurangzeb's prejudice was treated as angularity rather than government policy. He had almost as much support from Hindu nobles as Dara Shukoh. It has been estimated that there were twenty-one Hindu nobles with a *mansab* of over thousand in his support, as against twenty-four for Dara.[77]

While in the Deccan, Aurangzeb came to an understanding with the rising Marathas, just as Shahjahan had in 1620. On his 19th birthday in November 1637, he met Linguji Bhonsle, an ally of Shahuji Bhonsale, the most powerful Maratha leader of that time, along with high-ranking officers in the army and allies in Aurangabad. They had fought alongside Aurangzeb in 1638 and had helped crush a revolt by the zamindars. Aurangzeb renewed contact with them in 1653. Among those who were in the front ranks in the battles of Dharmat and Samugarh against Dara were Jadu Rai, Rustam Rai, Babaji Bhosale, Netuji Bhosale, Damaji, Beas Rao and Manuji, all of whom received *mansab*s.

But he destroyed this relationship by bigotry, a confrontation that undermined his strength. Instead of accommodation, he sought to defeat the Marathas, a war that weakened his military capability.

Shivaji, eight years younger than Aurangzeb, was the first king to establish an independent realm out of Mughal territory. After the tribulations of their engagement, Aurangzeb recognised him as king in 1668. Shivaji's achievements are not the subject of this work; suffice it to note that if Aurangzeb had recognised the validity of Shivaji's arguments against *jizya*, history might have followed a different course.

Aurangzeb did not cloak his antagonism towards Shias, which culminated in the 'holy wars' against Bijapur and

Golconda, exhausting his life and emptying the remnant goodwill of the empire. As a young governor of Gujarat, he targeted the powerful Shia sect of Ismaili Bohras, executed one of their leaders and persecuted them throughout his reign. He dismissed Shia Muslims as *rafizi* or heretic. This was hardly the sole contradiction in a ruler who professed to be a good administrator. It was impossible, however, to remove the Shia Persian contingents in his armies, who were formidable fighters, as he admitted on his deathbed. In 1666, he ordered them to change their style of prayer to the Sunni methods of *namaaz*.

In one letter, he praises a Sunni who escaped to Turkey after murdering a Shia in Isfahan. In another, he calls his personal dagger *rafizi kush* (killer of heretics) and orders a few more. The Shia are always, in his correspondence, *ghul-i-bayabani* (corpse-eating demons) or *batil mazhaban* (apostates). He tried to pass off his campaign against Bijapur and Golconda, which had Shia sultans, as a holy war. In protest, the chief qazi Shaikh-ul-Islam resigned his post and ignored all efforts to bring him back.

Shia Persia had always kept an ambassador in the Mughal capital, and its envoys were adept at sweetening their insults. Aurangzeb had little time for them beyond protocol engagements. For Aurangzeb, faith became the basis for assertion of supremacy, not equity. Being a *hafiz*, or someone who could recite the holy book from memory, he was fully aware of the Quranic verse *La qum deen-o-qum wa il ya deen* (For you, your religion; for me, mine). He cited the verse only when convenient. When, in 1698, Muhammad Amin Khan, a petitioner seeking high office, complained that two paymasters were 'heretical Shia' or 'accursed misbelievers' and he would strengthen the Sunni faith if approved, Aurangzeb, now in his eighties, wrote on the petition: 'What connection have worldly affairs with religion? And what right have matters of religion to enter into bigotry? *For you is your religion and for me is mine.*⁷⁸ This was chicanery. It was common knowledge that in Medina, the Prophet had entered into contractual agreements with other communities, guaranteeing their right to maintain their way of life, but Aurangzeb preferred imposition to co-operation.

Islamic law leaves room for interpretation. Where the Quran is not explicit, jurists take recourse to precedents set by the Prophet. When this, too, becomes insufficient, a lawgiver uses individual judgement, *ijtihad*, or *ijma*, consensus. The very fact that there are different schools of jurisprudence means there is no uniformity in interpretation of the law. Four principal schools found broad support among Sunnis: Maliki, Hanafi, Shafi and Hanbali. Aurangzeb proclaimed loudly and often that he was a Hanafi. Theory aside, in practice, the establishment was happy to twist the law to suit its behaviour. Prof. Mujeeb records some strange judgements: a drunk found staggering and stumbling through streets could not be considered eligible for marriage to a virtuous woman. But if a courtier who drank concealed the fact and was treated with respect by the people, this would not be held against him.⁷⁹

Apologists for Aurangzeb's argue that he should not be judged by the standards of the 20th or 21st century. That is semantics, if not sophistry. He is guilty when judged by the standards of the 16th century, set as policy by his great-grandfather to promote *akhlaq* and *adaab*, ethics and harmony. His father, Shahjahan, celebrated the spring Hindu festival of Holi as *Eid-i-Gulabi,* or the pink Eid, and described it as *Aab-e-Pashi,* the shower of flowers. Nobles in court sprinkled one another with rose water from specially designed metal bottles to the beat of drums, *nagara,* on Holi day. The king's forehead was touched with colour in a display of *tehzib-i-akhlaq* (etiquette of harmony). In a decision that disrupted administration and revenue collection, Aurangzeb changed the official calendar from the Persian twelve-month span beginning with Nauruz in March to the rotating lunar Arabic year.

Aurangzeb's life ended not in the triumph of a pious man waiting to go to heaven but in the despair of a disjointed ruler who had triggered the ruin of a majestic empire.

Testament of Despair

By 1690, after more than three decades on the throne, Aurangzeb became strangely concerned about the official record of his reign.

Previous Mughal rulers had taken care to set down their narratives. Babur's memoirs, in Chagatai Turkish, are justly renowned. Humayun asked his court historian Ghiyas-al-din Khwandamir to produce an account of 'the inventions of my auspicious mind and the improvements of my enlightened understanding'. Akbar sent a *firman* to his aunt Gulbadan Begum to write down what she knew of events about Babur and Humayun and established a department under Abul Fazl to compile what became a classic history of his reign. Akbar also commissioned biographies of Genghis Khan and Taimur and a history of a thousand years, *Tarikh-i-Alfi*.

In 1618, Jahangir began gifting copies of his memoirs to be 'used by rulers as guides for ruling'. Shahjahan got the first copy, with an inscription expressing the hope that the contents would be acceptable to God and satisfactory to the people. Shahjahan's scholars produced three texts: the *Amal-i-Salih* by Muhammad Salih Kambu; the *Padshahnama* by Muhammad Amin Qazwini and the *Shahjahannama* by Sadiq Khan.

Qazwini's son Mirza Muhammad Kazim chronicled the first ten years of Aurangzeb's reign. In 1690, Aurangzeb banned all histories after hearing a summation of this account, *Alamgirnama*. He claimed that inward piety was preferable to ostentatious display of achievements. As an excuse, it was specious. There is nothing in Islamic doctrine that forbids the historical narrative. Lisa Balabanlilar finds it difficult to understand the rationale and notes that by this time, Aurangzeb had begun to regret many of his actions.[80]

A principal source of information on Aurangzeb's reign is the *Maasir-i-Alamgiri*, written by Muhammad Saqi Mustaid Khan in secrecy over four decades of Aurangzeb's rule and published with the help of Inayatullah Khan, vizier of Bahadur Shah (1707–1712). Aurangzeb's surviving letters and commentaries, collected in five volumes by his courtiers, confirm the ageing ruler's deep distress at his record.

In the early years, Aurangzeb was conscious of the deleterious temptations of power. In a letter to his captive father, which Bernier quotes from the part he had read, Aurangzeb mentions that their 'great ancestor' Akbar had recommended 'serious attention' to the excellent memoirs of Amir Taimur. Aurangzeb cites the encounter between the Ottoman Caliph Bayazit and Amir Taimur after the former's defeat in the battle of Ankara in 1402. Bayazit reprimands Taimur for laughing, saying that the God who had given victory today could put him in chains tomorrow. Heaven forbid, Taimur replied, that he should insult a fallen enemy. He had laughed because Bayazit was blind in one eye and he was a cripple in one foot. Heaven had provided the 'baubles' of empire to 'such ill-favoured mortals'.[81]

Stanley Lane-Poole notes that, by nature, Aurangzeb was not a generous person, but when, soon after his accession, the combination of drought and war led to famine, he established free kitchens and remitted 'about eighty taxes, including the vexatious highway and ferry tolls, the ground cess on houses and shops etc'.[82]

Aurangzeb regretted that his education had been flawed by too great a stress on Arabic. He blamed one teacher, called 'Mullah Sale' by Bernier. The Mullah had retired to Kabul. When he learnt that his former pupil had become monarch, he hastened to Delhi in search of promotion to the rank of a noble. He was kept waiting three months before being granted an audience. Hakim Danishmand and two or three other officials were present at the encounter. Bernier heard the details from the Hakim, who was his patron.

Aurangzeb was acerbic:

Let us then examine your title to any mark of distinction. I do not deny you would possess such a title if you had filled my young mind with suitable instruction. Show me a well-educated youth, and I will say that it is doubtful who has the stronger claim to his gratitude, his father or his tutor. But what was the knowledge I derived under your tuition? You taught me that the whole of Franguistan [Europe] was no more than some inconsiderable island, of which the most powerful Monarch was formerly the King of England. In regard to the other sovereigns of Franguistan, such as the King of France and him of Andalusia [Spain], you told me they resembled our petty Rajas, and that the potentates of Hindoustan eclipsed the glory of all other kings; that they alone were Humayuns, Akbars, Jahangirs or Shahjahans; the Happy, the Great, the Conquerors of the World, and the Kings of the World; and that Persia, Uzbek, Kachgar [Kazak], Tartary and Cathay, Pegu, Siam, China and Matchine [Maha Chin], trembled at the name of the Kings of the Indians. Admirable geographer! Deeply read historian! Was it not incumbent upon my preceptor to make me acquainted with the distinguishing features of every nation of the earth; its resources and strength; its mode of warfare, its manners, religion, form of government, and wherein its interests principally consist; and, by a regular course of historical reading, to render me familiar with the origin of States, their progress and decline; the events, accidents, or errors, owing to which such great changes and mighty revolutions, have been effected? Far from having imparted to me a profound and comprehensive knowledge of the history of mankind, scarcely did I learn from you the names of my ancestors, the renowned founders of this empire. You kept me in total ignorance of their lives, of the events which preceded, and the extraordinary talents that enabled them to achieve their extensive conquests. A familiarity with the languages of surrounding nations may be indispensable in a King; but you would teach me to read and write Arabic; doubtless conceiving that you placed me under an everlasting obligation for sacrificing so large a portion of time to the study of a language wherein no one can hope to become proficient without ten or twelve years of close application. Forgetting how many important subjects ought to be embraced in the education of a Prince, you acted as if it were chiefly necessary that he should possess great skill in grammar, and such knowledge as belongs to a Doctor of law; and thus did you waste the precious hours of my youth in the dry, unprofitable, and never-ending task of learning words!

If, Aurangzeb continued, he had been taught the 'philosophy which adapts the mind to reason, and will not suffer it to rest satisfied with anything short of the most solid arguments', lessons that fortified the soul against the assaults of fortune, producing equanimity that was neither insolently elated by prosperity nor basely depressed by adversity, if he had learnt science and geography, governance and history, the origin, progress and decline of states, 'I should be more indebted to you than Alexander was to Aristotle'. Instead, he had received an overdose of Arabic, filling his pupil's brain with 'idle and foolish propositions' that seldom mattered in real life. The Mullah was ordered out of sight.[83]

By the last year of his life, the empire of 'Paradise-like Hindustan' stretched from Kabul to Bengal and from Vijayanagar to Sindh. Little Tibet (Baltistan) sent an embassy when Aurangzeb visited Kashmir, and Great Tibet sent a jade stone of extraordinary size, greenish with white veins. The wealth of India can be estimated by the trade of one province alone: Bengal supplied rice to Ceylon, the Maldives and Egypt, and sugar to Arabia and Mesopotamia through Basra. Portuguese merchants sold Bengal's products and praised its sweetmeats. Fish was profuse. Bernier is amazed at the vast quantity of its cotton and silk that reached the world from Japan to Holland. Bernier's only complaint was about the quality of its *arrack*, distilled from molasses, mixed with lemon juice, water and nutmeg, pleasant to taste but injurious to health.[84]

The crown jewels of Aurangzeb contained a unique diamond that weighed 756 English carats when found in the Kolar mines of the Deccan. It had been presented to Shahjahan by Mir Jumla in 1656 or 1657. Tavernier saw the gem at the invitation of the emperor. It had been cut by jewellers to a little more than 268 carats. In 1739, the Persian invader Nadir Shah carried off this gem after devastating Delhi and renamed it Kohinoor, or Mountain of Light. The Kohinoor, ever in search of a home in the mightiest power of the time, ended up with the British.

Jadunath Sarkar, a sharp critic, analyses the character of 'the last of the Great Mughals': in spite of 'his religious intolerance, narrowness of mind, and lack of generosity and statesmanship, he was great in the possession of some qualities which might have gained for him the highest place in any sphere of life except the supreme one of ruling over men.[85]

Aurangzeb had some qualities that could have placed him in the ranks of the greats. He was brave to an unusual degree, cool when making decisions and led by personal example in battle. He prepared for power with 'self-reverence, self-knowledge and self-control.' He was extremely well-read and a master of Persian poetry and sacred Arabic literature. His contemporaries described him as a 'dervish clad in the imperial purple'. His memory was remarkable until his death in his 90th year, and his physical powers were intact apart from deafness in one ear.[86]

Aurangzeb feared that 'the least deviation from the strict and narrow path of Islamic orthodoxy' would endanger his soul. He regarded 'danger as the legitimate risk of greatness'.[87] His debilitating flaw was a passion for micro-management, robbing governors and generals of initiative and judgement, leaving them hesitant in any emergency. His suspicious nature crushed the latent ability of his sons. He was matchless in diplomacy, intrigue and secret manipulation but a cold intellectual who chilled the love of those who came near him.

Aurangzeb lacked sympathy, imagination, vision, elasticity in the choice of means and that warmth of the heart that atones for a hundred faults of the head. These limitations of his character undermined the Mughal empire, so that after his death it suddenly fell in a single downward plunge.[88]

The Last Prediction: After Me, Chaos! 215

In early February 1707, the eighty-eight-year-old Aurangzeb realised that his life was over. In his last letter to Azam Shah, he wrote:

> I came alone and am going away alone. I know not who I am and what I have been doing ... I have not at all done any [true] government of the realm or cherishing of the peasantry ... I brought nothing with me and am carrying away with me the fruits of my own sins. I know not what punishment will fall on me.

A letter to Kam Baksh is soaked in similar despair: 'I shall carry away with myself the fruits of all the punishments and sins that I have done ... Set your feet within the limits of your carpet.' A statement said to be written in his own hand and left under his pillow, now with the India Office Library in Britain, urges his sons not to slaughter mankind in pursuit of the throne but to share power. He proposed a formula. This being the Mughal dynasty, the sons ignored his advice.

Hamiduddin Khan Bahadur's *Ahkam-i-Alamgiri* contains Aurangzeb's last will and testament, written in 12 points because 'twelve is blessed among numbers'. He sought mercy for 'this sinner sunk in iniquity' and 'drowned in sin'. His personal wealth, he said, amounted to 4 rupees and 2 annas earned from prayer caps he had sewn, and 305 rupees from copying the Quran. The first would buy a coarse white shroud. The second should be distributed among the poor on the day of his death. He sought burial in the Valley of Deviation from the Right Path with bare head, for God would be merciful to the humble. He left some advice for the heir: conciliate the Persians, even if this required subterfuge, because they never abandoned the field of war. (His first wife and chief consort, Dilras Banu Begum, was a Safavid Persian princess; they were married in 1637.)

The Turanis, or those of Turkic origin, were excellent soldiers and deserved due favour. Aurangzeb was wary, however, of an Indian clan that had risen to high office from the obscurity of Muzaffarnagar, a rural town north of Delhi, the Sayyids of Barha. They were worthy of honour and favour, but a king had to be extremely cautious in dealing with them. Their rank should not be increased, for they would become 'predominant partners in the government, nay more, they would demand the kingdom for themselves. If you let them take the reins ever so little, the result will be to your disgrace'. This was prescient. In the decade after his death, they became kingmakers and, briefly, masters of a flailing kingdom. Government, Aurangzeb had said, functions on accurate information.

It reveals a great deal about Aurangzeb's troubled state of mind that his last thoughts also featured the mistakes he had made in dealing with Shivaji.

His eleventh commandment was precise: never trust your sons, nor play favourites.[89]

Aurangzeb summoned his heir, Bahadur Shah, in prison from 21 February 1687, for an audience after he was released on 9 May 1695. He justified his long years in confinement. They had been as salutary as prison had been to Prophet Joseph before he became ruler of Egypt: 'In this hope I have in my lifetime entrusted to you Paradise-like Hindustan.'

Aurangzeb then revealed a startling fact to his son: every prediction made in his horoscope drawn by Fazil Khan 'from the day of my birth' had been 'verified by actual experience'. The horoscope was completely accurate. More: the horoscope had also forecast what would happen 'after my death'.

There would be chaos after he was gone. *Az mast hamah fasad-i-baqi!*

Aurangzeb was brutally honest about the impending misfortune:

> In that horoscope it is written that after me will come an emperor, ignorant, narrow-minded, overpowered by injuries, whose words will be all imperfect and whose plans will be immature. He will act towards some men with so much prodigality as almost to drown them, and towards others with so much rigour as to raise the fear of destruction. All these admirable qualities and praiseworthy characteristics are found in your nature! Although I shall leave behind me a competent *vazir* [Asad Khan] who has come to the front in my reign and whom I have secured, yet what good will it do, as the four pillars of empire, my four sons, will never leave that poor man to do his work?[90]

Many officials were secretly begging for his death now, he said, but once he was gone, they would be pleading before God for death to themselves. He advised Bahadur Shah 'out of fatherly love' not to be so salty that his subjects would spit him out of their mouths, nor so sweet that they would swallow him.

Aurangzeb became emperor at the age of forty. Babur was twenty-one when he conquered Kabul, Humayun twenty-two when he inherited the throne, Akbar thirteen when coronated, and Jahangir and Shahjahan both thirty-six. Aurangzeb's heir, Bahadur Shah, was sixty-four when he became king.

Aurangzeb was in Ahmadnagar on 20 February 1707. He finished his morning prayer and began to recite the *shahada*, the Islamic declaration of faith, on his rosary:

> there is no God but Allah, and Muhammad is His Messenger. His breathing slipped into a rasp. He died

at eight that morning. It was a Friday. He had sought death on a Friday. His prayer was answered.

His simple grave in Khuldabad, a few inches high, measured nine feet by seven feet, with a cavity in the middle for plants.

7

The Rise of Suhail

ALLAH IS MENTIONED thirty-four times in Babur's memoirs, *Vaqai*, mostly in quotations from the Quran or references to religion. The term he uses for God far more often is Tengri, the blue-sky deity of the Mongols, adding *taala* (highest) as a suffix in the manner of Allah-taala. Babur thanks Tengri-taala for the historic victory at Panipat in 1526. He

> ascribes his Panipat victory to God's plan ... when he invokes God in this passage, he uses the name of the Turco-Mongol deity Tengri, 'the blue sky' of Central Asian pastoral nomadic societies. He uses this word for God throughout the [*Vaqai*] far more than the Arabic-Islamic Allah, which occurs only 34 times, often in Quranic quotations and frequently in the writings of clerics and scholars, such as his companion Shaikh Zain.[1]

What Tengri has fixed, he writes, cannot be changed. The dead go to Tengri's mercy. For Babur, there was no conflict between his ancestral culture and his Islamic faith. He attributes earlier conquests like Badakhshan, Qunduz, Kabul and Qandahar also to Tengri's kindness and compassion. He adds, ruefully, that none of these regions were profitable, unlike Hindustan.[2]

His Majesty Giti-Sitani Firdaus-Makani Zahiruddin Muhammad Babur Padishah Ghazi is introduced in the

Akbarnama, the official history of his grandson, with the grandiloquence of astral acclaim, as an emperor of the seven belvederes, prince of the heavenly throne and celestial crown, and one who increases the felicity of a lucky ascendant.

Babur was born in 1483, the eldest son of Omar Shaikh Mirza, a favourite of his beloved maternal grandmother, Aisan Daulat Begum, descended from Genghis Khan through maternal blood and Amir Taimur through Miran Shah Mirza, Sultan Muhammad Mirza and Abu Said Mirza, Babur's grandfather.

Life was short, so life began early. Babur was ten when he took over as the governor of his hometown, Andijan, in today's Uzbekistan, after his father's sudden fall from the rampart of a fort into a ravine at the age of thirty-nine. Babur describes the death with poetic brevity: on 4 Ramadan [8 June, ad 1494], his father flew with his racing pigeons and became a falcon. A Mughal prince was treated as an adult before his teens. Humayun rebuked a ten-year-old Akbar for racing pigeons and watching camel races instead of ruling his appanage, Ghazni, a responsibility meant to test his son and teach him the art of administration.

Astrologers were consulted on all important occasions. When Babur, then seventeen, was compelled to confront his lifelong enemy, the warlord Muhammad Shaibani Khan Uzbek, he asked astrologers to find the propitious moment:

> The reason why I was so eager to fight was that on the day of battle, the Eight Astronomical Stars [seven stars of the Plough or Great Bear constellation and the Pole Star] were between our two armies. If I had postponed the battle, these stars would have shifted to the enemy's rear [and helped him].

On this occasion, the stars faltered. He was badly defeated and condemned to years of nomad poverty during which he came frequently close to death. He was in such despair that he decided to go to China but was deterred by circumstances. He cites a rueful couplet:

> He who lays his hand on the sword with haste,
> Shall lift to his teeth the back hand of regret.

The four lean years that followed became a learning period, succinctly summed up in an old aphorism: ten dervishes can sleep under one blanket but two kings cannot find room in one clime.³

> If a man of God eats half a dish,
> He gives the other to a dervish;
> But let a king grip the rule of a realm,
> He dreams of another to overwhelm.

In 1504, after years of turbulence, sometimes a ruler, sometimes a fugitive, Babur saw the promise of good fortune in the rise of a star. He was travelling through the Hupian Pass, a few miles north of Charikar, on his march to Kabul when he saw a star low on the horizon and wondered if it was Suhail. His companion Muhammad Baqir Chaganiani conveyed that the glimmer of Suhail was a sign of good luck.

The happy omen changed his life. In October 1504, the commander of Kabul fort preferred a negotiated surrender and was allowed to leave with dependants and goods. A brief uprising by the populace was literally cut to pieces. Babur sat on the throne of Kabul, a great trading centre whose merchants made profits of 300 to 400 per cent from trade with India, Turkey and China. Caravans from India brought cloth, sugar and aromatic roots; from the west and north came 8,000 to 10,000 horses.

In June 1505, Babur was deeply affected by the death of his mother, Qultuq Nigar Khanum; at the same time came news that his grandmother Aisan Daulat Begum had passed away. The grief, he writes, was extreme. On 5 July, there was a major earthquake in Kabul. Ramparts, walls and houses collapsed, and dust rose from the top of the mountains. The earth quaked thirty-three times on the first day, and tremors continued for a month. The death toll was heavy.

Babur records that the Sun was in Pisces when Humayun was born on the night of 6 March 1506 in the repaired citadel of Kabul to his third wife Mahim Begum. According to Gulbadan Begum, his daughter, Babur ordered his nobles to call him Padishah or king of kings that year. Babur proved a successful ruler, building alliances with tribes who had been alienated by the previous kings and taking care to protect friendships by sharing the spoils of raids. His enemies learnt that he could be ferocious in war: he erected pyramids of skulls after victory and employed scorched-earth tactics.

He was still a teetotaller, although family history indicated a different temperament. Babur's grandfather Abu Said was famously fond of wine and *majun*, a concoction of crushed *bhang*, milk, sugar and spices, but Babur remained abstemious until he was over twenty-nine, excusing himself even when his father offered wine. He narrates stories of resisting temptation. In 1506, he was taken to a wine party in Herat where the guests drank wine as if it were water. He noted that the party became cordial when the wine rose to their heads. There was much drunken dancing, but the men danced well. Babur was inclined to indulge but did not. Later, the desire for wine came with a young man's growth of sexual passion, but it took more time for the appropriate opportunity to arise. He took his first sip in October 1511 when celebrating the reconquest of Samarkand. It was a pyrrhic victory; Babur returned to Kabul in 1512. But alcohol had taken hold. He was soon drinking *araq* in copious quantities and eating *majun*. During the heady years of *bazm-u-razm*, feasting and fighting, he would wait for the end of Ramadan, the month of fasting, to resume drinking. He wrote these lines in June 1519, while recovering from a high fever:

Ramadan came and I a pious wine-sot,
Eid arrived and with it remembrance of wine
Neither fasting nor prayer [but] years, months,
Nights and days with wine and *majun*, crazy and drunk.

One cannot easily think of a king's autobiography so full of carefree carousel. A painting in opaque watercolour, ink and gold included in a manuscript of *Baburnama* dated 1589, now in the Arthur Sackler Gallery at the Smithsonian, is captioned, succinctly and accurately, *A Drunken Babur Returns to Camp at Night*. He described in detail an evening on the river when he left the boat roaring drunk and galloped 'free-reined' to camp. He did not remember a thing the next morning and vomited a lot. All through the long dominance of the Mughal Empire, European merchants knew that a case of wine was a passport to many a princely home. As the British ambassador Sir Thomas Roe, who came to India in 1616, noted, alcohol could breach hierarchies and smooth negotiations.

A 15th-century European travelogue of India gives a glimpse of the land before Babur's invasion. Afanasy Nikitin was a Russian horse-dealer who came down the Volga, crossed the Caspian, rode through Iran and sailed from Hormuz to Muscat, from where he took a ship to Gujarat, some three decades before Vasco da Gama made landfall in the deep south in 1498. Nikitin, who returned home in 1473, wandered through the Deccan.

Visitors, he writes, could rent a room in an inn and persuade the landlady to do more than offer food. He is amazed by the merchandise in Bidar: horses, goods, silks, eatables, handicrafts and slaves, for that was a dark and despicable part of international commerce in that era. He is impressed by war elephants: 'Large scythes are attached to the trunks and tusks of the elephants, and the animals are clad in ornamental plates of steel. They carry a citadel, and in the citadel twelve men in armour with guns and arrows.'[4]

These moving citadels would be the biggest military threat to Babur as his ambitions shifted east.

Babur identified the seven kingdoms that dominated the contemporary political map of India: Delhi's Lodi Sultanate (1451–1526), descendants of the Tughluq dynasty's water-carriers (*saghgha*); Rana Sangha of Mewar (1484–1528), who had become the most powerful ruler of central India; the Muzaffarids of Gujarat (1391–1583), Rajput converts to Islam; the Bahmanis of Deccan (1347–1527), now weakened; Malwa (1392–1562), which had lost most of its territory to Rana Sangha; the Husain Shahi dynasty in Bengal (1494–1538); and the Tuluva dynasty of Vijayanagar (1503–1614).

His target was the Afghan Ibrahim Lodi in Delhi.

Panipat: The Sign of the Archer

Astrologers fixed the day on which Babur began his fifth expedition to Hindustan: Friday (17 November), when the Sun was in the sign of the Archer. Abul Fazl confirms that the Sun was in Sagittarius. The previous four attempts had withered around the Indus.

Prophecy through dreams was a familiar element of Mughal cosmology. In 1502, Babur became suicidal after the rout at Akhsi in Fergana, when all seemed lost, and he readied himself for the death that was inevitable, whether one lived to be a hundred or a thousand. He was offering a prayer when he fell asleep.

He dreamt that Khwaja Yaqub, grandson of Khwaja Ubaydullah Ahrar, a family protector and patron, was riding towards him on a dappled horse with a message that triumph was near at hand, and he would be seated on a royal throne. Babur awoke feeling happy, only to find that he was on the verge of becoming a hostage. He challenged those who had betrayed him. As he did so, there came the sound of approaching hooves. Babur was certain that they were enemies as the riders crashed through a hole in a part of the wall that had crumbled. Instead, it was a posse led by the faithful Qutlugh Muhammad Barlas. He felt as though God had granted him a new lease of life. For Babur, dreams were a divine message.

Babur made his first incursion into India soon after his conquest of Kabul, in January 1505, when the Sun was in the sign of Aquarius. He reached Adinapur after six days and discovered, to his astonishment, the heat of Hindustan, along with different plants, trees, animals, birds, tribes, people, manners and customs. He visited a cave called Gurh Kattri, a holy place for Hindu yogis and Hindus who came from long distances to get their hair and beards cut. He camped at Jam and celebrated Eid on the banks of the Gumal River but returned to Kabul after a plot was discovered to kill him. It was too early for expansion. The only notable thing about the second expedition, in September 1507, was a river ride on a raft near Nangarhar.

The decisive march towards Delhi began in the winter of 1525. When a count of the army was taken in Peshawar in 1526, Babur had some 12,000 men, including *naukar* (soldiers), *chakar* (servants) and *saudagar* (traders). Humayun, then at Badakhshan, would join later. Discipline was imposed on the army: drinking days were restricted to

Saturday, Sunday, Tuesday and Wednesday, although *majun* was permitted on all days. Babur proclaimed his right to rule Delhi as Taimur's descendant; in December 1398, Taimur had defeated Sultan Nasiruddin Shah. There was a happy start to the campaign when, on 26 February 1526, eighteen-year-old Humayun rode out from Ambala against Hamid Khan Lodi, a commander in the army of Ibrahim Lodi, and returned with a hundred prisoners and seven or eight elephants. This was Humayun's first experience of battle, which Babur considered an excellent omen.

From mid-March, news began to come through that Ibrahim Lodi was proceeding at a pace of 2 to 4 miles a day. Skirmishes began on 2 April. Babur called a meeting at which it was decided that Panipat would be the preferred site of battle, as a crowded city would be on one side, and other flanks could be protected by carts and mantlets behind which infantry and matchlock men could take their position. They camped at Panipat on 12 April.

When a final count was taken, Babur's forces did not add up to the 12,000 at Peshawar. The odds were heavily against them. People estimated Ibrahim Lodi's army at 1,00,000 men and 1,000 elephants, financed by the treasure of three generations. Stephen Dale suggests this is an exaggeration, but there is no dispute that Babur was vastly outnumbered. He records that some of his soldiers were full of fear. He was more nonchalant. What God had fixed could not be changed.

Babur had carts tied together and placed about 20 or 25 feet apart, with space left every 50 yards or so ('an arrow's flight') for 100 to 150 horsemen to charge. On 20 April, news came at dawn that the enemy was advancing in fighting array. Humayun was given command of the right wing. There were two 'turning' units, on the extreme right and left, contingents versed in the *tulghamah* or encircling manoeuvres that could attack the enemy's rear during close combat.

The Sun was spear-high when fighting commenced in earnest at eight in the morning. The Afghan line broke early, and soon the enemy was able to neither advance nor retreat in the melee. Babur used two types of cannons, *Farangi* and *zarb-zanan Rumi*, from the centre and left of centre. His archers were more effective, particularly against elephants. The wheeling parties pressed from the sides, while archers showered arrows on the surrounded enemy. At noon, after fierce fighting, the enemy was crushed. Ibrahim Lodi's body was found during the time of the afternoon prayer.

Humayun rode quickly to Agra, site of the treasury, and won possession of a diamond valued, according to Babur, at the price of two-and-a-half days' food for the whole world. Humayun offered the famous diamond to his father at Agra. Babur gave it back to his son.

Babur repeatedly invokes the name of Tengri in gratitude: 'We sent the army to Hindustan, and the fifth time, God, may He be exalted, Tengri-*taala*, in wisdom and mercy, made such an enemy as Sultan Ibrahim, defeated and worthless, and [left] such a country as Hindustan accessible and conquered for us.' He adds: 'We placed our trust in God the most high, Tengri-*taala*.' Victory had been granted by the kindness and compassion of Tengri rather than the strength of the Mughal army.[5]

On 24 April, Babur offered prayers at the shrine of Nizam al-Din Auliya and the next day at the shrine of Khwaja Qutbuddin in Delhi. He followed this with some political tourism, visiting the graves of Ghiyasuddin Balban and Alauddin Khilji before boarding a boat on the Jamuna to drink *araq*.

India's wealth had been neatly defined by the Persian poet Ashraf Mazandarani: 'Whoever comes to Hindustan from

Iran imagines/That in India gold is scattered like stars in the evening sky.' Babur praised its other attractions: craftsmen (whose work was visible in the Registan of Samarkand), the air after monsoon rains, calibrated weights and measures, and gold and silver coins. India's economy was reflected in its numeral system, with values as high as a lakh, or 1,00,000, and a crore, 1,00,00,000. The revenue from Agra alone in 1526 was 29,00,000 *shahrukhis*, while that from the fourteen districts of his Kabul domain was only 8,00,000.

The people were hostile, with the local peasantry running away in fear as the Mughals approached. Conquest was not easy. Every fortified town, apart from Delhi and Agra, strengthened its defences, and each had to be taken. Aware that a single battle could not assure a stable kingdom, Babur reached out to the Afghans, giving Ibrahim Lodi's mother a generous estate worth 1 crore rupees, downstream on the Jamuna River. Her response was venomous. She conspired to poison Babur and refused to accept her son's defeat.

The Poisoned Kitchen

Babur records the full story of a 'strange event' on 21 December 1526 in a letter to his wife, included in his memoirs.

Ibrahim Lodi's mother, 'an ill-omened woman', heard that the new ruler had employed four cooks from Ibrahim Lodi's kitchen, as he wanted to taste Hindustani dishes [Lodi had fifty or sixty cooks on his staff). Lodi's mother sent a *tola* of poison, wrapped in a square of paper, through a slave woman to a food-taster from Etawah called Ahmad; a *tola* was equivalent to the weight of a silver rupee. Ahmad was to give the poison to the four cooks, promising them a province each if they succeeded. Ibrahim Lodi's mother sent another slave woman to confirm that the poison had reached the cooks.

Ahmad and the cooks, who knew the drill, put the poison not in the food but on a serving dish because there were strict instructions that all dishes had to be tasted by any Hindustani present, including the cook, a subordinate taster and a head taster. Ahmad realised that he might become a victim if the poison were put in the pot. On 21 December, they sprinkled half the poison on thin slices of bread placed on the porcelain plate, covered with buttered fritters. Nervous, they threw the rest of the poison into the fire.

It was a Friday. After the afternoon prayer, Babur ate a good deal of cooked hare and then took a few mouthfuls of the poisoned food without noticing any unpleasant flavour. He felt sick and thought the nausea was from dried meat. He got up, retching all the way to the 'water room'. He had never vomited after food before. He became suspicious. The cooks were put under guard, and the vomit was given to a dog, whose belly swelled although it did not die. Two or three warriors who had shared the meal with Babur also fell ill. They survived. Babur thought the evil was over, and God had given him a new birth. The antidote given to Babur was a bowl of milk on Saturday and *araq* in which stamped clay had been dissolved, along with a laxative the following day. On Monday, there was milk mixed with a laxative.

Mughal retribution was immediate. Torture induced quick confessions from the cooks. Babur presided over the court on Monday in the presence of nobles. The slave women gave evidence. Justice was swift: the taster Ahmad was cut into pieces, and one cook was skinned alive. A slave woman was thrown under an elephant, another shot with a matchlock. Ibrahim Lodi's mother was put under guard, stripped of her possessions and banished to Kabul. Her infant grandson, who had been treated with respect and delicacy, was sent to Qandahar.

But the perils of Hindustan were not over. The resistance had found another leader, and within three months, Babur would fight another battle for survival.

Star-Crossed: A Prediction Goes Wrong

The astrologer Muhammad Sharif had not accompanied his master to Panipat, but he arrived just before the encounter that determined the fate of north India: the Battle of Kanwah in 1527 between Babur and the powerful ruler of Mewar, Maharana Sangram Singh Sisodia, popularly known as Rana Sangha. The Lodi Afghans made common cause with the Rana.

Babur's ambitions were not unknown. From Kabul, he had corresponded with Rana Sangha over a peaceful division of territory, by which the latter would extend Mewar to Agra while Babur ruled on an axis from Kabul to Lahore to Delhi. The proposal was a non-starter.

Babur lists the nine small principalities whose support would be crucial in the coming confrontation: Qasim Sambhali, Nizam Khan of Bianah, Muhammad Zaitun of Dhulpur, Tatar Khan Sarang-Khani of Gwalior, Husain Khan Nuhani of Rapri, Qutb Khan of Etawah, Alam Khan Kalpia and Hasan Khan of Mewat, whose family had ruled the crucial route from Delhi to Agra for more than a century. He was annoyed but helpless as some of his Begs decided that they had come to India for plunder and would return to Kabul with it. Khwaja Kalan and Khwaja Mir Maran, roasted by the heat and piqued by unfamiliar people and customs, left for the cool of Kabul and Ghazni before battle. Babur decided that he had come to stay. In late August, he ordered the construction of a garden on scrubland near Agra. The signal brought allies. Other Indian princes rallied alongside Rana Sangha.

By August 1526, Rana Sangha had reached Kandar in Rajasthan. In November, Babur received information that Rana Sangha had 'assembled a large force of Hindus and Muslims and made bold advances'. On 30 November, Babur summoned Humayun from Jaunpur, Nizam Khan from Bianah, Tatar Khan from Gwalior and Muhammad Zaitun from Dholpur.

Babur mobilised on 11 February 1527, establishing camp outside Agra. Nerves were strained when they learnt that the Rana had defeated Abdul Aziz's garrison at Bianah Fort. Those who escaped brought stirring stories of Rajput valour. A scouting party was badly mauled. Babur's daughter Gulbadan Begum describes the ground reality:

> [The] Rana had the support of a countless host. Amirs and Rajas and Ranas, every one of those who had come earlier and paid duty to His Majesty [Babur], now became an enemy and went and joined the Rana, until Kul-jalali and Sambhal and Rapri—every *pargana*—and Rais and Rajas and Afghans became hostile...[6]

As reports spread of Rana Sangha's success in preliminary clashes, Afghans and Rajputs occupied forts at Gwalior, Rapri, Chandawar and Koil. Babur quoted Firdausi's 11th-century *Shah Nama* to instil some confidence among his troops: it was better to die with a good name, for the body was certain to die in any circumstance.

Babur was constructing his battle defences near the Sikri lake when the astrologer Muhammad Sharif arrived, along with 500 men and 3 camel loads of 'reasonable' Ghazni wine. As if the mood was not sufficiently gloomy, Sharif predicted doom. Gulbadan Begum quotes Sharif telling soldiers: 'It would be best for the Emperor not to fight, for the constellation *Sakkiz Yildoz* [Eight Stars] is opposite.' She adds: 'Amazing perturbation fell upon the royal army. They became increasingly anxious and troubled and showed signs of cowardice.' Babur confirms the negativity of Muhammad Sharif, who kept insisting that Mars was in the west, and whoever came from the eastern side would be defeated.

Babur's resolve remained steady. He ignored wild reports and words, made no change in plans and prepared in earnest for the battle. He assembled his officers and troops, high and low, plebeian and noble, and told them a simple truth. The distance between Agra and Kabul was a journey of some months. There was no hope of peaceful return. If they died, they would be martyrs; if they lived, there was glory. He had to practise what he preached. Wine was hardly the perfect drink for a holy war. Two days before the battle, he renounced alcohol, broke the 'vessels of gold and of silver, goblets and flasks etc., and he gave them to the poor and needy'.[7]

Muhammad Sharif's three camel-loads of wine were converted to vinegar with salt. The next day, a Mughal Beg Shaikh Zain issued an edict saying that Babur had won the greater *jihad*, or *jihad-i-akbar*, with his victory over wine, and it was now left to the army to win the lesser *jihad*. No mention was made of the fact that a large part of Rana Sangha's forces were Muslims.

On Saturday, 17 March 1527, between nine and ten in the morning, Rana Sangha moved forward at the head of a magnificent host. His main allies, according to the *Akbarnama*, were Hasan Khan Mewati and Rawal Udai Singh of Nagaur with 12,000 cavalry each; Mahmud Khan Lodi, Ibrahim's brother, with 10,000 men; Nirpat Hada with 7,000; Sthirvi Kechi of Jarhal with 6,000; and Dharm Deo of Meerut. The numbers are exaggerated, but Babur was as heavily outnumbered as in Panipat. He retained, to a large degree, the Panipat battle plan. Mustafa Rumi's carts, guns and mortar played a punishing role. The flanking cavalry was deployed, but Rana Sangha's forces remained formidable on the field. Babur, riding directly into battle, ordered the royal guard (*tabinan-i khasa-i padshahi*) into action. Mustafa Rumi brought forward his chained carts, while Ustad Ali Quli's guns unleashed fire in a set-piece known as *tir u tufaq*, bow and gun. The flanking detachments played a key role but, as Stephen Dale points out, this was the first battle in which gunpowder began to exert a significant effect on the outcome.

Muhammad Sharif, the doomsdayer, had got it wrong. Babur accused the clairvoyant of deliberate mischief, castigated him as an evil wretch and sent him back to Kabul. Rana Sangha returned to Chittor, where he passed away in January 1528. Mahmud Lodi fled to fight another day. He was eventually vanquished in 1529 at Ghagra, near Chhapra in Bihar, and then found sanctuary in the court of a new Afghan leader, Sher Shah, in his capital at Sasaram.

Humayun returned to Badakhshan. In his father's fond estimate, he had now become a 'companion without equal'. In the summer of 1529, Babur was in Agra, engaged in conversation one evening with Humayun's mother when, suddenly, a brilliant star rose over the direction of Badakhshan and shone with the glory of a lucky star. Humayun returned to Agra that day.

Babur's vow of abstinence, made by a contrite warrior in search of divine assistance, soon became reason for private regret. As he wrote to his friend Khwaja Kalan:

I am distraught to have given up wine,
I do not know what to do, and I am perplexed.
Everybody regrets drinking and then takes the oath,
But I have taken the oath and now regret it.

He decided that *majun*, the sweet intoxicant that increased the pleasure of innumerable boat rides on the Jamuna or evenings in camp, would be less injurious to his spiritual health. Babur's memoirs are an eloquent testament to a temperament that balanced aristocratic inclinations with unpretentious (*bitaqalluf*) habits. Outside the contemporary demands of war and government, he was generous, good-humoured, eloquent (*shirin zaban*), congenial and capable of holding his liquor.

Music and dance were integral to the culture of the Mughal dynasty. An artist in the court of Humayun painted idealised scenes from Akbar's birth in a triptych of the mother, astrologer Maulana Chand doing his calculations and women dancing to music. The *Padshahnama*, an illustrated imperial manuscript now in the possession of the Royal Library at Windsor Castle, offers exquisite evidence of these arts during the reign of Shahjahan. Musicians play from the ramparts, and ten women dance in the courtyard while Shahjahan is weighed against gold and silver on his forty-second lunar birthday, 23 October 1632, in the presence of the Iranian ambassador Muhammad Ali Beg. The most stunning pictures are from Dara Shukoh's wedding, each face in the procession etched in classic detail. Women dance in the torchlight at the wedding of his brother Shah Shuja. In another painting, Aurangzeb is bathed in a shaft of light while women with tambourines and men with drums, kettledrums and clarinets enliven his wedding procession.[8]

Babur's memoirs become more mellifluous as he settles down to rule. He is astounded by India's acrobats. One of them spun seven rings: one on the forehead, two around the knees, and the remaining four on two fingers and two toes, with ease. Another stood on one hand, like a peacock's foot, and spun three rings on the other hand and two feet.

Babur admired the verse of Maulana Nur-al din Jami and Mir Ali Shir Navai, and learnt the poetry of Amir Khusrau Dihlavi (1253–1325), the first major Indo-Persian poet who also wrote in Hindawi. Khusrau was an astrologer in addition to being a great poet.

He marvelled at the qualities of Indian medicine. In 1502–1503, Ataka Bakhshi (the surname for doctors) healed Babur's thigh wound without applying a dressing, rubbing it with an animal's foot. His salves and herbs worked for a range of ailments, from head injury to a shattered bone.

Babur was often nostalgic for the land he had left behind, but he returned to Kabul only in a coffin. He took comfort in the successful plantation of Afghan fruits like melons and grapes in his *Hasht Bihisht,* or Garden of Eight Paradises, just outside Agra. After experiencing his first monsoon in 1526, Babur praised the rainy season, adding that the air was excellent in the cold and hot seasons as well.

Destiny had a final, and fatal, twist.

In 1530, Humayun fell perilously ill. Gulbadan Begum, who was with him as he swayed close to death, says that Humayun asked for his sisters each time he recovered consciousness. Babur was filled with dread. Humayun's mother, Maham Begum, told Babur: 'Do not be troubled about my son. You are a king; what griefs have you? You have other sons. I sorrow because I have only this one.' Babur replied: 'Maham! Although I have other sons, I love none as I love your Humayun. I crave that this cherished child may have his heart's desire and live long, and I desire the kingdom for him and not for the others, because he has not his equal in distinction.'[9] There is a painting included in Gulbadan's history of Babur praying on the floor at his son's bedside. He kept circumambulating the bed, beseeching God to take his life in exchange for that of Humayun. Humayun recovered, and Babur's health began to deteriorate. Babur died on Monday, 26 December 1530.

His doctors had a more rational explanation for the death, as recorded by both Gulbadan and Abul Fazl. Gulbadan writes: 'When they felt His Majesty's pulse, they came to the opinion that there were symptoms of the same poison as that given him by Sultan Ibrahim's mother.'[10]
The poison of Afghan enmity ran deep.

When Fate Descends, Caution Is in Vain

The powerful hold of astrology was not restricted to the Mughals. Sher Shah Suri, the Afghan who nearly aborted the Mughal dynasty before it had matured, was equally certain that his destiny was written in the stars.

Babur's military genius had converted an uncertain expedition into a kingdom. Under Humayun, the realm withered and cohesion within the family and nobility degenerated into intrigue. Humayun's younger brothers, Kamran Mirza and Hindal Mirza, abandoned their king; a hot-tempered brother-in-law, Khwaja Muazzam, was arrested for sedition. Humayun's domain shrank with the secession of Gujarat, Malwa and Bengal and disappeared when he was defeated by Farid Khan, the grandson of a horse trader Ibrahim Sherakhel, son of Hasan, a mercenary who moved through the lesser states until he settled down in the village of Juna in Sasaram, Bihar. Farid, better known as Sher Shah Suri or Sher Khan (Tiger Lord) because of his reputation for ferocity, broke from his father and joined the service of Sultan Junaid Barlas, who took him and two other Afghans to Babur. Abul Fazl notes that when Babur first saw Farid Khan, he said that the Afghan's eyes indicated trouble and sedition. Farid Khan graduated from brigandage and extortion to a regional power centre after the successful conquest of Patna in Bihar. He then turned his attention to Bengal.

Abul Fazl narrates a strange story about the ambitious Afghan. Sher Shah heard of an outstanding astrologer in the service of the raja of Orissa and summoned him to find out the propitious time for a march on Bengal. The astrologer was not allowed to leave Orissa but sent a letter to Sher Shah with a prediction: Bengal would fall but not for one year and only if he crossed the Ganges River at a particular time. This proved to be correct.

Abul Fazl calls Sher Shah a blackguard, brigand and trickster, seditious and corrupt, citing as evidence the siege of Rohtas, held by Raja Chintaman Brahman and considered impregnable. Sher Shah sent word to the raja proposing an alliance, the suggestion laden with flattery and charm. The raja made the mistake of trusting Sher Shah. The Afghan put two armed warriors in each of three hundred sedan chairs, placed maidservants around the sedans and sent them as a gift to the raja. The trick got his soldiers inside the fort, which they seized.

The Greeks could have picked up a few lessons from this ploy of the Trojan chairs. As almost everyone he dealt with discovered, a promise from Sher Shah was nebulous. Bahadur Shah of Gujarat sent him substantial funds to open an eastern front against the Mughals when he was under pressure from Humayun. Sher Shah kept the money and left Bahadur Shah to his fate.

The 19th-century Scottish scholar-administrator William Erskine describes how Sher Shah cheated the Rajput Raja Puran Mal of Chanderi in 1543 during the blockade of Raisen. The impasse was resolved by a truce in which Puran Mal agreed to surrender the fort in exchange for the safety of his family, secure passage for the 4,000-strong army and their possessions. The moment he took the fort, Sher Shah attacked the Rajput camp. The men fought until death; the women committed sati.[11]

In 1539, the naïve Humayun also believed that terms had been settled with Sher Shah, despite a warning from one of his officers, Shaikh Khalil. Complacency cost him the Battle of Buxar on 26 June 1539. As Humayun's long-serving ewer-bearer Jouher said, when fate descends, caution is in vain:

> The King would not believe the information, or that Sher Khan would be guilty of such a breach of honour or religion; but just as the sun rose next morning, the Afghans entered the rear of our encampment, made a dreadful uproar, and caused the greatest confusion both among the troops and followers.[12]

The surprise was complete. Humayun lost control and was fortunate to escape.

In 1540, Sher Shah won a comprehensive victory over Humayun at Kannauj. Abul Fazl points to the skies: the Sun had entered Cancer, which was not propitious for Humayun. Courage was impotent against the schemes of stars. Humayun's personal bravery in battle could not save him from defeat.

Mughal reliance on astrology was not unique. Arab caliphs were also believers. In 762, the second Abbasid caliph, Abu Jafar al-Mansur, laid the foundation of his new capital Baghdad at an auspicious hour determined by his leading astrologer, a Persian Muslim Naubakht Ahvazi, an Arab-Jew Mashallah and Muhammad ibn Ibrahim Fazari, who is known for a translation of a Sanskrit text on astronomy. The time was 2:40 in the afternoon of 31 July 762 because, according to Benson Bobrick,

> Jupiter at the time was rising and exactly conjunct the ascendant, which happened to be in Sagittarius, its own sign. The Sun, in trine to Jupiter, was then in its own sign, Leo, in the ninth house, in a sextile to Mars in the seventh, even as it moved away from a square to Saturn

in the sixth. This augured well for Baghdad's early glory as the seat of learning throughout the Arab world.[13]

Astrology was accepted as a credible science in Persia and Central Asia. One of the great intellects of his era, Muhammad bin Ahmad al-Biruni (born near Khiva in 973, died at Ghazni in 1048), served a range of rulers as astronomer and astrologer. In 1022, al-Biruni came to India in the entourage of Mahmud of Ghazni and stayed back to study Sanskrit and write a sociological study of the country that is still in print. His *Instruction in the Elements of the Art of Astrology*, written in 1029, became a textbook.

Astrology's disciples were spread across the known world. Marco Polo reported that there were 5,000 astrologers in Kublai Khan's court. According to Benson Bobrick:

> By the reign of Charlemagne's successor, Louis the Pious [ruler between 814 and 840], it was said that 'every Carolingian lord had his own astrological adviser'... By the 12th century, astrology had openly returned to the West enriched by a number of Arab concepts ... Latin translations of Arabic works [derived in part from the Greek] enthralled the learned community, and for five centuries thereafter, astrology pervaded European culture, just as it once pervaded that of imperial Rome ... Scarcely a figure of importance—pope, general or king—could be found without his court astrologer to advise him: Henry II and Charles IX of France; Catherine de Medicis [herself proficient in the art, which she practiced at an observatory near Paris]; the Holy Roman Emperor Charles IV; Charles V of France, and so on. When Charles V of France died in 1380, almost a tenth of his vast library was found to consist of

astrological works. At least 12 popes were also votaries of the art.[14]

Pope Sixtus IV (1471–1484), the warrior Pope Julius II (1503–1513), Leo X (1513–1521) and Paul III (1534–1549) calculated auspicious moments from the stars for important events, just as their Mughal contemporaries were doing in India. Leo X founded a chair for astrology at Sapienza. By the late Middle Ages, the universities of Paris, Padua, Milan, Bologna, Florence, Vienna and Oxford recognised astrology as an academic subject.

Leo X's favourite astrologer, Franciscus Priulus, became so depressed at his own predictions that he committed suicide. Under Pope Urban VIII (pontiff between 1623 and 1644), street vendors in Rome sold prediction sheets called *Avvisi*. In Byzantine Rome, Manuel Comnenus, who ruled between 1143 and 1180, defended astrology on the basis of natural science and scripture. His coronation chart has survived. Andronicus II made his astrologer Theodorus Metochites (1282–1328) prime minister. There are many more examples in *The Fated Sky*. Incidentally, there is a reason for 52 playing cards in a pack, often used to indicate your fortunes. There are 52 weeks in a year. The 4 suits, spades, hearts, diamonds and clubs, are based on the 4 fixed signs, Taurus, Leo, Scorpio and Aquarius. There are 13 cards in each suit. If you add up the numbers from 1 to 13, you get 91; multiply that by 4 to get 364. Add a joker to reach 365, the number of days in a year.

We owe our extensive knowledge of the true founding father of the Mughal Empire, Jalaluddin Akbar, to the authorised biographer, the scholar Abu al-Fazl or Abul Fazl, and his large team of researchers. Abul Fazl believed in *sulh-i-qul*, the philosophy of harmony that became the official policy of his master and monarch. Abul Fazl's father, Shaikh Mubarak Nagauri (1506–1593), a respected scholar and Sufi, died just before the first volume of the history was presented to the emperor in 1596 (the event is portrayed in a painting that has survived). Abul Fazl claims that he began to speak at the age of one, learnt to read and write Arabic by five and began studies with his father at seven. He immersed himself in books for ten years. He was precocious, by his own account, and honest. He acknowledges that at the age of fifteen, the higher he went on the rungs of learning, the more the intoxication of knowledge confused him.

Abul Fazl was appointed head of the translation department, which, in addition to compiling a momentous history, commissioned Abdul Rahim Khan-i-Khanan's translation of *Baburnama* from Chagatai to Persian. Abdul Rahim, a remarkable warrior-poet whose couplets are a highlight of Hindi literature, wrote two books on astrology, *Khetakautukan* and *Dwatrimshadyogavati*. Abul Fazl's brother Abul Faiz (1547–1595), proficient in Persian, Arabic and Sanskrit, joined the government as a teenager and rose to become tutor to three princes, Salim, Murad and Danyal, born in 1569, 1570 and 1572. A polyglot, he wrote poetry under the name Faizi: odes (*qasida*), four-line stanza verse (*rubai*), love poetry (*ghazal*) and elegies. In 1577, he began work on a Persian version of the epic tale of Nala and Damyanti, *Nal-o-Daman*, from the Mahabharata. By 1587, he had translated Bhaskaracharya's Sanskrit study of mathematics, *Lilavati*, written in 1150. (This is a second Bhaskara [1114–1185], from Karnataka, who also did innovative work on calculus half a millennium before Isaac Newton; the earlier Bhaskara formulated the decimal system with zero in 629.) Faizi's eclectic work ranged from *Haft Kishvar* (The Seven Zones of Earth) to a translation of Valmiki's *Yogvashista* with the assistance of Sanskrit scholars. By 1588, Faizi had been promoted to *Malik-ush-Shuara* or poet laureate.

The last horoscope recorded in *Akbarnama* is that of Danyal Mirza, Akbar's third and youngest son, born on 11 September 1572 'under the sign of Aries by the calculation of Greek metaphysicians and under the sign of Aquarius according to the sages of India, in Ajmer, the longitude of which is 111 degrees 5' and the latitude of which is 26 degrees'. God, says Abul Fazl, had bestowed upon the emperor 'a lucky-starred child and placed all souls in the world under obligation for the rising of this luminous star'. The diagrams of his horoscope are included in the history. Akbar prostrated in prayer upon hearing the news and hosted a massive celebration. When Danyal was a month old, he was on the orders of his father 'entrusted to the bosom of the *rani*, the wife of Raja Bihari Mal'.[15]

Babur ruled for two decades in Kabul and four years in Delhi; Humayun for fifteen years in Kabul and eleven in Delhi. Both Babur and Humayun would have been forgotten even by the footnotes of history but for Akbar, a reflection of the 'dazzling light ... of that Venus of fortune', the goddess Alanqoa. Eternity had celebrated Akbar's birth with a holiday in heaven and a feast on earth, for he was born at a conjunction of stars that took place but once in a thousand years, according to his faithful chronicler. His life was evidence that the stars were correct.

Acknowledgements

Thank You, My Friends

FRIENDS, GOES THE ADAGE, are those who eat together, travel together and face danger together. I hope they also read your books.

Writing is never easy. This book was particularly difficult, although so much factual material was hidden in plain sight within primary sources. About two-thirds of the first volume of Abul Fazl's *Akbarnama* is a narrative of horoscopes and differences of interpretation between astrologers. It is amazing that little attention was paid to personal belief, whose roots lay in pre-Islamic culture. Contemporary texts confirm that while emperors had different characters and value systems, faith in astrology did not abate. The last word is not the last event in the creation of a book. Delivery needs expert editorial gynaecologists at the publishing house. My debt to my editor and friend Paul Vinay Kumar is immense. His knowledge and tact were essential in the nurture of the process. We always had the gentle advice of our common friend Prabir Bhambal, a sage of the Indian book industry. My gratitude also to Rahul Srivastava, who now heads Bloomsbury India, for the calm and quiet with which he took vital decisions. Thanks once again to Rajiv Beri, his predecessor, who brought me into the Bloomsbury fold.

The love and care of one's family is an indescribable blessing, from siblings in distant cities to the immediate constellation: Mallika, heart, head and lodestar; Mukulika and Carl Nordenberg; Shanta and Prayaag; and the infinite joy of three grandchildren, Julian, Kayan and Agastya. My sister, Ghazala, and brother-in-law, Lokesh Sharma, have given me the love that enhances life.

I can proudly assert that Ajit Doval and Nripendra Mishra have given me the affection of elder brothers; words do not suffice to convey my feelings towards them. Sunil Gujral is older but not elder, so let's settle for twin. Sunil and Geeta have been dearest friends for more years than we want to reveal, as has Rani Mitra. There are other old and valued friends: Subhash Chandra for over three decades; Arif Vazirally, Manjushri and S.M. Basu from College Street in the 1960s; and Tapan Chaki from Park Street in the 1970s.

Alas, the list becomes shorter with every book, but death is the final passage to the unknown. It has been my immense good fortune that the perimeters of brotherhood have kept growing: the consummate editor S. Prasannarajan; the immaculate Raian Karanjawala, whose perennial smile sits easily with a brilliant mind and generous heart; twinkle-eyed Devesh Kumar, a boon companion; and the irrepressibly generous Jamshed Zaidi. There are no hierarchies among friends. Each friend is special: in Delhi, Ashok Swaroop (we share a birthday and a world view), Ashok Mittal, Abhijit Halder, Anil Rajput, Naresh Gujral, Rajeev Chandrasekhar, Awanish Dwivedi, Akash Chopra, Gunu and Ranjan Bhattacharya, Gugu Singh, Joyeeta Basu, Kumkum Chadha, Mukhtar Abbas Naqvi, Maulana Mahmood Madani, Nitin Gokhale, Naved Qureshi, Partha Bhattacharya, Preet Malik, Praveen Saini, Ronen Sen, Anil Bhasin, Rajni and Shyam Bajpai, Ranjan Mukherjee, Rajiv Kapoor, Dr Siddhartha Mehta, Sandeep Kapur and Veenu Sandal. It has been a pleasure to know and admire Shobhana Bhartiya for more than four decades. As for that irrepressible man for all seasons, Rajeev Shukla, it seems surprising that I have known him for over four decades, given that he does not know how to age. It has been a privilege to befriend Rajiv Nayar, proud lawyer-son of a great journalist-author-father, Kuldip Nayar. Ram Madhav somehow finds time for a stream of books and a think-tank, India Foundation.

From lands outside Delhi: Satish Gupta and Y.S. Chowdary are warm and constant friends, as are Gopal Hosur and Vishveswar Bhat from Bengaluru; Chuti Ray (I miss Utpal), Tayyab Khan and K.K. Bhaumik from Kolkata; Kiran Vadodaria from Ahmedabad; and E.M. Haridas from Kochi. I do not know quite where to place Rahul Bhatia geographically, since he lives so often in the air. Mohandas Pai is firmly grounded in Bengaluru, but his multinational brain is always awash with ideas.

The Goa gang began as a quad and developed organically into a squad: Apurva and Archana Jasraj, Charu and Pankaj Mehra, Rose and Omer Haider, Rina and Kishore Rao, Apu and Shashi Srivastava, Gaurapriya and Atul Pai Kane, Ralph de Sousa and Alok Kumar.

An eleventh book resurrects memories of the first, published by Penguin in 1985. That was hard work too, and thank you, Shekhar Bhatia, my colleague in the *Telegraph*, whose quiet command of the office enabled me to find time for *India: The Siege Within* and *Nehru: The Making of India*. Thank you again, Shekhar. My abiding gratitude to Aveek Sarkar: we faced danger together, no doubt about that—the danger of bringing to life radical concepts in media that challenged the establishment in both magazines and newspapers. We have shared a warm, if continual rather than continuous, relationship that has survived the pitfalls of geography and the inevitable swerve into different directions.

To every one of my friends, wherever you are, land, seaside or sky, thank you from an overwhelmed heart.

Notes

PREFACE: BELIEF, BEHAVIOUR, DESTINY

1 *The Caliph's Splendor: Islam and the West in the Golden Age of Baghdad*, Benson Bobrick, Simon & Schuster, 2012, page 15.
2 *The Indian Muslims*, Mohammad Mujeeb, Munshiram Manoharlal Publishers, reprint 2017, page 379.
3 *The Indian Muslims*, page 230; the quotation is from Ziyauddin Barani's *Tarikh-i-Firuz Shahi*
4 *History of Tipu Sultan*, Mohibbul Hasan, The Bibliophile Ltd, 1951.
5 *Episodes in the Life of Akbar: Contemporary Records and Reminiscences*, Shireen Moosvi, National Book Trust, page 12.

CHAPTER 1 BIRTH OF AN EMPIRE: THE STARTLING MYSTERY OF A HIDEOUS FACE

1 *The History of Akbar, or Akbarnama*, Abul Fazl, Vol. 1, page 81, edited and translated by Wheeler M. Thackston, Murty Classical Library, Harvard University Press; henceforth *Akbarnama*.
2 *Akbarnama*, Vol. 1, pages 215, 217.
3 *Akbarnama*, Vol. 1, page 239.

CHAPTER 2 THE TABLET OF DIVINE SECRETS

1 *The History of Akbar, or Akbarnama*, Abul Fazl, Vol. 1, edited and translated by Wheeler M. Thackston, Murty Classical Library of India, Harvard University Press, page 75. 'There is no choice before the chosen,' wrote Shaikh Abul Fazl ibn Mubarak Allami to justify a lifetime of service to Abul-Fath Jalaluddin Muhammad Akbar Padishah. The courtier-historian served the emperor from 1574 till his assassination on the orders of Salim

(later Jahangir) in 1602. This was neither the inertia of fatalism nor the weakness of indecision on Abul Fazl's part. It was a scholar's recognition of the best option before him. He began his career as a scribe in the department of diplomatic correspondence, a high art form, and rose to become one of the 'nine jewels' in the court of a great king.

Born on 14 January 1551, during the interregnum in Mughal rule, Abul Fazl was a son of the renowned theologian Shaikh Mubarak, who wanted him to become an academic in his influential Sufi seminary in Agra. By the age of fifteen, Abul Fazl had studied all the existing branches of the sciences known as *hikami, naqali, maqul* and *manqul* (difficult knowledge, revelations from holy books, philosophy and transcription, respectively). But the twenty-three-year-old Abul Fazl preferred 'imperial service, which is the elixir of the intelligent' (*The History of Akbar, or Akbarnama*, Vol. 3). All kings, however, are not the elixir of the intelligent; some are dull, many are whimsical and others are tyrannical. Abul Fazl believed he was fortunate to have served a monarch who was recognised in his lifetime as a great ruler. For a bureaucrat with an academic inclination, no honour could be higher than the commission to write a history of this monarch's reign with the help of a team of researchers.

He establishes his academic credentials in the opening pages of this multi-volume work:

> Consequently I began to exert myself to the utmost to gather narratives and accounts of the events in His Majesty's life, and I spent a long time questioning members of the court and intimates of this illustrious family—both truthful and alert elders and honest and aware youths—and reducing their accounts to writing. Imperial decrees were dispatched to all parts of the realm, to some whose truthfulness, by virtue of long service, was above suspicion and to others who were questionable, asking them to send to the imperial court copies of their journals and memoirs ... Based on that imperial edict, which is a translation of divine decree, as thoughts emerged from the recesses of my mind, I began to write a rough draft free of rhetorical embellishment ... Much effort was expended to obtain either the originals or copies of most imperial decrees ... Much labour also went into collecting the many reports

that nobles and officials had written describing events and incidents throughout the realm, and with their verification my mind, which is difficult to please, was put at ease. (*Akbarnama*, Vol. 1, pages 33, 35)

In 1589, the emperor, then at the height of his power and fame, visited Abul Fazl's home to console him on the death of his mother and said:

> If the people of this world lived for ever and did not only once die, kind friends would not be required to direct their hearts to trust in God and resignation to His will; but no one lives long in the caravanserai of the world, and hence the afflicted do well to accept consolation. (*Ain-i-Akbari*, Vol. 1, translated by H. Blochmann, Low Price Publications, page xxxix)

2 *Akbarnama*, Vol. 1, page 95.
3 *Akbarnama*, page 103.
4 The constellation of Leo consisted of a segment of the zodiac that had moved into space originally occupied by Virgo at the time of Akbar's birth; Virgo had shifted to that extent into Libra. Modern research has established that the rate of the precession of the equinoxes is 1 degree in 72 years, making a complete revolution in about 26,000 years. *Akbarnama*, Vol. 1, page 582.
5 *Humayunnama: The History of Humayun*, Gulbadan Begum, translated by Annette Beveridge, Idarah-i Adabiyat-i Delli, page 158.
6 *Akbarnama*.
7 *Akbarnama*, Vol. 1, pages 509, 511, 513.
8 *A History of India under the Two First Sovereigns of the House of Taimur, India under Baber and Humayun*, Irish University Press, 1854, Vol. 2, pages 530, 531.
9 Humayun believed that he had been defeated by deceit, since terms between him and his adversary Sher Shah, the then ruler of Bengal, had been settled after the Battle of Chausa on the Ganges at Buxar on 26 June 1539. But Sher Shah had merely tested the character of his target and prepared for the next battle, which would make him the king of north India. Humayun was warned about him by one of his officers, Shaikh Khalil, but as Humayun's long-serving ewer-bearer, Jouher, notes ruefully, when fate descends, caution is in vain:

> The King would not believe the information, or that Sher Khan would be guilty of such a breach of honour or religion; but just as the sun rose the next morning, the Afghans entered the rear of our encampment, made a dreadful uproar, and caused the greatest confusion both among the troops and followers. (*Jouher*, page 18)

The surprise was complete. Humayun lost control of the kingdom and was fortunate to escape. Jouher narrates the story of the water-carrier who saved a wounded Humayun's life during his escape from Chausa in 1539. Such was Humayun's plight in that battle that Mir Bejke, celebrated for his valour, and his sons Gurk Ali and Tetta Beg, who carried the king's double-barrelled gun and spear, refused to protect Humayun from a charging war elephant. Further, an enemy archer wounded Humayun in the arm, and his troops would not obey orders. It represented a collapse of leadership. A loyal follower caught the bridle of his horse and said, 'There is no time to be lost; when your friends forsake you, flight is the only option.' As if this were not enough, Humayun's horse sank as they were crossing the river. Jouher writes:

> On seeing this event a water carrier who had distended his leathern bag (*musek*) with air, offered it to His Majesty, who by means of the bag swam the river (Karamnasa). On reaching the northern bank he asked the man his name; he said, 'Nizam'. The king replied, 'I will make your name as celebrated as that of Nizam-addyu-Aulia (the celebrated sufi saint of Delhi Nizamuddin Auliya), and you shall sit on my throne.' (*Tezkereh Al Vakiat*, translated by Major Charles Stewart, Gyan Publishing House, first published 1832, pages 18, 19)

Jouher writes that Humayun made the water-carrier king for two hours; Gulbadan believes it was for two days. Humayun's brother Kamran, disgusted, wondered at this kind of frivolity when the threat from Sher Khan was palpable. Servants, he said, should receive rewards, not power.

10 *Akbarnama*, Vol. 1, page 47.
11 *Humayunnama*, page 145.
12 *Akbarnama*, Vol. 1, pages 53, 65.
13 *Akbarnama*, Vol. 1, page 57.

The goddess Alanqoa inspired honour for women, which was unusual in that age. Jack Weatherford, who held an honorary position at Chinggis Khaan University in Mongolia in addition to his academic duties as the DeWitt Wallace Chair of Anthropology in Minnesota, noted that the term *khatun*, which has entered more than one language, conveys regal, unbreakable strength combined with grace and beauty in the Queen-Hero, so much so that many men have been given names like Khatun Temur ('Queen Iron').

> The Mongols recognized the role of the father as the provider of the sperm, which created the bones of a new child, but the mother gave meat and blood. Thus, male lineages became known as yas, meaning 'bone of the father', while the larger kinship system was known as the urug, meaning 'the womb'. Genghis Khan gave his royal family the name Altan Urug, the Golden Womb.

Weatherford spelt Alanqoa as Alan Goa, 'from whom all Mongol clans traced descent'. The male and female spiritual balance was the essence of Mongol belief; Genghis Khan attributed his success to this: 'While the Eternal Blue Sky offered inspiration, only the Mother Earth could offer success and fulfilment of the endeavor.' (*The Secret History of the Mongol Queens*, Broadway Paperbacks, New York, pages 38, 198). In 2007, Weatherford was honoured with the Order of the Polar Star, the highest award for service in Mongolia.

14 *Humayunnama*, pages 147–151.
15 *Humayunnama*, pages 147–151; *Akbarnama*, Vol. 1, page 535.
16 *Akbarnama*, Vol. 1, page 49.
17 *Akbarnama*, Vol. 1, page 555.
18 *Jouher*, pages 36–51.

The dangers of bar conversation while indulging in potent arrack should never be underestimated, or perhaps overestimated. Jouher tells an amusing story of the time Humayun was in Jun, helping Rana Prasad expand his domain:

> During the period that the King laid siege to Sehwan, it was observed that a soldier in the fort made so good use of his musquet [sic] that he never failed to hit some of our people; on which his Majesty [Humayun] said, 'I hope I shall one day get hold of that fellow'; he also said, 'I wish I

could catch the person who took the sword from under my head, and drew it halfway out of the scabbard.' By chance it now happened that these two men were both in Jun when we took it; and having met in an arrack shop were boasting of their feats of bravery; their conversation having been overheard, they were seized and brought before the King, who, after inquiry, ordered the musqueteer to be put to death, but forgave the thief, and made him a handsome present.

One reason why Humayun found support even when seemingly lost in a maze was his persistent belief that destiny was on his side. Shah Hussain, unable to face the alliance of Humayun and Rana Prasad in Sindh, tried to buy off the latter with costly presents. The Rana showed them to Humayun, who suggested that they be placed on a dog and sent back to Shah Hussain. Hussain was more successful in managing the defection of a Mughal Chieftain, Tersh Beg. Writes Jouher:

> This news greatly affected the King, and he said, 'May a speedy death overtake him!' and it really so happened that the arrow of Fate did suddenly strike him ... One of his slaves, enraged by injustice, killed Tersh Beg. Upon hearing this, 'the people all declared that the King was a worker of miracles'.

19 *Akbarnama*, Vol. 1, page 53.
20 *Humayunnama*, page 157.
21 *Jouher*, page 44.
22 *Sher Shah Suri 1540–1545*, Dr Hussain Khan, Ferozsons (Pvt.) Ltd, pages 155, 162.
23 *Jouher*, page 26.
24 *Akbarnama*, Vol. 1, page 149.
25 *Akbarnama*, Vol. 2, page 19.
26 *Akbarnama*, Vol. 2, pages 17, 19.
27 *Akbarnama*, Vol. 1, page 143.
28 *Jouher*, pages 54–79
29 *Jouher*, page 54.
30 *Jouher*, page 61.
31 Jouher, who was among the five persons who accompanied their king on the visit to the tomb of Imam Ali ibn Musa al-Rida, the eighth Imam of the Twelver Shias, narrates how Humayun handled the situation when the doorkeeper blocked

their entry by claiming that it was impossible to unlock the chain on the door. Humayun stepped back and prayed: 'O Imam, every person who has ever offered up his vows at your shrine has obtained the object of his wishes; your slave has also come with similar hopes to your tomb, in expectation of succeeding in his request.' The doorkeeper relented. Humayun walked around the shrine, and then sat down to read the Quran. Before he left, he suspended one of his bows there as an offering. News of this homage was communicated to Shah Tahmasp. 'Soon after this another letter arrived from the sovereign of Persia, inviting the King to proceed to Cazvin' (*Jouher*, pages 60, 61). Before he returned to Afghanistan in the winter of 1545, Humayun visited Tabriz to see its famous astrolabes, globes and astronomical instruments, hoping to satisfy his 'intense' interest in astronomy (*Akbarnama*, Vol. 2, pages 89, 91).

32 *Jouher*, page 62.
33 Major Charles Stewart writes about the cap:
   Taj, properly Taji Hyder, a tiara of crimson silk, wrought with gold, and richly ornamented with jewels, worn by the kings of Persia, so called from Hyder, the father of Shah Ismael, by whom it was first adopted. It is of a high conical shape, and divided into twelve segments, in honour of the twelve Imams from whom he claimed descent. In the course of time the Persian officers and soldiers were ordered to wear caps of this pattern, from which they were nicknamed by the Turks Kuzel Bash, red heads. (*Jouher*, page 64)
34 *Jouher*, page 70.
35 *Jouher*, page 66.
36 *Akbarnama*, Vol 2, page 83.
37 *Akbarnama*, Vol. 2, page 83.
38 *India under Baber and Humayun*, Vol. 2, William Erskine, Irish University Press, page 295.
39 *Travels in the Mogul Empire AD 1656–1668*, Francois Bernier, S. Chand & Co., Delhi, 1968, page 152.
40 *Akbarnama*, Vol 2, page 89.
41 *Akbarnama*, Vol. 2, page 107.
42 *Akbarnama*, Vol. 2, page 111.

43 *Akbarnama*, Vol. 2, page 117.
44 *Akbarnama*, Vol. 2, page 133.
45 *Akbarnama*, Vol. 2, page 153.
46 *Jouher*, Page 83.
47 *Akbarnama*.
48 *Akbarnama*, Vol. 2, pages 125, 127.
49 *Akbarnama*, Vol. 2, page 211.
50 *Akbarnama*, Vol. 2, pages 209, 211, 213, 219.
51 *Humayunnama*, pages 183, 184.
52 *Akbarnama*, Vol. 2, page 221.
53 *Jouher*, page 90.
54 *Humayunnama*, page 201.
55 *Jouher*, page 106.
56 *Akbarnama*, Vol. 2, page 227.
57 *Akbarnama*, Vol. 2, page 19.
58 *Tarikh-i Akbari*; translated by Tasneem Ahmad, 1993.
59 *Akbarnama*, Vol. 2, page 421.
60 *Akbarnama*, Vol. 2, pages 433, 463.
61 *Akbarnama*, Vol. 2, pages 481–493.
62 *Akbarnama*, Vol 2, pages 497, 499.
63 *Akbarnama*, Vol. 2, page 501.

Construction on Humayun's Tomb near the city of Dinpanah in Delhi began in 1564, when Akbar was just twenty-two years old, under the supervision of Hajji Begum, Humayun's widow. The principal gateway of the first great Mughal monument is to the west, 'the walls flanking the arch of the doorway have been placed at an angle', which gives 'the whole gateway the appearance of a screen lowered from heaven, with an opening through which one sees the mausoleum as a vision of grace and beauty'. Prof. Mujeeb writes in an eloquent passage:

> There is something definitely Persian about this mausoleum—the large, bulbous dome, the recessed alcoves on each of the four sides, which seem to take away all the impression of weight and mass, the arrangement of rooms and corridors around the tomb chamber. There is also something definitely Indian Muslim about it—the restrained but striking use of marble inlay for

ornamentation, and the domed kiosks at the corners of the main structure, which give it a fluid skyline. But the blending of the foreign and indigenous elements is so perfect, the proportions of all the parts so harmonious, that any analysis of its design or embellishment seems pedantic.

The great scholar and academic icon also understands that this was a son's homage to his father:

[Humayun's] tomb is much greater than he, because it is an idealization of his person and his qualities by someone who loved him. Culturally, the value of Humayun's tomb is magnified a thousandfold by this love, which has here demonstrated its power to create out of wrecked plans, fugitive living, deception and disaster an image of strength and grace and poetic lucidity. (*The Indian Muslims*, page 338)

Akbar was one of history's great builders, although his grandson's monument symbolising love, the Taj Mahal in Agra, is far better known than the nearby fort built by Akbar, called Fatehpur Sikri, the city framed around an intellectual concept more than living space. Akbar built more than 500 edifices, mainly in red stone, using artisans from all over his empire, inspired by the architectural styles of Bengal and Gujarat.

64 *Akbarnama*, Vol. 3, pages 19–43.
65 *Akbarnama*, Vol. 2, pages 427, 429.
66 *Akbarnama*, Vol. 3, pages 59, 61.
67 *Akbarnama*, Vol. 3, page 87.
68 *Akbarnama*, Vol. 3, pages 83–93.
69 *Akbarnama*, Vol. 3, page 95.
70 *Akbarnama*, Vol. 3, page 97, 99.
71 *Akbarnama*, Vol. 3, pages 99, 101.
72 *Akbarnama*, Vol. 2, page 431.
73 *Akbarnama*, Vol. 3, pages 109, 111, 113, 127.
74 *Akbarnama*, Vol. 3, page 107–127.
75 *Akbarnama*, Vol. 3, pages 109, 111, 113, 127.
76 *Akbarnama*, Vol. 3, pages 109, 111, 113, 127.
77 *Akbarnama*, Vol. 3, pages 109, 111, 113, 127.
78 *Akbarnama*, Vol. 3, pages 109, 111, 113, 127.
79 *Akbarnama*, Vol. 3, page 135.
80 *Akbarnama*, Vol. 3, page 135.

81 *Akbarnama*, Vol 3, page 107.

CHAPTER 3 AKBAR: SUN OF FELICITY AND FORTUNE

1 *Akbarnama*, Vol. 5, pages 525, 527.
2 The six directions are *puratthima-disa* (east), *dakkhina-disa* (south), *pacchima-disa* (west), *uttarima-disa* (north), *hetthima-disa* (nadir) and *uparima-disa* (zenith).
3 *Akbarnama*, Vol. 3, pages 11, 19, 21.
4 *Akbarnama*, Vol. 3, pages 23, 25, 27.
5 *Akbarnama*, Vol. 3, page ix, preface.
6 *Culture of Encounters: Sanskrit at the Mughal Court*, Audrey Truschke, Allen Lane, page 38.
Abul Fazl attributes four texts of Sanskrit astronomy to divine origin (*Brahma Siddhanta, Surya Siddhanta, Soma Siddhanta* and *Brihaspati Siddhanta*) and five to human intellect (*Garg Siddhanta, Narada Siddhanta, Paras Siddhanta, Paulis Siddhanta* and *Vasishtha Siddhanta*).
7 His exact forecast said:

> Since the regent of the cusp of the seventh house is Saturn, which is at exaltation, those taken in marriage in the Native's early youth will be from the ruling families of India. Since Saturn is the second house, it is indicative of the fact that these chaste ladies will come from tribute-paying rulers who keep the treasury full. Since the Part of Intimacy and Affection is in this house, it indicates much pleasure in intimacy and affection, particularly since the Part of Intimacy is in Pisces, which is the house of Jupiter and Venus's exaltation. (*Akbarnama*, Vol. 1, pages 129, 131)

8 Khwaja Muinuddin Hasan Chishti (1141–1236), known as Gharib Nawaz ('Benefactor of the Poor'), was a mystic from Seistan, in Persia, who founded the Chishti order in India, which became a dominant influence on Indian Islam. His most famous disciples are Nizamuddin Auliya and the poet-disciple Amir Khusrau, both buried at Nizamuddin in Delhi. Gharib Nawaz is believed to have been blessed with *Karamat* or marvels like clairvoyance. The devotional music he inspired diversified into many forms including the qawwali, a popular lyrical song that celebrates adoration.

9 *Akbarnama*, Vol. 3, page 471.
10 *Akbarnama*, Vol. 3, page 477.
11 *Akbarnama*, Vol. 3, pages 479, 481.
12 *Akbarnama*, Vol. 3, page 63.
13 *Ain-i-Akbari*, Vol. 1, pages 57, 58.
14 *Akbarnama*, Vol. 4, pages 3, 5.
15 *Ain-i-Akbari*, Vol. 1, page 198.
16 *Akbarnama*, Vol. 3, page 587.
17 *Ain-i-Akbari*, Vol. 1, pages 193, 215.
18 A good instance of upward mobility in the Mughal hierarchy is the career of Rai Pitr Das, who began as an accountant in the emperor's elephant stables. He came to attention in 1568 when he distinguished himself in the battle of Chittor. He was appointed joint diwan of Bengal in 1580. In 1586, he became diwan of Bihar and was sent to Kabul in 1599. When Abul Fazl was murdered on the instructions of Salim, Akbar ordered Pitr Das to hunt the assassin, Bir Singh. The next year, Akbar raised his rank to commander of 5,000 and gave him the title of Raja Bikramjit. Jahangir made him Mir Atish (head of artillery) with 3,000 gun carts and 50,000 men under his command (*Ain-i-Akbari*, Vol. 2, pages 523, 524). The acquisition of Panna between 1563 and 1564 is an instance of a policy that sought to be both expansionist and accommodative. Panna had provoked the empire by giving sanctuary to a rebel, Ghazi Khan Tannuri. Panna's Ram Chand, one of the 'renowned rajas of Hindustan', was offered a deal: he could 'pay tribute to the Protected Realm', hand over Ghazi Khan and enjoy 'safety and security'. Raja Ram chose war, lost and holed up in Bandho Fort, 'the greatest stronghold of his territory'. Intermediaries negotiated a deal. Ram Chand 'kissed the imperial ground' and continued to rule his fief as part of the empire. (*Akbarnama*, Vol. 3, pages 563, 565)
19 *Akbarnama*, Vol. 5, pages 517, 519, 521.
20 *The Indian Muslims*, pages 262, 360, 361.
21 *Akbarnama*, Vol. 4, page 177.
22 *Akbarnama*, Vol. 6, page 553.
23 *Akbarnama*, Vol. V, page 91.
24 *Tuzuk-i-Jahangiri*, translated by Alexander Rogers, edited by Henry Beveridge, Atlantic, Vol. 1, page 37.

25 *The Emperor Jahangir*, Lisa Balabanlilar, pages 83, 84.
26 *Akbarnama*, Vol. 6, page 13.
27 *Akbarnama*, Vol. 6, pages 88, 89, 103, 129, 137.
28 Persian terms are used. Venus is Zohra, the Sun is Shams, the Moon is Qamar, Mars is Bahram and the Dragon's Head is Anabikazon. The Dragon's Tail is Dhanab. A third part of a sign is Darijan. The period during which a planet exerts its maximum influence is Sharaf; 180 degrees opposite to the exaltation is Suqut. One-seventh of a division is Haftbahr, and a ninth division of a sign is Nubahr. Shirazi's calculations are meticulous:

> The cusp of the ascendant in this royal horoscope, which is a transcript of the revolutions of the fixed stars and planets, lies at 28 degrees 36' Leo, and it has occurred with angles in fixed signs. Since the cusp of this felicitous ascendant is in the Sun's house, no planet rules its house. It is the term of Mars; its lord of triplicity is Jupiter in partnership with the Sun and the attendance of Saturn; it is the face and darijan of Mars; the nubahr of Jupiter; the adarjan and haftbahr of Mars; the dodecatemory of the Moon; and the detriment of Saturn. It is a masculine degree, lucid and devoid of infelicity. Dominant over this ascendant is the Sun, with an intent to form an alliance with Saturn. Venus is at 26 degrees 23' 37" Virgo. (*Akbarnama*, Vol. 1, page 109)

29 *Akbarnama*, Vol. 1, page 105.
30 *Episodes in the Life of Akbar: Contemporary Records and Reminiscences*, Shireen Moosvi, National Book Trust, pages 14, 15. Moosvi's source is *Zubdatut Tawarikh*, a history written by Nurul Haqq Dihlawi, commissioned by Shaikh Farid Bukhari, who served as Mir Bakhsi under Akbar and Jahangir. Shireen Moosvi was teaching at Aligarh Muslim University when this charming collection of vignettes was published.
31 *Ain-i-Akbari*, page 207.
32 *Ain-i-Akbari*, Vol. 1, page 194.
33 Freedom: The Jesuits, seeking freedom of religion in Mughal India, were at that very time inflicting the horrors of the Inquisition in God, while the order became a battering ram of Spanish and Portuguese cruelty towards Jews and Muslims.
34 *On Hinduism*, Wendy Doniger, Aleph, pages 15, 133.
35 *Akbarnama*, Vol. 2, page 50.

36 *Ain-i-Akbari*, Vol. 1, pages 50, 51, 192, 193.
37 *The Indian Muslims*, pages 262, 263, 264.
38 *Ain-i-Akbari*, Vol. 1, pages 181, 182.
39 *The Indian Muslims*, pages 260, 261.
40 The orthodox accused Akbar of heresy. His foster brother Khan-i-Azam Mirza Aziz Koka (Koka is an abbreviated form of Kukaldash or foster-brother in Turkish), veered away from him after the ban on beef in 1591. 'Between me and Aziz is a river of milk which I cannot cross,' Akbar used to say. But that river went dry. Aziz Koka began to sneer at the brothers Abul Faizi and Abul Fazl, saying they thought they were Hazrat Usman and Imam Ali (two of the first four caliphs) of a new faith. Around 1595, Aziz sidestepped a summons by the emperor and, in protest against 'religious innovations', left for Portuguese Diu on the pretext of conquest. He boarded a Portuguese ship to Arabia for Hajj from Balawal near Somnath, accompanied by six sons, six daughters and a hundred attendants. He was cured of excessive piety by touts in the holy land. According to the *Ain-i-Akbari*:

> Aziz spent a great deal of money in Makkah; in fact, he was so 'fleeced' that his attachment to Islam was much cooled down; and being assured of Akbar's good wishes for his welfare, he embarked for India, landed again at Balawal, and joined Akbar in the beginning of 1003 [Al Hijri].

He was appointed governor of Bihar. Koka was to play a losing part in the politics of succession. He supported his son-in-law Khusrau against Jahangir. Jahangir produced a letter written by Aziz Koka to Raja Ali Khan of Khandesh in which the late emperor Akbar had been disparaged. Koka acknowledged its veracity and was sent to prison but was released two years later. Koka's coarse wit is unrepeatable half a millennium later (*Ain-i Akbari*, Vol. 1, pages 342–346).
41 *Akbarnama*, Vol. 5, page 219.
42 *Akbarnama*, Vol. 5, page 663; *Ain-i Akbari*, pages 318, 319.
43 *Ain-i-Akbari*, pages 113, 114, 115; *Akbarnama*, Vol. 1, pages 567, 569.
44 *Akbarnama*, Vol. 3, pages 283–289, 303, 305, 307.

45 *Akbarnama*, Vol 1, page 87, 101, 103.

CHAPTER 4 JAHANGIR: NO ONE IS A RELATION TO THE KING

1 *The Emperor Jahangir: Power and Kingship in Mughal India*, Lisa Balabanlilar, I.B. Tauris, page 37.
2 *The Tuzuk-i-Jahangiri; Or, Memoirs Of Jahangir, From the First to the Twelfth Year of His Reign*, translated by Alexander Rogers, edited by Henry Beveridge, Atlantic Publishers & Distributors, first published in 1909, Vol. 1, page 1.
3 *Akbarnama*, Abul Fazl, Vol. 4, edited and translated by Wheeler M. Thackston, Murty Classical Library of India, Harvard University Press, pages 459, 461, 463; the horoscopes are reproduced.
4 *Akbarnama*, Vol. 4, pages 431, 433.
5 *Tuzuk*, Vol. 1, page 1.
6 *Akbarnama*, Vol. 4, pages 441, 443.
7 Abul Fazl gets grouchy at this point: 'Now that I am so occupied day and night with service to the emperor that it is impossible to carry out my tasks satisfactorily, where would I find the time to do anything else?' Jahangir was a young man when this official history was being written, so this seems evidence of distance between Abul Fazl and the prince. Fazl showed more enthusiasm when recording the birth charts of Salim's brothers.
8 *Tuzuk*, Vol. 2, pages 76, 77.
9 *Akbarnama*, Vol. 4, pages 459, 463, 467, 517, 519, 521.
10 *Tuzuk*, Vol. 1, page 85.
11 *Tuzuk*, Vol. 1, page 34, 35.
12 *Akbarnama*, Vol. 4, pages 451, 457, 471.
13 *Akbarnama*, Vol. 5, page 227.
14 *Akbarnama*, Vol. 6, pages 123–124.
15 *Akbarnama*, Vol. 6, page 491.
16 *The Princes of the Mughal Empire, 1504–1719*, Munis D. Faruqi, Cambridge University Press, page 189.
17 *Tuzuk*, Vol. 1, page 23. But Jahangir had something good to say about Hemu, who nearly aborted the Mughal Empire. Hemu, he writes, was a remarkable strategist who 'collected a wonderful force after King Humayun's death, with a stud of elephants such as no ruler of Hindustan had at that time' and defeated the Mughals to take Delhi. He cites 'pride' as

the reason for Hemu's defeat at Panipat on 5 November 1556 although he had '30,000 brave fighting horsemen' against the 4,000 or 5,000 with Akbar.
18 *The Emperor Jahangir,* page 20.
19 *Tuzuk,* Vol. 1, page 2.
20 *Tuzuk,* Vol. 1, page 36.
21 *Tuzuk,* Vol. 1, page 140.
22 *Tuzuk,* Vol. 1, pages 4–10.
23 *Tuzuk,* Vol. 2, pages 6, 7.
24 *Tuzuk,* Vol. 1, pages 237, 239.
25 *Culture of Encounters,* page 237.
26 *Tuzuk,* Vol. 2, pages 161, 162.
27 *Tuzuk,* Vol. 2, pages 161, 162.
28 *Tuzuk,* Vol. 2, pages 161–162.
29 *Tuzuk,* Vol. 2, page 169.
30 *Tuzuk,* Vol. 2, page 211.
31 *Tuzuk,* Vol. 2, pages 214, 215.
32 *Tuzuk,* Vol. 2, pages 227, 228.
33 *Tuzuk,* Vol. 2, page 249.
34 *The Princes of the Mughal Empire,* page 83.
35 *The Emperor Jahangir,* pages 29, 30.
36 *Tuzuk,* Vol. 1, page 54.
37 *Tuzuk,* Vol. 1, page 12.
38 *Tuzuk,* Vol. 1, pages 50, 51.
39 *Tuzuk,* Vol. 1, pages 65.
40 *Tuzuk,* Vol. 1, pages 65, 66.
41 *Tuzuk,* Vol. 2, page 106.
42 Even a saint could not escape tragic consequences. The Sikh patriarch Guru Arjun Singh, according to Jahangir's version, had blessed and financed Khusrau. In what would evolve into a serious rupture with the rising Sikh community, the Guru was imprisoned and then martyred when he refused to pay a fine.
43 *Tuzuk,* Vol. 1, page 66.
44 *Ain-i-Akbari,* page 345.
45 *Tuzuk,* Vol. 1, page 251.
46 *Tuzuk,* Vol. 1, page 62.
47 *Tuzuk,* Vol. 1, page 314.
48 *The Indian Muslims,* page 267.
49 *The Emperor Jahangir,* page 58.

50 *Tuzuk*, Vol. 1, page 116.
51 *Tuzuk*, Vol. 1, pages 163, 164, 165.
52 *The Princes of the Mughal Empire*, page 35.
53 *Tuzuk*, Vol. 1, pages 58, 59.
54 *Tuzuk*, Vol. 1, page 36.
55 *Tuzuk*, Vol. 1, page 15.
56 *Tuzuk*, Vol. 1, page 134.
57 *Ain-i-Akbari*, Vol. 1, page 363.
58 There is no mention of Birbal's progeny. We can gauge the degree of Akbar's affection for Birbal by this paragraph:
    The raja was one of the emperor's most intimate confidants, and by imperial command palaces of stone had been constructed for him. When they were finished he requested a visit by the emperor ... [on 27 January 1583, Birbal] gave a marvellous banquet and was the object of much imperial favour. (*Akbarnama*, Vol. 6, page 501)
59 *Tuzuk*, Vol. 1, page 123.
60 *Tuzuk*, Vol. 1, page 134.
61 *The Emperor Jahangir*, page 23.
62 *Tuzuk*, Vol. 1, page 214.
63 *Tuzuk*, Vol. 2, page 1.
64 *Tuzuk*, Vol. 2, pages 1, 2, 26, 27.
65 *Tuzuk*, Vol. 2, page 57.
66 *Tuzuk*, Vol. 2, page 112.
67 *Tuzuk*, Vol. 2, page 127.
68 *Tuzuk*, Vol. 2, pages 112–114, 242.
69 *Culture of Encounters*, page 266.
70 *Tuzuk*, Vol. 2, pages 112, 113, 114.
71 *Tuzuk*, Vol. 1, pages 248, 249, 250.
72 *Tuzuk*, Vol. 2, page 36.
73 *Tuzuk*, Vol. 2, page 42.
74 *Tuzuk*, Vol. 1, page 359.
75 *Tuzuk*, Vol. 1, pages 215, 216.
76 *Imperial Identity in the Mughal Empire*, Lisa Balabanlilar, Bloomsbury, page 97.
77 *Culture of Encounters*, page 43.
78 *Culture of Encounters*, page 43.
79 *Culture of Encounters*, page 15.
80 *Culture of Encounters*, pages 210, 211, 212.

81 *The Emperor Jahangir*, page 173.
82 *Tuzuk*, Vol. 2, page 224.
83 *The Indian Muslims*, pages 360, 361.
84 *Imperial Identity*, page 68.
85 *Tuzuk*, Vol. 2, pages 55, 56.
86 *Tuzuk*, Vol. 1, pages 7–10.
87 *Akbarnama*, Vol. 6, page 189.
88 *Tuzuk*, Vol. 1, page 72.
89 *Tuzuk*, Vol. 2, page 8.
90 *Tuzuk*, Vol. 2, page 192.
91 *Tuzuk*, Vol. I, pages 140, *141*.
92 *The Emperor Jahangir*, page 176.
93 *Tuzuk*, Vol. 2, pages 204, 211.
94 *Tuzuk*, Vol. 1, page 33, 34.
95 *Tuzuk*, Vol. 2, page 89.
96 *Tuzuk*, Vol. 1, pages 140, 141.
97 *Tuzuk*, Vol. 2, pages 100, 101, 114.
98 *Tuzuk*, Vol. 2, page 135.
99 *Tuzuk*, Vol. 1, page 8.
100 *Tuzuk*, Vol. 2, page 197.
101 *Tuzuk*, Vol. 2, page 242.
102 *Tuzuk*, Vol. 2, pages 262, 263.
103 *Tuzuk*, Vol. 2, page 310.
104 *Tuzuk*, Vol. 2, page 67.
105 *Tuzuk*, Vol. 138–202.
106 *Tuzuk*, Vol. 2, pages 12, 38, 126.
107 *The Emperor Jahangir*, page 202.

Chapter 5 Second Lord of the Auspicious Conjunction

1 *Shahjahan: The Rise and Fall of the Mughal Emperor*, Fergus Nicoll, Penguin, pages 27, 28.
2 *Tuzuk*, Vol. 1, page 46.
3 *The Princes of the Mughal Empire*, page 70.
4 *Tuzuk*, Vol. 1, page 47.
5 *The Princes of the Mughal Empire*, page 125.
6 *Tuzuk*, Vol. 1, pages 109, 110.
7 *The Princes of the Mughal Empire*, pages 117, 118, 125, 126.
8 *The Princes of the Mughal Empire*, page 93.

9   *The Princes of the Mughal Empire*, page 113.
10 *Tuzuk*, Vol. 1, pages 355, 366, 368.
11 *Tuzuk*, Vol. 1, pages 285–288.
12 *Tuzuk*, Vol. 1, page 285; the British bureaucrat translator uses Victorian idiom.
13 *Tuzuk*, Vol. 1, page 103.
14 *Tuzuk*, Vol. 1, page 249.
15 *Tuzuk*, Vol. 1, page 171.
16 *The Emperor Jahangir*, pages 177, 178.
17 *The Princes of the Mughal Empire*, page 100.
18 *Tuzuk*, Vol. 2, pages 227, 228.
19 *Tuzuk*, Vol. 2, pages 268, 269, 270, 271.
20 *Culture of Encounters*, pages 30–32, 51–54, 58–60, 65, 74–78, 82, 83, 89, 90, 109–110, 178, 196–200, 222.
21 *Culture of Encounters*, pages 30–32, 51–54, 58–60, 65, 74–78, 82, 83, 89, 90, 109–110, 178, 196–200, 222.
22 *Tuzuk*, Vol. 2, page 53.
23 *Tuzuk*, Vol. 2, pages 240, 241.
24 *Travels in the Mogul Empire 1650–1668*, Francois Bernier, Asian Educational Services, 2010, pages 161, 162, 163.
25 *Travels in the Mogul Empire*, Page 244, 245.
26 *Aurangzib and the Decay of the Mughal Empire*, first published in 1896; reprinted by L.G. Publishers in 2022, page 16.
27 *Imperial Identity*, page 48.

CHAPTER 6   THE LAST PREDICTION: AFTER ME, CHAOS!
AZ MAST HAMAH FASAD-I-BAQI

1 *Tuzuk*, Vol. 2, pages 51, 52.
2 *Tuzuk*, Vol. 2, page 51.
3 *Tuzuk*, Vol. 2, pages 51, 54.
4 *Tuzuk*, Vol. 1, page 262.
5 *Tuzuk* Vol. 1, 263.
6 *Ahkam-i-Alamgiri*, Hamid-ud-din Khan Bahadur, translated by Jadunath Sarkar, Gyan Press, Delhi, 1925.
7 *History of Aurangzib Mainly Based on Persian Sources*, Jadunath Sarkar, pages 77–81; *Anecdotes of Aurangzib*, pages 35, 36, 56.

8 'Learned Brahmins and the Mughal Court', in *Religious Interactions in Mughal India*, Christopher Minkowski, Oxford University Press, pages 114, 115.
9 *Religious Interactions in Mughal India*, pages 122, 123.
10 *Travels in The Mogul Empire 1656–1668*, Francois Bernier, Asian Educational Services, page 161.
11 *Travels in the Mogul Empire AD 1656–1668*, Francois Bernier, Archibald Constable and Company, pages 161, 162.
12 *Travels in the Mogul Empire AD 1656–1668*, Francois Bernier, Archibald Constable and Company, page 243, 244.
13 *The Indian Muslims*, pages 229–230.
14 *The Indian Muslims*.
15 *Anecdotes*, pages 32, 33.
16 *Travels in The Mogul Empire 1656–1668,*, pages 182, 183.
17 *Religious Interactions in Mughal India*, pages 89, 90.
18 *Dara Shikuh: Life and Works*, Bikrama Jit Hasrat, Munshiram Manoharlal, pages 101, 102.
19 *The Indian Muslims*, page 309, citing *Maktubat-i-Shah Muhibullah Ilahabadi*, Azad Library, Aligarh Muslim University.
20 *Anecdotes*, page 37.
21 *The Princes of the Mughal Empire*, page 126.
22 *The Princes of the Mughal Empire*, pages 38, 40.
23 *The Princes of the Mughal Empire*, page 127.
24 *The Princes of the Mughal Empire*, page 172.
25 *The Princes of the Mughal Empire*, page 200.
26 *Anecdotes*, pages 33, 34.
27 *Travels in The Mogul Empire 1656–1668*, Francois Bernier, Asian Educational Services, page 6.
28 *Travels in The Mogul Empire 1656–1668*, Francois Bernier, Asian Educational Services, page 13.
29 *Travels in The Mogul Empire 1656–1668,*, pages 6–13.
30 *The Princes of the Mughal Empire*, page 38.
31 *The Princes of the Mughal Empire*, pages 38, 39.
32 *Imperial Identity*, page 131.
33 *Anecdotes*, pages 43–46.
34 *A Pepys of Mogul India*; abridgment by M.L. Irvine of *Storio do Mogor*, by Niccolao Manucci, Shristi Publications, page 65.
35 *A Short History of Aurangzeb*, Orient Blackswan, pages 48–57.

36 *A Short History of Aurangzeb*, pages 92, 93.
37 *A Short History of Aurangzeb*, pages 92, 93.
38 *History of Aurangzib*, pages 80–85.
39 *Travels in The Mogul Empire 1656–1668*, Francois Bernier, Asian Educational Services, page 71.
40 *Travels in The Mogul Empire 1656–1668*, Francois Bernier, Asian Educational Services, page 72.
41 *Travels in The Mogul Empire 1656–1668,*, pages 70–73.
42 *Anecdotes*, pages 46, 47.
43 *Travels in The Mogul Empire 1656–1668,*, page 99.
44 *Travels in The Mogul Empire 1656–1668,*, pages 102, 103.
45 *Travels in The Mogul Empire 1656–1668,*, page 166.
46 *The Princes of the Mughal Empire*, 41.
47 *Anecdotes*, pages 46, 47.
48 *History of Aurangzib*, pages 291–296.
49 *History of Aurangzib*, pages 291–296.
50 *History of Aurangzib*, page 107.
51 Translated by Abdullah Yusuf Ali, published by Amana Corporation.
52 *Aurangzib and the Decay of the Mughal Empire*, pages 65, 67.
53 *Travels in the Mogul Empire*, page 351.
54 *Travels in The Mogul Empire 1656–1668,*, pages 359–374.
55 *Travels in The Mogul Empire 1656–1668,*, page 271.
56 *Travels in The Mogul Empire 1656–1668,*, Appendix, pages 471–473.
57 *Anecdotes*, pages 23, 38–41.
58 *Tuzuk*, Vol. 1, pages 340–342.
59 *Anecdotes*, page 61.
60 *Anecdotes*, page 71.
61 *Anecdotes*, pages 72–74.
62 *The Princes of the Mughal Empire*, page 207.
63 *Travels in The Mogul Empire 1656–1668,*, pages 83.
64 *Storio Do Mogor: Or, Mogul India, 1653–1708*, Niccolao Manucci, Atlantic.
65 *Storio Do Mogor*, Vol. 3, pages 288–291.
66 *Shivaji and His Times*, Jadunath Sarkar, pages 251–253, Orient Blackswan.
67 *Anecdotes*, pages 132, 133.
68 *Aurangzeb: The Man and the Myth*, page 89.

69 *A Short History of Aurangzib*, Orient Blackswan, pages 123, 124, 125.
70 *A Short History*, pages 86, 87.
71 *Anecdotes*, page 11.
72 *Travels in The Mogul Empire 1656–1668,*, page 134, 137.
73 *A Short History*, pages 144–145.
74 *Aurangzib and the Decay of the Mughal Empire*, pages 69, 75.
75 *Travels in The Mogul Empire 1656–1668,*, pages 30, 173.
76 *Storio Do Mogor*, page 266, 267.
77 *Culture of Encounters*, page 72.
78 *Anecdotes*, page 91.
79 *The Indian Muslims*, page 60.
80 *Imperial Identity*, pages 55, 56.
81 *Travels in The Mogul Empire 1656–1668,*, page 167, 168.
82 *Aurangzib and the Decay of the Mughal Empire*, page 81.
83 *Travels in The Mogul Empire 1656–1668,*, pages 154–161.
84 *Travels in The Mogul Empire 1656–1668,*, pages 437–442.
85 *Anecdotes*, page 25.
86 *A Short History of Aurangzeb*, pages 365–366.
87 *Anecdotes*, page 26.
88 *Anecdotes*, page 28.
89 *Anecdotes*, pages 48–51, Jadunath Sarkar, Forgotten Books

CHAPTER 7 THE RISE OF SUHAIL

1 *Babur: Timurid Prince and Mughal Emperor, 1483–1530*, Stephen Dale, Cambridge University Press, pages 130, 131.
2 *Babur: Timurid Prince and Mughal Emperor, 1483–1530*, pages 130, 131.
3 *Babur Nama: Journal of Emperor Babur*, Penguin Classics, pages 74, 90, 116.
4 *Beyond the Three Seas: Travellers' Tales of Mughal India*, Random House, page 19.
5 *Babur: Timurid Prince and Mughal Emperors, 1483–1530*, pages 130, 131.
6 *Humayun Nama*, Gulbadan Begum, translated by Annette Beveridge, Idarah-i-Adabiyat, Delhi, 1972, page 98.
7 *Humayun Nama*, pages 100, 101.

8 *King of the World*, Milo Cleveland Beach and Ebba Koch, Azimuth Editions, Sackler Gallery, 1997; pages 12, 13, 21, 22, 23, 24, 25, 26, 124; figures 42, 43, 44, 45.
9 *Humayun Nama*, pages 104, 105.
10 *Humayun Nama*, page 108.
11 *A History of India under the Two First Sovereigns of the House of Taimur Baber and Humayun*, Irish University Press, 1854, Vol. 2, page 434.
12 *Tezkereh al Vakiat*, page 18.
13 *The Fated Sky: Astrology in History*, Benson Bobrick, Simon and Schuster, New York, 2005, page 75.
14 *The Fated Sky: Astrology in History*, pages 82–84.
15 *Akbarnama*, Vol. 4, pages 517, 519.

Index

A
Abbas, Shah, 110, 127, 166
Abdullah Khan, 59
Abdur Rahman, Shaikh, 115
Abedin, Zaynal, 159
Abul Faiz, 241
Abul Fazl, 2, 6–7, 9–11, 13, 16,
   18, 22, 26–27, 29, 30, 33, 36,
   38–46, 50–51, 55, 59, 60,
   64, 66, 69–72, 75–77, 79,
   81–83, 85, 86, 92, 95, 98, 104,
   105, 125, 127, 133, 137, 139,
   160, 162, 209, 224, 236, 238,
   240–241
Adam, 7, 9–10
Afghanistan, 15, 21, 25, 28, 39, 131
Afghans, Mughals and, 108–109
Agra, 5, 8, 23, 36, 50, 51, 75, 76,
   78, 81, 83–85, 102, 104–108,
   123, 148, 167, 192, 228, 230,
   233
Ahkam-i-Alamgiri, 171, 215
Ahmedabad, 60–62, 93, 164, 202
Ahvazi, Naubakht, xii, 238
Ahwal-i Shahzadagi, 159
Ain-i-Akbari, 76, 77, 90, 96, 162
Ajmer, 50, 61, 65, 92, 95, 100, 104,
   140, 157, 242
Akbarasahisrngaradarpana, 160
Akbar, Jalaluddin, ix, xv–xvi, 7–9,
   13, 21, 28, 33, 35, 37, 40, 47,
   56–57, 64–75, 86–88, 91,
   97, 104, 121, 127, 133–134,
   139–140, 145, 155, 160–162,
   167, 200–201, 209, 240, 242
   affection for Birbal, 54
   art and painting, interest in,
      77–78
   Bairam Khan and, 80–84
   battle against rebels in Malwa,
      59–60
   belief in astrology, 45, 47–49,
      81, 133–134, 172–173
   birth of, 1–3, 6, 20
   bravery incidents, 58–63
   cards playing, interest in, 77
   circumcision at age of four, 136
   death, 88, 183
   divine favour/protection, 22,
      32, 43, 57, 59, 64, 65, 79
   drinking, indulgence in, 55
   dyslexic child, 68
   economic reforms, 51–52, 54
   elephants, fascination with,
      57–58, 74–75
   empire and reputation, 5, 56
   fearless from childhood, 56–57
   first marriage, 49
   formal education, 33
   Hamida Begum, xv–xvi, 1–3, 5
   Hemu, battle against, 41–44
   Hindu luminaries in court, 53
   horoscope, 3–5, 56, 66–68
   interest in music, 74
   Jahangir revolt against,
      104–106
   jharoka on ramparts, 76
   jizya revocation, 51
   justice in administration, 78–79,
      84
   karmi abolition, 52
   love for foster mothers, 33, 79,
      148
   magic knife as gift, 85
   Maham Anaka and, 22, 28, 33,
      37, 50, 79–85, 148

Mughal fleet for rivers, 75
Rajput alliances, ix
re-conquest of Gujarat, 60–63
religious interest, 69–74, 161
Salim, birth of, 93
sayings of, 88–90
second marriage, 49
separation from parents, 21, 28, 29
Shahjahan, birth of, 134
slavery abolition, 52–53
social reforms, 52–53
sons and daughters, 55, 93–95
spiritual dimension, 78
stars position at birth time, 3–5, 9, 74, 85
third marriage, 49–51
Timurid–Rajput association, 50–51
title of mujtahid, 64
trauma early in life, 31, 33, 79
upbringing, 21–22
wardrobe, 76
weighing ceremony, 138
wet nurse for, 21–22
Akbar, Muhammad (Aurangzeb's son), 199
Akbarnama, 24, 38, 72, 148, 220, 232, 242
Alamgirnama, 210
Alanqoa, Goddess, 7–9, 17, 48
Al Biruni (Abu Rayhan Muhammad ibn Ahmad al-Biruni), xi, 239
Alcohol/alcoholism, 55, 95, 126–128, 132, 137, 139, 145–147, 149, 153, 205, 223
Allahabad, 104, 105, 113, 121
Al-Mansur, Abu Jafar, 238
Amal-i-Salih, 210
Ambar, Malik, 152
Amber, 50

Aml-i-Salih, 194
Amuli, Talib, 132
Andronius II, xiii, 240
Aram Banu Begam, 95
Askari, Mirza, 21, 22, 28–29
Astrologers, 166–167, 174–176.
    See also Astrology
    influence of, xii, xiii, xv, 220, 224
    position in Mughal court, 48–49, 172–173
Astrology, xi, 10–11, 13, 165, 175, 236, 238–240
    Adam creation, 9
    Arab caliphs, 238
    attraction among powerful, xv, 1, 236, 237
    Baghdad, building of, xii
    chairs for, xiii
    coronation time of Akbar, 47–48
    historical perspective, xii–xvi
    Indian faith in, xiv–xv
    Islamic doctrine, xi–xii
    Mughal kings, ix, xvi, 1, 38–39, 47–49, 64–65, 93, 99–103, 133, 159, 172, 220
    in Persia and central Asia, 239
    prevalence in Europe, xii–xiii
Auliya, Nizamuddin, 108
Aurangabad, 180, 185, 206
Aurangzeb, ix, x, xvi, 135, 139, 168, 172, 176, 178–180, 182–184, 186, 187–190, 198, 208–209, 234
    Arab Syeds in army of, 181
    astrologers, belief on, 192–196
    birth of, 170
    bitterness with father, 180, 181, 183, 187
    coronation, 192–195
    corruption after jizya imposition, 201

Index

crown jewels of, 213–214
death of, 217–218
early studies, 179
empire after death, x, 217
faith for, 207
free kitchens by, 210
gender discrimination, 202
Hanafi school of thought, 208
hatred for Dara, 188, 189
horoscope, 171
intra-faith consolidation,
  180–181
jharoka darshan and Hindu
  rituals, end of, 202
jizya, imposition of, 199–200
last will and testament, 215–216
last year of life, empire in, 213
letter to captive father, 210
majestic empire, ruin of, 209
Marathas and, 206
marriage, 197
overconfidence in, 202–203
plots and wars, 183–194
prediction in horoscope of,
  216–217
qualities of, 214
Rajputs, alienation of, 204
relations with sons, 197–199
Shahjahan confined to Agra
  Fort, 191
Shah Shuja, battle with, 189–190
Shias, aversion to, 207–208
Shivaji advice to, 200–201
stress on Arabic in education,
  211–213
Tegh Bahadur's execution, 203
temples and Hindu schools,
  demolition of, 202
victory against Dara, 184–187,
  190–191
war by Sikhs against empire,
  203–204

Aurangzebnama, 188
Avvisi (prediction sheets), xiii,
  240
Azam, Muhammad, 198
Aziz Koka, Mirza, 53, 60, 61, 86,
  91, 106, 110

B

Babur, 6, 7, 22, 23, 42, 50, 126,
  127, 139, 144, 145, 154, 209,
  219–200, 233–236, 242
  alcohol/drinking, 222–223
  astrologers, belief on, 220, 221,
    224
  battle of Kanwah, 230–233
  birth of, 220
  death, 183, 235
  father, death of, 220
  Humayun, birth of, 222
  Ibrahim Lodi, battle with,
    226–228
  India, wealth and attractions of,
    227–228
  on Kabul throne, 221
  love for Humayun, 235
  march towards Delhi,
    225–226
  mother, death of, 222
  poison by Lodi's mother,
    228–229
  prophecy through dreams,
    224–225
  Tengri's kindness, 219, 227
  Vaqai, 219
Baburnama, 145, 223, 241
Badauni, 72, 73
Badshahnama, 164
Baghdad, xii, 238
  astrological schools, xii
  building of, xii
Bahadur Shah, xvi, 171, 210, 216,
  217

Index

Baksh, Dawar, 158
Bakshi Banu Begum, 28, 81
Balabanlilar, Lisa, 111, 127, 132, 149–150, 210
Balzac, Honoré de, xiii
Baqir, Muhammad, 137
Baqlani, Muhammad Baqi, 81
Battle
  of Buxar, 238
  against Hemu, 41–44
  with Ibrahim Lodi, 226–228
  of Kannauj, 1, 15
  of Kanwah, 230–233
  with Shah Shuja, 189–190
Bayazit, Ottoman Caliph, 210
Beg, Husain, 109
Beg, Jamil, 109
Bengal, 1, 40, 47, 53, 54, 75, 104, 105, 157, 173, 184, 188, 190, 192, 205, 236, 237
Ben Tariq, Jacob, xii
Bernier, Francois, 27, 161, 166, 168, 173–174, 181, 183, 188, 190, 191, 195, 203, 205, 210, 211, 213
Bhagwant Das, Raja, 58
Bhalta, Narayan, 172
Bhonsle, Linguji, 206
Bicha Jan Anaka, 79
Bidaulat, 129–130, 155
Bihari Mal Kachchwaha, Raja, 45, 50
Birbal (Maheshdas Brahmabhat), 54, 86
Bir Singh Deo, Raja, 98
Bobrick, Benson, xii, 238, 239
Bodhonchar Qa'an [Khan], 8
Buland Darwaza, 63

C
The Caliph's Splendor (Benson Bobrick), xii

Capital punishment, 53
Catherine of Medici, xiii
Chamkora diamond, 143
Charles V of France, xii
Child marriage, 53
Chishti, Khwaja Muinuddin, 49, 92, 118, 140, 190
Colossal Elephant, 16, 27
Comnenus, Manuel, xiii, 240

D
Dale, Stephen, 226
Daniyal Mirza, 95, 104, 134, 147, 155, 158, 242
Dara Shukoh, 136, 164, 168, 177–179, 182–191, 197, 206, 234
Das, Rai Sundar, 141–142
Delhi, 12, 34, 40–42, 45, 81, 83, 106, 108, 175, 189, 192, 198, 224, 226, 228, 230, 242
Dildar Begum, 17
Doniger, Wendy, 71
Drinking, Mughal kings and, 126–132, 145. *See also* Alcohol/alcoholism
Dwatrimshadyogavati, 241

E
Erskine, William, 14–15, 237

F
Family wars, in Mughal history, 154–155
Farid Bukhari, Shaikh, 110–111
Farrukh Fal, Mirza, 86
Faruqui, Munis, 138, 151, 179–181
The Fated Sky (Benson Bobrick), xii, 240
Fatehpur Sikri, 63, 93, 167
Fathnama-i Nurjahan, 157
Fatuhat-i-Alamgiri, 194

Index

G

Ghazi, Khwaja, 20
Ghaznawi, Imam, 38, 47, 48
Gilani, Hakim Ali, 86–88
Gobind Singh, Guru, 204
Gujarat, 60–63, 71, 116, 198
Gulbadan Begum, 14, 16, 17,
    19–20, 31, 32, 70, 96, 209,
    222, 231, 235, 236
Gulrukh Begum, 21
Gwalior Fort, 75, 110, 191, 199

H

Haalat-i-Alamgiri, 188
Habash Khan, Sidi Miftah, 181
Hajji Begum, xvi
Hakim, Mirza, 53, 86, 155
Hakim, Muhammad, 139, 153
Hamida Banu Begum, xv–xvi, 1,
    17–18, 21, 29, 33, 74, 79, 81,
    97, 105, 106, 120, 148, 161
    birth of Akbar, 1–3, 20
    divine benediction during
        pregnancy, 18–19
    H.H. Maryam Makani, 18
    marriage with Humayun, 17–18
    mother of emperor, 1, 5
    titles, 79
Harkha Bai, 50, 51, 92
Hasrat, Bikram Jit, 178
Hemu, 39–45, 79
Henry II of France, xiii
Hindal Mirza, 17, 236
Hiravijaya, 160
Humayun, ix, xv, 1, 6–7, 13–15,
    19–23, 34, 48, 79, 127, 136,
    139, 145, 154–155, 209, 220,
    225, 226, 233–238, 242
    Ahmad of Jam's caveat in
        dream of, 16, 17
    Akbar, birth of, 1–3, 6, 13, 20,
        22–23
    Akbar's horoscope and, 30
    battle of Kannauj, 1, 15
    belief in astrology, 1, 6, 14–15,
        28, 33–37
    circumstances at son's birth,
        6–7, 15
    conquest of Kabul, 29
    death, 37–38, 183
    defeat in 1540, 1, 7, 13, 14, 238
    divine protection, belief in, 16,
        19, 22
    dream in Lahore, 15–16
    inventions, 36
    marriage with Hamida Banu,
        17–18
    news of son's birth, 6
    Persian monarchs and, 23–28
    personal astrologer, 1
    separation from son, 21, 28–30
    siege of Kandahar, 28, 30
    stars position at his child's
        birth, 3–5
    stepbrothers as enemies, 21
    victory in Delhi and
        administration, 34–35
Humayun's tomb, Delhi, 79, 106
Hussain, Muhammad, 59, 122

I

Ibrahim Farazi, Muhammad ibn,
    xii
The Indian Muslims (M. Mujeeb), xiv
*Instruction in the Elements of the
    Art of Astrology* (Al Biruni),
    xi, 239
*In the Shadow of the Gods: The
    Emperor in World History*
    (Dominic Lieven), 87
Iqbalnama-i Jahangiri, 159

J

Jadrup, Gosain, 116–117, 164

Index

Jahanara, 182–183, 191, 192, 200
Jahangir (Salim), ix, x, 53, 57, 60, 62, 69, 91, 110–111, 134, 137, 140, 141, 144, 145, 147, 155–157, 164–165, 167, 169, 197, 198, 201, 209
  Abul Fazl killing, 98, 105
  administration manual, 123–124
  Akbar's philosophy of amity, 99, 113–114
  animal slaughter, ban on, 161
  astrologers, faith in, 95, 116, 129, 132
  Aurangzeb, birth of, 170
  belief in astrology, 99–103, 110
  benevolent neutrality, 113
  birth of, 93
  books, interest in, 113
  coronation, 98, 107
  court language, 119
  Dara Shukoh, birth of, 170–171
  death, 132, 183
  education, 96
  engagement with intellectuals/religious scholars, 119–120
  expansion of chain of food kitchens, 124
  faith as healer, 117–118
  favour to Khurram, 141–144
  first guardians, 97
  good governance, interest in, 125–126
  help to poor, 124–125
  Hindi poets in court, 120–121
  ill health, 151–153
  jharoka darshan, 121
  justice and social reforms, 124, 125
  Kashmir, visits to, 100–102, 130–132
  knowledge from hermits, 116–117
  love with nature, 100–101, 111, 130
  lunar eclipse of 1621, impact of, 129
  marriage and children, 97–98
  meetings with Jadrup, 116–117
  military campaign to Kabul, 96
  Nurjahan and, 149–154
  opium and drinking, 126–132, 145–146
  painting, liking for, 121
  participation in Hindu festivals, 118–119
  rebel son (Khusra), 106–109
  revolt against father, 104–105
  Sanskrit texts, translations of, 162
  sons of, 134
  transactional diplomacy, 115–116
  treasury, 98–99
  veneration of Sun, 119
Jahan, Khwaja, 82
Jain monks, 119, 120, 160, 161
Jain seers, at Mughal court, 160
Jai Singh, 189, 190, 204
Jaisingh, Raja, 184
Jang, Firuz Khan, 201
Japeth, 10
Jaswant Singh, Raja, 189, 190, 204, 205
Jaunpur, 51
Jharoka darshan, 121, 139, 154, 202
Jiji Anaka, 28, 60, 79, 110, 148
Jizya, abolition of, 51
Jodh Bai (Manmati), 134, 147
Jotik Rai (Jyotish Raja), 13, 15, 48, 67, 74, 85, 87, 100–103, 153, 159
Jouher, 24, 27, 29, 32

Index

K

Kabul, 5, 21, 28, 29, 31–32, 80, 111, 128, 137, 139, 145, 147, 157, 221, 229, 230, 235, 242
Kafur, Malik, 11
Kalim, Abu Talib, 144
Kam Baksh, 197, 198, 215
Kamran, Mirza, 21, 25, 27, 28, 30–33, 57, 85, 236
Kandahar, 5, 22, 28, 30, 80
Kashmir, 100–102, 130–134, 139, 151, 165, 213
Khan, Abdur Rahim, 49, 53, 61, 84, 97, 120, 156, 163, 173, 241
Khan, Adham, 81, 83, 84
Khan, Asaf, 49, 142, 158
Khan, Ataka, 84
Khan Azam, 141
Khan, Bairam, 20–21, 24, 25, 29, 34, 41–45, 58, 80–84, 148
Khan, Chaghatai, 50
Khan, Dilawar, 109
Khan, Farid, 236
Khan, Fazil, xvi, 171, 172, 187, 216
Khan, Genghis, 7, 8, 10–11, 209, 220
  belief in astrology, 10
  rule, 11
  Yasa, 11
Khan, Hajji, 40
Khan-i-Khanan. *See* Khan, Abdur Rahim
Khan, Jafar, x, 204, 205
Khan, Kamal, 128
Khan, Mahabat, 157, 158, 188
Khan, Mahdi Qasim, 82
Khan, Muhibbul Hasan, xiv
Khan, Najabat, 185
Khan, Qulich, 104
Khan, Shahquli, 44
Khanzada Begum, 28

Khetakautukan, 241
Khilji, Alauddin, 11
Khurram, 107, 112, 167
Khusrau, Amir, 104, 106–110, 112–114, 117, 134, 140, 142, 148, 153, 155, 167, 234–235
Kohinoor, 214
Krparasakosa, 161
Kumis, 126

L

Lahore, 108, 110, 117, 148, 152, 158, 189, 230
Lal, Baba, 177–178
Lane-Poole, Stanley, 168, 204, 211
Leo X, xiii, 240
Lilavati, 241
Lodi, Hamid Khan, 226
Lodi, Ibrahim, 224, 227

M

Maasir-i-Alamgiri, 199, 202, 210
Maasir-i Jahangiri, 159
Mahabharata, 161
Maham Agha Anaka, 21, 22, 28, 31, 33, 37, 50, 79–85, 148
Maham Begam, 23
Mah Chuchuk Begum, 86
Majma al-Bahrayn, 164
Malwa, 59–60
Man Singh, Raja, 53–55, 63, 86, 97, 104, 114–115, 142, 149
Mansur, Abu Nasr, xi
Mansur, Caliph, xii
Manucci, Niccolao, 186
Manucci, Nicolo, 165, 188, 200, 205
Mariam-uz-Zamani, 50, 92
Maryam Zamani, 148
Masha-allah Athari, xii
Masihuzzaman, Hakim, 132
Masir-i-Alamgiri, 194

Masir-ul-umra, 197
Masum, Muhammad, 51
Mauizah-i Jahangiri (Muhammad Baqir), 137
Maulana Chand, 1–3, 6, 85, 93, 234
   horoscope of Akbar, 3–5, 9
   personal astrologer of Humayun, 1
Mazandarani, Ashraf, 227
Mecca, 23, 26, 33
Metochites, Theodorus, xiii, 240
Minkowski, Christopher, 172
Mir Jumla, 185, 189, 192, 205, 213
Mir, Miyan Shaikh Muhammad, 117
Mirza, Muhammad, 60–63
Mirza, Sam, 25
Misra, Vamsidhara, 134
Misri, Hakim, 140
Muazzam, Khwaja, 18, 198, 199, 236
Mughal coins, 100
Mughal empire, ix. *See also* Mughal kings
Mughal kings. *See also specific ruler*
   ancestry, x, 9
   belief in astrology, ix–xi, 1 (*see also* Astrology)
   Sufi saints and syncretic values, x
Mughal prince, 135–139, 176
Muhammad Hadi, Mirza, 129
Mujeeb, M., 54, 69, 121, 175, 208
Mulk, Muizzul, 51
Mulla Muhammad, 52
Mumtaz Mahal, 158, 184
Murad, 104, 137, 148, 182–184, 188, 191
Music and dance, in Mughal dynasty, 234
Muzaffar, Hakim Jalaluddin, 88
Muzaffar, Saiyid, 56

N
Nadira Banu, 121
Nadira Begum, 180
Najoomee (stargazers), xv
Nal-o-Daman, 241
Nasiruddin, 197–198
Nikitin, Afanasy, 223–224
Nityananda, 49
Noah, 10
Nurjahan, 118, 127, 129, 140, 144, 149–154, 157–159
Nuskha-i-Dilkasha, 194

O
Observations on the Mussulmauns of India (Meer Hassan Ali), xiv–xv

P
Padmasundara, 160
Padshahnama, 210, 234
Panditraja, Jagannatha, 164
Panipat, 42, 45, 108, 226, 230
Paramananda, 49
Patna Fort, 112
Persia, 23–27
Poetry, in Mughal culture, 68–69
Pope Urban VIII, xiii
Prince, Mughal, 135–139, 176
Priulus, Franciscus, xiii, 240
Punjab, 83, 128

Q
Qandahar, 179, 229
Qandhari, Arif, 33–34
Qanun-i-Humayuni (law of Humayun), 35
Qaqshal, Majnun Khan, 45
Quli Khan, Murshid, 189
Qutbuddin, Khwaja, 227

R
Raghunatha, Raja, 204–205

Index

Rahim. *See* Khan, Abdur Rahim
Raja of Cochin, 85
Rakhi, 119
Ramayana, 113, 120
Ram Das Kachchwaha, 142
Rana Sangha, 230–233
Rasagangadhara, 164
Rayke Begum, 29
Rehman, Abdur, 109
Risalo (Shah Abdul Latif Bhittai), 5
Roshanara Begum, 194, 196
Royal horoscopes, 48
Rudrakavi, 162–163
Ruggieri, Cosimo, xiii
Ruhallah, Hakim, 132
Ruqaat-i-Alamgiri, 179
Ruqaiya Sultan Begum, 49, 135

S
Saad Akbari (child of Jupiter), 34
Sahib-i-Qiran, 47
Salima Sultan Begum, 49, 105
Salim Chishti, Shaikh, 78, 92, 94
Sannyasi Moti, 165
Sarasvati, Kavindracarya, 162–163
Sarkar, Jadunath, 193, 200, 202, 214
Sarma, Kesava, 100
Scholarship works, Mughal emperors and, 159
Shab-i-barat, 119
Shah al-Hind, 144
Shah, Azam, 215
Shah Hussain Arghun, 19, 21
Shah Ismail, 23
Shahjahan (Khurram), ix, 27, 79, 87, 97, 113, 126, 129, 133, 140, 147–148, 151, 157–159, 168, 176, 179, 183, 184, 187, 198, 201, 204, 206, 209–210, 213, 234
    Aurangzeb, birth of, 170
    belief in astrology, 134, 158, 159
    birth of, 134
    bond with Akbar, 134–135
    celebrations on son's birth, 135
    children of, 182–183
    circumcision at age of four, 136
    confined to Agra Fort, 191
    conspiracy by Nurjahan, 152, 154
    coronation, 158
    death of, 191–192
    drinking, abstinence from, 146–147
    education, 136–137
    feast of victory at Nurjahan's home, 144–145
    influence of, rise of, 141–144
    life as prince, 135–139
    marriage to Mumtaz Mahal, 140–141
    Mewar campaign, 141–142
    military assignments, 140
    royal incarceration, 168
    Sanskrit, Sufis and Sanyasis, 159–168
    Taj Mahal for Mumtaz, 141
    war on father, 154
Shahjahanabad, 166, 175
Shahjahannama, 210
Shah Murad, 94–95
Shahrukhi, 6, 7
Shahryar, 129, 152, 154, 158
Shah Sarmad, 178
Shah Shuja, 101, 234
Shah Tahmasp, 21, 23, 25–27, 32
Shaibani, Aliquli, 44
Shaikh Ahmad, 18
Shaikh Muhibullah, 178–179
Shaikh Tajuddin, 73
Shajahannama, 159
Shakarunnissa Begum, 95
Shamla, Kara Sultan, 24
Shamshuddin Muhammad (Ataka Khan), 28

Sharab-i-marhamat, 145
Sharif, Muhammad, 231–233
Sharifuddin Husain, Mirza, 50, 81
Shihabuddin Ahmad Khan, 82
Shirazi, Azududdaula, 49, 56, 59, 66–67, 86
Shivaji, 200–201, 206
Shuja, Shah, 182, 184, 189–190, 192
Sikri, 92
Silsila-i-gurkaniyya, 10
Singh, Bhagwant, 53
Singh, Rana Prasad, 1, 19, 20
Sirr-i-Akbar, 178
Sulaiman Shukoh, 184, 191
Sultan Begum, 110
Sultan Khwaja, 65
Sultan, Muhammad, 198
Sultanum Khanum, 26
Sumbul Khan, 31
Sumbul, Mihtar, 6
Sun, veneration of, 119
Suri, Sher Shah, 1, 34, 236–238

T
Tahqiq ma li-l-Hindi min maqulah maqbulah fi al-aql aw mardhulah (Al Biruni), xi
Taimur, Amir, 7, 9, 20, 209, 210, 220, 226
Taj Mahal, 191
Tansen, 74, 86
Tardi Beg, 6, 8, 20, 40, 41
Tarikh-i-Alfi, 209
Tarikh-i-Shah-Shujai, 194
Tavernier, Jean-Baptiste, 167–168, 195, 196

Tegh Bahadur, Guru, 204
Thomas Roe, Sir, 114, 128, 142, 151, 223
Timurid–Rajput association, 50–51
Tipu Sultan, xiv
Todar Mal, 53, 54, 86, 172
Travels in India (Jean Baptiste Tavernier), 168
Truschke, Audrey, 119, 201, 205
Tuladaan, 138
Tuzuk-i-Jahangiri, 92

U
Umarkot fort, 1, 5, 19

V
Vaqai, 219
Virgin birth, 7
Viswanath temple, 172

W
Wahab, Abdul, 205
Wine, by Muslim aristocrats, x. *See also* Alcohol/alcoholism
Wolsey, Cardinal, xiii

Y
Yasa, 11

Z
Zij-i-Gurkani (Ulugh Beg Mirza), 3
Zij-i-Shah Jahani, 49
Zille-Ilahi, 47

Selected Bibliography

THIS IS A HISTORY of personal belief, assimilative values and varied temperaments that shaped two centuries of Indian history. Such a narrative must of necessity be based on primary sources, such as a monarch's memoir or official chronicles. We are fortunate that two of the six Mughal kings who mattered, Babur and Jahangir, kept a candid diary. A third, Akbar, commissioned an exhaustive study of his reign by an astute intellectual assisted by a large department. The life of a fourth, Humayun, was recorded by two persons who knew him intimately: his educated sister Gulbadan and a faithful valet Jouher. Court historians were part of the establishment by the time of Shahjahan, and while the puritan Aurangzeb stopped his historians after the first decade of his reign had been chronicled, his personal correspondence, official communications and accounts by others have survived.

The epic narrative of the Mughal Empire is *Akbarnama*, written in Persian by Abul Fazl ibn Mubarak Allami with the help of assistants. A three-volume English translation by the scholar-bureaucrat Henry Beveridge was published by the Asiatic Society of Calcutta in the first decades of the 20th century, titled *The Akbar Nama of Abu-l-Fazl*. The most recent edition, *The History of Akbar*, is by Wheeler M. Thackston (Murty Classical Library of India, published in 2014 by Harvard University Press). I have used both, for pioneers should not be forgotten. *Akbarnama* has etched an indelible place in academic knowledge and popular memory.

The *Ain-i-Akbari* was translated into English in 1873 by Heinrich Blochmann, a German orientalist who spent much of his life in India and became the principal of the Calcutta Madrassa. The Asiatic Society of Bengal sponsored a second edition, edited by Lt Col D.C. Phillott, in 1927. The copy in my possession was brought out by Low Price Publications in 1989,

1994, 1997, 2001, 2006 and 2008, testimony not to the price, which is not low, but to its popularity. *Ain-i-Akbari* is treated as a separate work from *Akbarnama*.

Abul Fazl, born on 14 January 1551, was five years old when fourteen-year-old Jalaluddin Akbar inherited a parlous throne. Within a decade, the young ruler had lifted an unstable realm into an expanding empire through strategic alliances, personal courage and exceptional leadership. Akbar became an icon, but what impressed intellectuals was the harvest of empire.

Construction of the Agra Fort and Humayun's Tomb began in 1565, and Fatehpur Sikri from 1569. The Mughal school of painting began to flourish with illustrations of *Dastan Amir Hamza*. Raja Todar Mal and Muzaffar Khan Turbati established a new revenue system. Social reforms unprecedented in the annals of Muslim kings were initiated. In 1562, Akbar ended the practice of enslavement of battlefield captives. Twenty years later, he freed his own slaves (renamed *chela*); by 1594, restrictions were imposed on the slave trade. In the 1570s, the emperor began efforts to achieve *Sulh-i Qul* or total peace between religions. The empire was restructured into twelve *subas*, creating a centralised administration that lasted for a century and a half.

Abul Fazl makes some effort to be fair to his mentor's opponents. He admires the brilliance of the meteoric general Hemu, who nearly destroyed the dynasty. He stresses his hero's exceptionalism, both as an invincible conqueror and as an idealist who sought to create harmony through 'cultural pragmatism' and assertive allegiance to India's ancient intellectual achievements. Abul Fazl attributes four texts of Sanskrit astronomy to divine origin, *Brahma Siddhanta*, *Surya Siddhanta*, *Soma Siddhanta* and *Brihaspati Siddhanta*, and five to human intellect: *Garg Siddhanta*, *Narada Siddhanta*, *Paras Siddhanta*, *Paulis Siddhanta* and *Vasishtha Siddhanta*.

The counternarrative to Abul Fazl is by Abdul Qadir Badauni bin Maluk Shah (1540–1615), who was compliant in court and caustic in private. Badauni indicts Akbar for dismantling the edifice of the true faith in *Muntakhab-ut-Tawarikh* ('A Selection of Historical Narratives'), first translated by W.H. Lowe, a lecturer in Hebrew at Christ College, Cambridge, and printed for the Asiatic Society of Bengal by the Baptist Mission Press in 1884. Badauni smirks that Akbar shows greater reverence for Sufis than he does for the Prophet and dismisses Abul Fazl as a liar but is impressed by Akbar's meditation and mysticism. He sets his stall without ambiguity; he castigates those who disown the sharia, the implicit reference being to the emperor and luminaries like Abul Fazl and his brother Abul Faizi. For him, such intellectuals were infidels, along with the 'accursed' Shia. History, in his view, was a noble branch of knowledge if used in the service of Islam. However, even Badauni notes that Akbar began his reign on Friday, the 2nd of Rabi-ul-Awwal, 'under an auspicious star'.

Shireen Moosvi of Aligarh Muslim University has put together a charming collection of vignettes (*Episodes in the Life of Akbar: Contemporary Records and Reminiscences*, National Book Trust), using sources such as *Zubdatut Tawarikh* by Nurul Haqq Dihlawi, commissioned by Shaikh Farid Bukhari, who served as Mir Bakshi under Akbar and Jahangir, and Bayazid Bayat's *Tazkira-i-Humayun-o-Akbar*.

While the emperor gets the headlines, the story of some nobles is vital to our understanding of that epoch. T.C.A. Raghavan's *Attendant Lords: Bairam Khan and Abdur Rahim, Courtiers & Poets in Mughal India* (HarperCollins Publishers India) combines meticulous research with lucid prose. After a successful career as a diplomat that culminated in his posting as high commissioner to Pakistan, Raghavan has been reminding us that he has a doctorate in history from Jawaharlal Nehru University. The Mughal elite valued high culture: Bairam Khan, whose father and grandfather had joined Babur, wrote poetry in Chaghatai and Persian. Bairam's son, the multilingual Abdul Rahim Khan-i-Khanan, became renowned for his poetry in Hindi.

A classic like *Baburnama*, written in Chaghatai Turkish, will inevitably invite more than one edition. I have used two: *The Baburnama: Memoirs of Babur, Prince and Emperor*, translated, edited and annotated by Wheeler M. Thackston (The Modern Library, New York) and *Babur Nama: Journal of Emperor Babar* (Penguin Classics), abridged by Dilip Hiro from Annette Susannah Beveridge's translation. Babur was a descendant of two world-famous conquerors, five generations from Taimur and twelve from his matrilineal forebear Genghis Khan. Despite the long gaps, from 1508 to 1519 and 1520 to 1525, the memoir is a mirror of its time.

Baburnama was lavishly illustrated in Mughal ateliers and preserved in royal libraries, but manuscripts became early victims of a dynasty's decay and dispersal. Europe discovered this work in India, of course, but also in Central Asia: a Tsarist mission to Turkistan bought a manuscript of *Baburnama* in 1721. In British India, John Leyden, working in Calcutta's Fort William College, began an English translation but died in 1811. William Erskine produced a complete translation from a Persian text in 1816, which was published in 1826 as *Memoirs of Zehir-ed-Din Muhammed Babar*. In 1900, the British orientalist Henry Beveridge found a manuscript that had belonged to Sir Salar Jung of Hyderabad. It was rendered into English by his wife, Annette. We owe a debt to the Beveridges for their rediscovery of Mughal texts. Dilip Hiro notes the number of words from *Baburnama* that have migrated into everyday Indian vocabulary, such as *bakshish* (gift), *hamesha* (always), *maidan* (plain, a word that remains alive in Eastern Europe), *julab* (laxative, which Babur took when he was poisoned) and *nimak-haram* (disloyal or false to one's salt).

Babur called his autobiography *Vaqai: The Truth*. Both Babur and his great-grandson Jahangir refused to brush out weaknesses and foibles, unburdened by the social morality that hides alcoholism or opium addiction. Among biographies, *Babur: Timurid Prince and Mughal Emperor, 1483–1530* by the Ohio State University academic Stephen Dale (Cambridge University Press) is excellent. *A History of India under the Two First Sovereigns of the House of Taimur, Baber and Humayun* by William Erskine (Irish University Press, 1854) has the meticulous touch of Victorian writing. British bureaucrats, fascinated by the regime they had replaced, did extensive work on the Mughal era, even as they ferreted away innumerable original documents to private and public collections in Britain.

Akbar asked his learned and long-lived aunt Gulbadan Begum (1523–1603) to write an account of his father's life. The result is *Humayunnama: The History of Humayun*, translated by Annette Beveridge (Royal Asiatic Society, 1902, and Idarah-i Adabiyat-i Delli, 1972). Annette dedicates this book 'To my husband, who set my feet upon the Persian way, and has strewed it with open-hearted largesse of help and counsel'.

Gulbadan went to Kabul after her marriage in 1540 but returned to Delhi with Hamida Banu in 1557. In 1575, she went on an arduous five-year Hajj pilgrimage. She died at the age of eighty and was buried beside Babur in Kabul. Women in the Mughal nobility were educated and many had a recognised role in court. Gulbadan means, literally, the body of a rose. Her mother, Dildar Begum, or one with a large heart, bore Babur three girls and two boys. The edition in my library has portraits of Amir Taimur (smiling, a sword in his right hand rising across his right shoulder); Babur in prayer, offering his own life for that of his son; Humayun against a backdrop of flowers and trees; celebrations after the birth of Akbar with Hamida Banu and child at the top right, while news is proclaimed with the sound of castanets and tambourines, the hour of birth being communicated by astrologers, and dancing when Humayun is given news of the birth by Tardi Beg.

An unusual primary source is *Tezkereh al Vaqiat or, The Private Memoirs of the Moghul Emperor Humayun, Written in the Persian by Jouher, a Confidential Domestic of His Majesty,* translated by Major Charles Stewart (first published in 1832; Idara-i Adabiyat-i Delli, 1972; Gyan Publishing House, 2022). Jouher disproves the adage that no man is a hero to his valet. Jouher never abandoned Humayun. Bayazid Bayat, author of *Tarikh-i-Humayun-o-Akbar,* written in 1590–1591, is another important source. Bayat served in the Persian army that helped Humayun recapture power.

Jahangir had copies made of his memoirs after he completed the first twelve years, and this constitutes the first volume of *The Tuzuk-i-Jahangiri,* translated by Alexander Rogers and edited by Henry Beveridge (Atlantic Publishers & Distributors, from an edition that first appeared in 1909). The second volume peters out when the emperor becomes seriously ill some five years before his death. Jahangir is confident enough to be honest. No commission of enquiry could reveal more than he does about the alcoholism that eroded his health, nor are expletives avoided when he is enraged by his son's rebellion.

Lisa Balabanlilar's *The Emperor Jahangir: Power and Kingship in Mughal India* (I.B. Tauris) is a portrait of a prince who grew up in a court with luminaries like Raja Man Singh, the mentor who checked but could not prevent his insurrection; the diplomat-wit Maheshdas Brahmbhatt (Birbal, the Great Mind), and Abdur Rahim Khan-i-Khanan. A volatile combination of bad advice and alcohol, the 'scourge of the Mughal dynasty', nearly cost Jahangir his inheritance and his life. He survived because he shifted from alcohol to opiates. The book extends our knowledge with a study of Jahangir's international diplomacy. Beni Prasad's *History of Jahangir* (Bhartiya Kala Prakashan; originally published by Oxford University Press in 1922) is dry and divided into too many sections; its footnotes are more interesting than the text. Beveridge, not a fan of Jahangir, thought that there was no need for another book about this 'poor creature', but Lisa Balabanlilar proves that Beveridge was wrong. *Imperial Identity in Mughal India: Memory and Dynastic Politics in Early Modern South and Central Asia* (Lisa Balabanlilar, I.B. Tauris) expands the focus to the Timurid tradition and explains the unique phenomenon of the 'peripatetic court' or the moving tent as a centre of power. The cover has a portrait of Babur in which his eyes are Mongol-narrow; by the generation of Shahjahan, the eyes and the features had become more Indian with the mix of Rajput blood.

Munis Faruqi's *The Princes of the Mughal Empire, 1504–1719* (Cambridge University Press) is a fascinating study of the making of a monarch through the careful, multi-dimensional education of a prince, who was sent to school at the age of four, to the battlefield before he was ten and to provinces as governor in his teens. At the heart of a royal upbringing was character: the best qualities of the *ashraf* (nobility) were *jud* (benevolence) and *sakhawat* (generosity), which ensured *ataat* (loyalty).

Shahjahan's contemporary chroniclers have left us *Amal-i-Salih* by Muhammad Salih Kambu, *Padshahnama* by Muhammad Amin Qazwini, *Shahjahannama* by Sadiq Khan and *Padshahnama* by Abdul Hamid Lahori. Lahori was a traveller who became Shahjahan's official historian.

In the popular genre, two books stand out: Waldemar Hansen uses dramatic phrases in search of impact, but *The Peacock Throne: The Drama of Mogul India* (Motilal Banarsidass) is a knowledgeable illumination of a life overshadowed by grandfather, father and son. Fergus Nicoll's *Shah-Jahan: The Rise and Fall of the Mughal Emperor* (Penguin) is eminently readable, while Banarsi Prasad Saksena's *History of Shah Jahan of Dihli* (Central Book Depot, Allahabad) is more academic. The Taj Mahal, a glorious, glittering, moonlit homage to lost love, establishes Shahjahan as the greatest architect-king since the pyramids (also a tomb) but that should not deflect from his ability as a sovereign.